*W*oolf *S*tudies *A*nnual

Volume 15, 2009

PACE UNIVERSITY PRESS • NEW YORK

Copyright © 2009 by
Pace University Press
41 Park Row, Rm. 1510
New York, NY 10038

All rights reserved
Printed in the United States of America

ISSN 1080-9317
ISBN 0-944473-93-8 (pbk: alk.ppr.)

Member

Council of Editors of Learned Journals

Paper used in this publication meets the minimum requirements of
American National Standard for Information
Sciences–Permanence of Paper for Printed Library Materials,
ANSI Z39.48–1984

Editor

Mark Hussey — Pace University

Editorial Board

Tuzyline Jita Allan	Baruch College, CUNY
Eileen Barrett	California State University, East Bay
Morris Beja	Ohio State University
Kathryn N. Benzel	University of Nebraska-Kearney
Pamela L. Caughie	Loyola University Chicago
Wayne K. Chapman	Clemson University
Patricia Morgne Cramer	University of Connecticut, Stamford
Beth Rigel Daugherty	Otterbein College
Louise DeSalvo	Jenny Hunter Endowed Scholar for Literature and Creative Writing, Hunter College, CUNY
Anne Fernald	Fordham University (Book Review Editor)
Sally Greene	Independent Scholar
Leslie Kathleen Hankins	Cornell College
Suzette Henke	Thruston B. Morton, Sr. Chair of Literary Studies, University of Louisville
Karen Kaivola	Stetson University
Jane Lilienfeld	Lincoln University
Jane Marcus	Distinguished Professor, CCNY and CUNY Graduate Center
Toni A. H. McNaron	University of Minnesota
Patricia Moran	University of Limerick
Vara Neverow	Southern Connecticut State University
Annette Oxindine	Wright State University
Beth Carole Rosenberg	University of Nevada-Las Vegas
Bonnie Kime Scott	San Diego State University
Brenda R. Silver	Dartmouth College
Susan Squier	Brill Professor of Women's Studies and English, Pennsylvania State University
Peter Stansky	Stanford University
Alex Zwerdling	University of California, Berkeley

Many thanks to readers for volume 15: Elizabeth Abel (U of California, Berkeley); Monica Ayuso (California SU Bakersfield); Emily Blair (Solano Community C); Mary Ann Caws (CUNY Graduate Center); Laura Davis (Kent SU); David Eberly (Independent Scholar); Ruth Hoberman (E Illinois U); Helane Levine-Keating (Pace U); Eleanor McNees (U of Denver); Deborah Roberts (Haverford C); Elisa Kay Sparks (Clemson U); Theresa Thompson (Valdosta SU).

Woolf Studies Annual is indexed in *Humanities International Complete*, *ABELL* and the *MLA Bibliography*.

The Society of Authors has been appointed to act for the Virginia Woolf Estate. Inquiries concerning permissions should be addressed to:

Mr. Jeremy Crow
The Society of Authors
84 Drayton Gardens
London SW10 9SB

Phone: 020 7373 6642
Fax: 020 7373 5768

Email: info@societyofauthors.org
URL: www.societyofauthors.org

Contents

Woolf Studies Annual

Volume 15, 2009

	vii	Abbreviations
Georgia Johnston	1	Virginia Woolf's Talk on the Dreadnought Hoax
Leah Leone	47	A Translation of His Own: Borges and *A Room of One's Own*
Vicki Tromanhauser	67	Animal Life and Human Sacrifice in *Between the Acts*
Jacqueline Doyle	91	Thinking Back Through Her Mothers: Judith Ortiz Cofer and Virginia Woolf
Jane Lilienfeld	113	"Success in Circuit Lies": Editing the War in *Mrs. Dalloway*
Leslie K. Hankins	135	Virginia Woolf's "The Cinema": Sneak Previews of the Holograph Pre-Texts through Post-Publication Revisions

GUIDE

| | 177 | Guide to Library Special Collections |

REVIEWS

| *Wendy Moffat* | 195 | *Imagining Virginia Woolf: An Experiment in Critical Biography* by Maria DiBattista |

Elizabeth Sheehan	200	*A Conversation with Julian Fry* by S.P. Rosenbaum; *Roger Fry, Apostle of Good Taste, and Venice* by John Lello, Illustrated by Sandra Lello; *Laura Stephen: A Memoir* by Hilary Newman; *Julian Bell: The Violent Pacifist* by Patricia Laurence.
Catherine Hollis	205	*Before Leonard: The Early Suitors of Virginia Woolf* by Sarah Hall
Iolanda Plescia	209	*Modernism and World War II* by Marina McKay
Erin Sells	213	*Narrative Form and Chaos Theory in Sterne, Proust, Woolf and Faulkner* by Jo Alyson Parker
Sarah Cornish	216	*Modernism and the Locations of Literary Heritage* by Andrea Zemgulys
Mark Hussey	221	*Modernism, Memory, and Desire: T. S. Eliot and Virginia Woolf* by Gabrielle McIntire
Jay Dickson	226	*The Letters of Lytton Strachey* Paul Levy, Ed.
Tonya Krouse	230	*Virginia Woolf, Jean Rhys, and the Aesthetics of Trauma* by Patricia Moran
Notes on Contributors	234	
Policy	237	

Abbreviations

AHH	*A Haunted House*
AROO	*A Room of One's Own*
BP	*Books and Portraits*
BTA	*Between the Acts*
CDB	*The Captain's Death Bed and Other Essays*
CE	*Collected Essays (4 vols.)*
CR1	*The Common Reader*
CR2	*The Common Reader, Second Series*
CSF	*The Complete Shorter Fiction*
D	*The Diary of Virginia Woolf (5 vols.)*
DM	*The Death of the Moth and Other Essays*
E	*The Essays of Virginia Woolf (6 Vols.)*
F	*Flush*
FR	*Freshwater*
GR	*Granite & Rainbow: Essays*
JR	*Jacob's Room*
L	*The Letters of Virginia Woolf (6 Vols.)*
M	*The Moment and Other Essays*
MEL	*Melymbrosia*
MOB	*Moments of Being*
MT	*Monday or Tuesday*
MD	*Mrs. Dalloway*
ND	*Night and Day*
O	*Orlando*
PA	*A Passionate Apprentice*
RF	*Roger Fry: A Biography*
TG	*Three Guineas*
TTL	*To the Lighthouse*
TW	*The Waves*
TY	*The Years*
VO	*The Voyage Out*

Virginia Woolf's Talk on the Dreadnought Hoax
Georgia Johnston

> "It was called the most daring hoax in history"
> --Virginia Woolf, from the *Talk*

In 1940, Virginia Woolf spoke to the Rodmell Women's Institute about the Dreadnought Hoax, a 1910 escapade starring her younger self, Virginia Stephen. Back then in 1910, she and her brother Adrian were sharing a house in Bloomsbury. The masterpiece novels, among them *Mrs. Dalloway, Orlando, To the Lighthouse,* and *The Waves*, were all in her future. Not yet a novelist, Virginia Stephen became an activist for one day, who thumbed her nose at the British Navy in 1910. Hermione Lee reads the hoax as both a joke and a political act, in its "ridicule of empire, infiltration of the nation's defenses, mockery of bureaucratic procedures, cross-dressing and sexual ambiguity" (279). Kathy Phillips also sees Woolf questioning the authority of Empire in this hoax, suggesting that Woolf "identified with the colonists" (248). Jean Kennard represents it as "a power game in which the traditional emblems of superiority, masculinity, and whiteness were the counters" (151). In her representation, however, Woolf deliberately evades, presenting the actions as more of a lark—as more a fast-paced and hilarious adventure—than as actions against authority. Not originally involved in the hoax, she signed on "at the last moment" when two of the planners had withdrawn, because "Either they were ill; or they were afraid; or they had urgent business elsewhere." Horace Cole, the ringleader, burst through the door, distraught, to tell Adrian Stephen that they needed to find two more "conspirators." Virginia Stephen stepped up: "'I'm quote ready to come' I said. 'I should like nothing better.'" Woolf is trying to make her audience laugh, while presenting an inherently political act.

Audience members remembered the 1940 talk anecdotally for its hilarity. But the memory is anecdotal, because only three pages could be found. Quentin Bell published them in an appendix to his 1972 biography of Woolf. The whereabouts of the rest of Woolf's speech were last known in 1955, more than a decade after Woolf's death. Then, memory was still firm enough that Dame Frances Farrer asked Leonard Woolf if she might see the talk. She represented the National Federation of Women's Institutes, and, since Woolf had given the talk at a Women's Institute meeting, Dame Frances thought it should have a place in their records. Leonard Woolf sent the Rodmell manuscript, but he also wrote Dame Frances that he had no other copy. He asked her to return the manuscript, "as there is no other, I think."

The Agricultural Organisations Society had initially formed Women's Institutes in 1915. After World War I, they came under the auspices of the Board of Agriculture. By the time Woolf gave her lecture, the institutes were self-governing units, part of a rural movement of education. The Rodmell Institute asked Woolf to speak about books.

She did not. Instead she talked about her part in the hoax, an autobiographical lecture unlike standard educational fare. The manuscript describes how friends darkened their skin, put on turbans and false beards, dressing up as an Emperor and his Princes from Abyssinia (now Ethiopia). They sent a false telegram from the War Office to give credence to the imposture, requesting a tour of the Navy's flagship warship, the *Dreadnought*. Admiral May, in charge of the *Dreadnought*, fell for it, and the young people viewed the most recent war technology in the British Navy, particularly the wireless equipment. Woolf states that it was "of course the newest and the most efficient kind."

The manuscript ended up in a box in the Women's Library of London Metropolitan University (5FWI/H/45 The Women's Library, London Metropolitan University). It is held in the Archive of the National Federation of Women's Institutes. Over the years, from 1955 presumably, the manuscript went with the library, in its archives, through the library's various manifestations. Begun in 1926, named Marsham Street Library (because it was housed in a converted pub on Marsham Street), it took on more feminist overtones with a new name, the Fawcett Library (after the suffragist Millicent Fawcett). Woolf had supported this library during her lifetime, particularly through donations of books (see Pawlowski). The library finally became the Women's Library, collecting books, pamphlets, and manuscripts pertaining to women's history. Today it is the most extensive collection on women's history in the United Kingdom. It moved, in 2002, to London's 25 Old Castle Street, taking the manuscript with it. In 2006, I uncovered the lecture. It was lying at the bottom of a box of papers about the Women's Institute.

Most of the box contained historical documents about the Women's Institute. I had assumed the lecture would be first and foremost, since the library had labeled this box "The Dreadnought Hoax," but it was not until I had reached the bottom of the box that I found the folder with the material by Woolf. This long-hidden typescript was Woolf's full twenty-four-page speech, minus the three pages published by Bell and the last paragraph housed in the Berg Collection. Along with the typescript were letters between Leonard Woolf and Dame Frances, with Dame Frances asking for and receiving the manuscript. Included is a letter from Minnie Decur (who had heard the lecture), in response to a query from Dame Frances in the "current number of 'Home & Country.'" Minnie Decur writes that she is an "old woman of 77 now" and has asked Leonard Woolf if she might write and tell Dame Frances the story of the lecture: "he was very pleased you asked." She states that the lecture had them "'helpless with laughter.'" Mary Somerset wrote, and the folder includes her letter as well. She responds to Dame Frances's query about Virginia Woolf by copying out a part of Woolf's *Writer's Diary*, 24 July 1940, in which Woolf refers to the talk at the Women's Institute. In addition, the folder contains a letter from an editor of *Home and Country*, Miss Mundy, who reports that she had been considering reproducing the lecture in *Home and Country* (the journal of the Women's Institute), but found it to be "somewhat too long a story to consider." The folder includes the copy of the typescript, typed at Miss Mundy's request by Miss Brander.

Adrian Stephen, Woolf's brother, had written a similar version of the hoax in 1936, published by Virginia and Leonard Woolf's Hogarth Press. The two texts with some discrepancies are similar in their accounts of the hoax. But, in Woolf's 1940 version, her insouciant voice pervades the tale. At one point during the tour, the officers begin to take the group to the officers' bathrooms. Woolf observes, "I suppose they were very proud of them." But then, "A horrid idea struck me. It came over me that this was a plot." She imagined that the officers had seen through their disguises, and that they planned to lure them into the bathrooms. There, they would strip and dunk the imposters.

Woolf's rendition of the aftermath to the hoax also makes use of her sense of a scene. After the successful hoax, Horace Cole, the ringleader, leaked the story to the press. Reaction was immediate. Outraged, a Member of Parliament "got up and asked whether His Majesty's government were aware that a party of irresponsible and foolish people had dressed themselves up as Abyssinians and gone on board the *Dreadnought*." While some members laughed, "the speaker went on to point out that it was a very serious matter." The young people might have been "German Spies"; they "had been shown secret instruments." The hoaxers could have been court-martialed.

Other responses show how the hoax became a cultural touchstone, causing even strangers to contact them. "By every post letters poured in upon us. We used to read them aloud to each other at breakfast and go into roars of laughter," Woolf reported. Family chimed in; many "were furious. They said we had degraded our family name; and were a disgrace to the parents who had borne us." Woolf highlights the assumptions of culture and gender in 1910, noting one letter that implores them, "'For God's sake keep Virginia's name out of it.'" And one cousin blamed religion—or lack thereof—for "the vulgar exploit," pinning Virginia Stephen's participation on her atheism, that she "had [not] found Christ."

"I did feel very queer," Virginia Woolf says in 1940, thinking back. And well she might have done, for she and her friends made history with their hoax. Their actions and the reactions expose the cultural and political changes that were taking place at exactly that time. Character changed in 1910, Woolf declared in "Mr. Bennett and Mrs. Brown." One cannot but assume she thought in small part of her own role in the Dreadnought Hoax.

The transcription of the typescript, which follows this introduction, retains line breaks, spelling errors, and deletions. That typescript takes up most of the right side of each page. Most of the last lines curve down, showing that the typewriter did not hold the ending of the page well. The typescript reveals a layering manuscript, not only of revision, perhaps, in the text itself, but of preparation for the lecture. For instance, in the left margins, on every page, jotted down words (some abbreviated) create a running outline, written primarily in red ink (a few times in black). These marginalia I place in italics to indicate handwriting instead of type. That outline also suggests intricate connections to Adrian Stephen's 1936 version of the story, as some of the notes reflect his version rather than the one Woolf has written down in this typescript. In some places on both left and right sides, Woolf emends the text, either in typing or in handwriting. Again, I have placed handwriting in italics. The last page has a good deal of extra handwritten commentary at its ending (a digital reproduction of that page is included as an example). Woolf's marginal comments (particularly at the very end of this piece) give another layer of textual construction.

In order to convey the vagaries of Woolf's typing, I have included the superscript and subscript characters, presumably revealing moments when Woolf did not hold the shift key down strongly enough. She generally excised words by placing x's over them, when that crossing-out was done by means of the typewriter. When her words underneath the x's can be read, I indicate cross-out with a strike through, simply so that the words can still be read in this transcript.

S.P. Rosenbaum has published a wonderful, readable, cleaned-up version of the lecture in his new edition of *The Platform of Time: Memoirs of Family and Friends* (2nd edition, Hesperus Press, 2008). It is a delight to read his superb rendition alongside Woolf's original.

I thank a number of people and institutions for making this presentation possible. My graduate Research Methods class of Fall 2008 excitedly took on a few murky moments in the manuscript to research as their first assignment, and I thank Amanda Barton, Candis Smith Bond, Julie Conway, Megan Lauer Demsky, Sarah Hoeynck, Jessica Krusemark, Una Seethaler, Cassandra Sheppard, Jennifer Stebick, and Margaret Sullivan for their work. My graduate student Kyle Crews brilliantly helped to proofread the typescript and research some of the notes. I was able to uncover and copy the manuscript with funds from a Saint Louis University Mellon Grant and (thanks to Sara van den Berg, my Chair of Department) with English Department travel funds. Mark Hussey, Bonnie Kime Scott, Ellen Jones, Murray Beja, Vara Neverow, and Sara van den Berg provided support and suggestions for this publication. Jeremy Crow, Mark Hussey, Pat Rosenbaum, and Stuart Clarke all gave essential support in helping me gain permissions to present this manuscript. And Anna Kisby at the Women's Library in London has been indefatigable in answering my queries. Many thanks to all.

Permission is gratefully acknowledged as follows:

Document 5FWI/H/45 The Women's Library, London Metropolitan University.

Copyright © 2009 Anne Olivier Bell and Angelica Garnett. Published by permission of the Society of Authors as the literary representative of the estate of Virginia Woolf.

Permission to reproduce and transcribe the final page of the typescript is gratefully acknowledged: The Henry W. and Albert A. Berg Collection of English and American Literature, The New York Public Library, Astor, Lenox and Tilden Foundations.

"The Dreadnought Hoax" from VIRGINIA WOOLF: A BIOGRAPHY by Quentin Bell, copyright © 1972. Reprinted by permission of Houghton Mifflin Harcourt Publishing Company. All rights reserved.

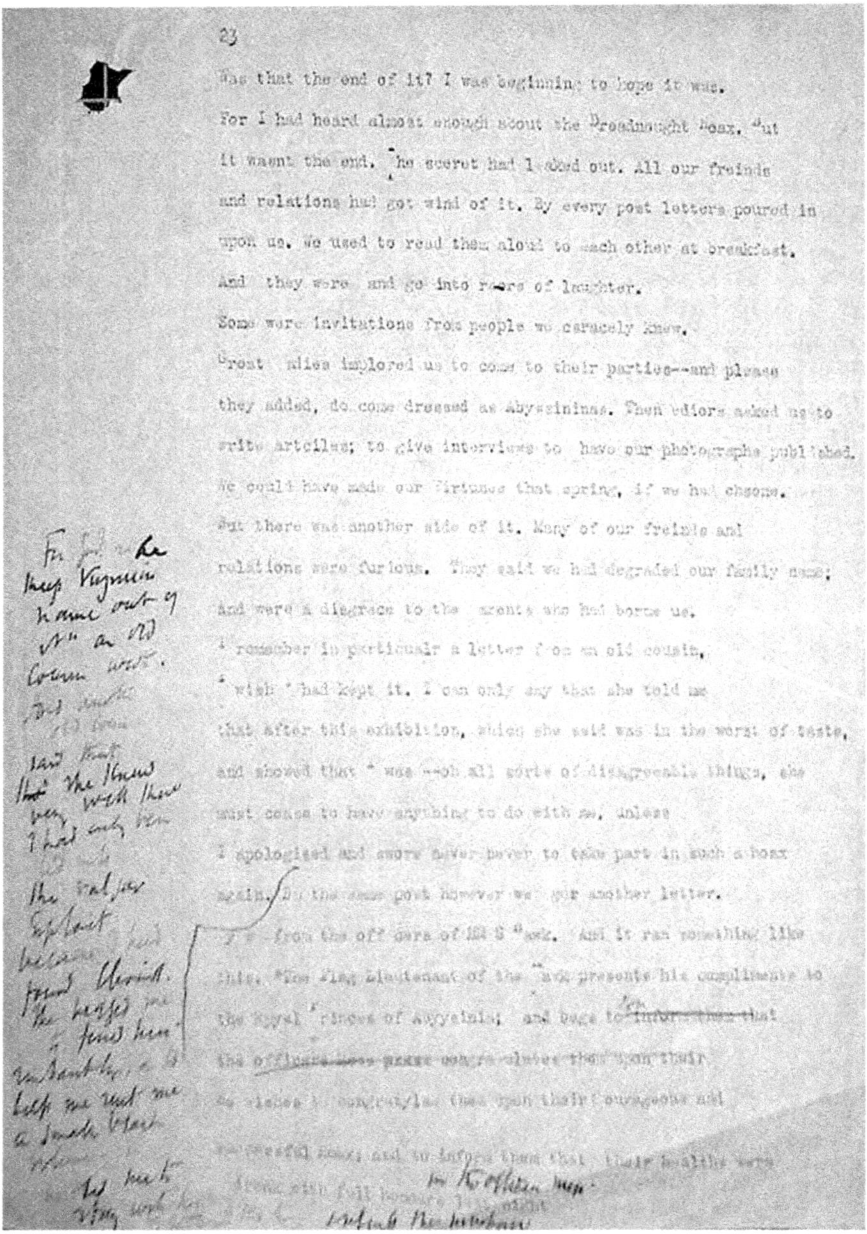

23

Was that the end of it? I was beginning to hope it was.
For I had heard almost enough about the Dreadnought Hoax. But
it wasn't the end. The secret had leaked out. All our freinds
and relations had got wind of it. By every post letters poured in
upon us. We used to read them aloud to each other at breakfast.
And they were and go into roars of laughter.
Some were invitations from people we scarcely knew.
Great ladies implored us to come to their parties--and please
they added, do come dressed as Abyssinians. Then editors asked us to
write artciles; to give interviews to have our photographs published.
We could have made our fortunes that spring, if we had choose.
But there was another side of it. Many of our freinds and
relations were furious. They said we had degraded our family name;
And were a disgrace to the ..rents who had borne us.
I remember in particualr a letter from an old cousin.
I wish I had kept it. I can only say that she told me
that after this exhibition, which she said was in the worst of taste,
and showed that " was --oh all sorts of disagreeable things, she
must cease to have anything to do with me, unless
I apologised and swore never never to take part in such a hoax
again. But the same post however we got another letter.

from the off cers of HMS Ԅawk. And it ran something like
this: "The Flag Lieutenant of the ..awk presents his compliments to
the Royal Princes of Abyssinia; and begs to inform them that
the officers .... .pon their
.. wishes t congratulate them upon their courageous and
...cessful ..... and to inform them that their healths were
drunk with full honours .... by the officers ..ss,
at ... . which the luncheon

[Handwritten marginalia in left margin, largely illegible]

Transcript of Virginia
Woolf's Rodmell Talk:
"The Dreadnought Hoax"

THE DREADNOUGHT HOAX *Johnston* 9

1

I wonder if nay of you happened to listen in last Aprils fools
day when some one gave an account of what he called
the greatest hoax in history? I listened in; because ¹ happen
to be ~~ratherx~~ concerned in that partuiclar hoax.
I took part in it. Well, my version of that hoax was rather
different from the wireless version. I thought it might amuse you
if ¹ told you the true story-- if ¹ told you what really
happaned. ᵀhe story is the story of how a party of
six wild young people went on board the Dreadnough
as the Emp of Avyssinia and his suite.

Horace Cole

To begin with ¹ must give you some account of Horace Cole,
for he was the ring leader. Horace Cole was a very charming ung man.
ᴴe was an ¹rishman; with beautiful blue eyes and a little moustache
and a perfect figure. He was as it happend the brother of Mrs neville
Cgamberlain. In those days she was called Annie Cole, and she was
very rpoud of her bother. I dont thonk though ahat she was proud
of him when she become the wife of a Prime Minister. For in truth
horace Cole was a wild young man. ᴴe was a bit of a scapegrace.
When he was boy he ran away from school; joined the army;
and went out to the South frcan war. And there he was shot rough the
head; but he recovered, ecept for this-- he was was deaf. The wound
somehow affected his hearing. And that perhaps was why he took up
practical joking. ᴴe couldnt take up any profession. And
fortunately for himself he had a ood deal of money. And so
he instead of going to the bar or becoming a man of business he made
It his bus ness simply to make people laiguh.   There were

2

a great ,any stories going the rounds about ᴴorace Cole.
Did you ever hear how he held up all the traffi at the ᵦank
of En land? ₕe strolled down into the city one day dressed as a
workman with a pick axe and a rope. And he roped off a space
in the middle of the street and proce ded to pick up the pavement.
And after he had made a big hole he put down his pick axe and
strolled off. And it wa nt for many hours that the pooice found that
t was merely a young man amusing himself. But I havent time to
tell you all his hoaxes. ᵀhe first time ¹ heard of Horace Cole
was from my brohter who was then an undergraduate at ᶜambr idge.

The
Zanzibar
Hoax

Horace turned up in his rooms one day and said, Hullo Stepehen,
what are you foin with all those books Reading or my exam, said
my brother. Oh nonsen se said Horace. ᴸets do something amusing.
Well as my brother was only to happy to throw awa his books.
And so they amused themselves. They s nt a wire to the ᴹayor of ᶜam
bridge telling him that othe Sultan of ᶻanzibar was coming to
ᶜambridhe. ᵀhen they rigged themselves up in trubrans and robes;
and took the train outside ᶜambridge; arrived
and much to their delight the ᴹayor received them in his wig and
go n; and showed them all the sights; and gave them a grand luncheon;
 and then when the hoax was discovered flew into a rage and thrarhed
to have them all sent down-- Well I can remember my brother
turning upin London, and telling us that story. And we all said,
 What a very silly thing to do; now youll be sent down; you wont
pass your exam; and how will oyou ever become a lawyer if you havent
got a degree? But that blew over. The The Vic Chancellor of the

3

of the ᵸUimv sity said it didnt matter hoaxing a Mayor. ᴴe said in private ᴹayors are rather ridiculous; they give them seles great air and we dont much mind if you do play practical jokes on them.

Cole at Fitzroy Sq.

So you can suppose that Hprace Cole was rather a dangerous freind for a young man to have. For he was ver charming. Like most ᴵrish eople he had a way with him. He had a beautiful soft voice; and a very whee dling way. An he had p enty of money; and any amount of time on his hands. One spring, just before the last war, he used to come and see us very often. I was living with my brother then in London. I liked Horace; but ᴵ admit ᴵ always wondered what he was up to. That spring ᴵ began to have my suspi ions. For whenever he came, my brother would make some excuse and take him off to his own room; and shut the door with a slam--by wayof a hint. I felt that ᴵ as not to follow them. I was certain something was up; but ᴵ didnt kno what; and perhaps ᴵ never should have known, if it hadnt been for an accident.

Cole comes in.

One night my broether and ᴵ were sitting quietly talking. It was a spring night; and as ᴵ happen to emember it was a Monday. My brother had come home from his chambers and we were talking quietly about the days doings. Then suddenly there was aring at the bell and in burst ᴴorace Cole. ᴴe was in such a state of escotement that he never noticed me. "My God he cried its all up."

"What cried my brother jumping up.

"Those damned fools said ᴴ race have let us down."

And then ti allcame out. They had to tell me the whole story. The story was this. It seems that ᴴorace Cole and my brother had been planning the greatest hoax of their lives. It was

4

nothing less than to hoax the ᴺavy.

I will tell it you as Horace ᶜole told it. He had a freind whowas
an officer on the ᴴawk. The Hawk was a battleship oin the

The
Plan

Channel Fleet. In those days the young officers had a gay time.
They were always up to some lark ; and one of their chief occupations
it seemed was to play jokes upon each other. There were a great many
rivalries; and intrigues in the navy. ~~Eachxahkyx~~ ᵀhe officers
liked csoring off each other. And the officers of the ᴴawk and
the Dreanought had a feud. The ᴰreadnought had got the btter of the
ᴴawk. And Coles friend who was on th ᴴawk had come to Cole,
and had said tohim; Youre a great hand at hoaxing people; couldnt
you do something to pull the p leg of the Dreadnought?
They want taking down a bit.. Couldnt you manage to play off one
of your jokes against them?

Cole
agrees

That was a red rag to a bull. There was nothing that ᴴorace
liked better. It put him on his mettle. Anyone can hoax a mayor
or a pipoliceman; but to hoax the gflag ship of the Channel Fleet
was ~~noxjokex~~ a very different matter. To cut the story short,
Cole and my brother had ~~takenx~~ laid very careful pnas. They had de
cdied had found that the Emerorr of Abyssinianwas in Europe;
he had been at Toulon, and the rench had taken him over the
ᴹediterranean Fleet. Therefore why not ta advanatge of that;
go down to Weymouth where the Fleet lay;
get on board the Dreadnought; dressed as Abyssinians;
and make the Admirla of the ᶠleet show them over?
~~Theyxhad~~ ᵀhis was their plan; and they had collected four of their
freinds. Suddenly at the last moment, on

	5
	Everything was arranged; they had got four freinds to come in; and the great hoax was to take place on Thursday. Now at the last
2 Conspirators fail	moment--for it was onday-- two of the conspirators had fubked it. Either they were ill; or they were afraid; or they had urgent business elsewhere. At nay rate, it was necessary to get two more people at once; or give the whole thing up.
	For the real Emperor would be in England at any moment; and then the chance of impersonating him would be m ch more dangerous. What were they to do? How could they find two people who could be trsuted;; two people who would be ready to take on the job at a moments notice?
I Agree	Here I interrupted. "Im quote ready to come " I said. I should like nothing better." At first they wouldnt have it. The they were de lghted. It would solve part of the problem. I was at tall; I was not likely to give them away; and there I was on the spot. Only GCole said to me; Can you swim? Ogf course I can, I said.
Duncan joins	*You'll want to know how to* But why? Well if were found out, he said theyll throw us over board. *swim* Before midnight we had it all settled. I was coming; and as luck would have it, another fre id of ours Duncan Grant happened to look in that night. And then my brother had bright idea ~~There was Duncan Grant a young painterxxx~~ and finding us all in a merry mood he joined in; and said hed come too. We And so it was settled in the early h urs of Monday morning. On T ursday we were all gojg down to Weymouth t hoax the Furaeno hg.

6

Clarkson

Then there followed two of the most hectic days Ive ever spent.
We only had Tuesday and Wednesday inw heth to transform ourseves into
Abyssinian princes. ~~Xexhmuhxtonmlmany~~ Early on ᵀuesday we went off to
Clarksons the theatrical costumier in ᴳarrick ˢteert.
We want to be made up as Abyssinian princes for a fancy dress ball
we said. And we rummaged through all his great trunks for the
clothes; and ¹ remember standing among jewls and trurbans and
splendid eastern dressing gowns and putting on one
after a nother. And then Mr ᶜlarkson had out wigs; and
then he painted our faces; and arms; and at last he said,
Is it a hoax Mr Cple? And Mr Cole swore him to secrecy.
And ᶜlarkson rubbed his hands and said; Now ¹ know its a hoax I'll
domy very best for you. ᴴe liked hozes too. He was a very great man
but he said he d do the dressing up with his own hands. ᴴe said when

The Language?

hed done with us, not even the Emperor himself would know the differcn.
Then there was another difficulty. ᵀhat was the language.

Eutaqui,
Mahai,
Kustufan

The plan was that Horace cole was to be a young man from the F O;
that my brother was to be the interpreter and that
What were we to talk? My We went to the ᶜharing ₓrsoss ᴿoad and
bought a Swahili grammer. Swahili is a very difficult langauge.
I can only remarmber two or three words---

Telling
Sophie

We spent Wednesady learning ˢwahili; and
in putting off our engagements and telling a variety of lies.
For of course nobody must suspect what we were after.
I remember telling my old cook who that I was going down to the county
on Thursday to see a freind.   And I should want my g breakafst very
early ¹ said. ᵀhe freind lived at W eymouth. I hoped

7

Breakfast
Nobody wd
take you for an
English lady. But
remember—if you
eat or drink the
dye
will
run

hoped she would think it natu al that and that she would stay in
the kitcehen. For I could think of no reason why, it was
neccesary to dress up in robes and have my face blackened,
because I was going down into the country to see a freind.
I had my breakfast at nix. At half past six Mr Clarkson himself
arraived. And he dyed my face and he put on my wig; and he dressed
me as though ₁ were a court lady going to aball. A

As
make up.

I must explian that my brother was going as intepreter.
His make up was comparatively simple. He had only to have a
little beard and a moustache; and a,long coat; and a little bowler
hat. Then a cab was called; and gathering my skirs under my
arm I made a dash for it. How ¹ hoped that old Sphie was busy

Sophie ..

But I couldnt help seeing my old cook peering round the
kitchen stiars. I just heard her cry what on earth M ss Virginia . . . .
and then ¹ vanished.

Goig to
Padd.

What on earthwas ₁ doing driving thro h London at e ght oclock
on a spring morning dressed in royal red saton witha truban on my head
People were going to work with their bags & baskets. The milk carts
I did feel very queer-- perhaps if it had been late at night one
were rattling along the road
wouldnt have felt so much like a an owl--Every body stared.
But
When we got to Paddington the porters and the-milmen-
gaped. But they didnt seem to see that ¹ was a young lady.
And when ¹ caught sight of the other ₚrinces waiting on the platform

The
princes

with Horace Cole in his tophat andx~~harmnhful~~ and saw our first class
reserved carriage--reserced for the Emperor of A and suite
I became another pseroen. Everybody took us seriously.
There was an o fffical to see us off. Cole acted as a F Office
officla we were bowed. We were shown to our seats. The station

8

master touched his hat. I saw people staring very respectfully at us. ⁱt was clear everybody belived we were Abyssininas; and one began to believe it too.

Then the train strated. Everything had been such a rush, that until this moment I d never realised who my companions were. Then I found that they were Tony Buxton; the Emperor; Guy ᴿidley; Duncan Grant and myself. were princes.

What the plan was

It had been such a rush that I hadnt really understood what the plan was. Now I admit when I did find out I was a little hat steps had been taken to ~~xplan~~ But as the jounrye went on the whole matter was fully discussed. And it then appeared that

The telegram

I had been rather vague as to what our plans were. Now I found ~~thatx~~ How were they certain to begin with that the Admiral of the Fleet would receive us? The answer to that was that they had sent a forged telegram; just as we left Paddington It ran thus; Please receive the Emp of A and suite and hos whtem all hopistality. This was signed ᴴardinge. Now Hradinge was the name of the for sec. The wire had been sent as we left ₚaddington. They planned that the Admiral would have no time to enqu e hether it was forged or genuine. Still there was a chance that he would telephone to the F O and if he learnt that they knew nothing about it of course we should be met by a pilicemna who would put us all in jail. It was no joke forging the f secrerayrs name to a tlegram. Still, We banked on the fcat that the ᴰamiral would not have time to take this step. The other possibility was that no not ce would be take of aus.

THE DREADNOUGHT HOAX   *Johnston*   17

us at all. Then we shoul dismply have to sljnk about
about Weymouth until the nest train for London -- a very
Weymou h
lame ending to all our escitemtn. But being in high spirits, we
deicded not to bother our heads with all this till we arrived.
But worse was to folow. For Horace Cole suddenly said;

Willy Fisher

By the way havent you a cousin in the navy called fisher?
I said Yes; ʰes my first cousin. "I thought so" said Cole,
Well, I thought Iｄ better tell you--Wiily ᶠisher is
the Commander of the Dreadnought.
That I confess did take my breath way. The first person we
should meet when we got on board was our own first cousin.
We knew him very well; he often spent his leave with us. I loo
ked at my brother. ᴴe as very slightly made up.
ₕe had only a false moustache and a beard. And to make matters w
worxe, he is ov r six foot five in height. What chnace was there
that he would escape recognition? Dressed up dyed and painted as I
was, I might be safe. But Still we made light of it. In for a penny
in for a pound. ᴹ eover, we were getting very hungry. Now Clarksons

Lunch

last words to me as he looked me up and down had been:
Madam youre the very image of an Abyssinian prince; but remember

                                                   food

this; if you eat or drink youre done. For any liquid or warmth
will make the dye run.   So on pain of our lives we couldn
neither eat nor drink. But that didnt apply to ᴴorace ᶜole and my
brother. When they got hungry--about one oclock--they went off to
the restaurant car and had a good meal. We princes remained
unfed.
    The n Horace and my brother came back and said;
now theres only fifteen minutes more... We watched the fields rush pat.

10

Fear on arriving

Wha was going to happen at the end of fifteen minutes?
Would there be an armed guard? Or would there be nothing?
It sometimes cheers me to remember my own state of mind
when ₁ read of people doing danegrous things; one simply feels
nothing. One feels its too late to begin thinking. Thus ₁ was in
a kind of trance, not fariad not anything, as the train slid into
Weymouth station. And as it came to a standstill,

Arrival at W.

a naval ofiver in full uniform stood at the sulate.
Tha was the greatest relief I have ever know.
And at once I became all over in my actions in my thoughts
              a Royal
in my gestures an A prince. No sooner had the train
stopped than a ;long coil of red carpetwas unfurled. And the

The Crowd

barriers were quickly run out to shut it off from the crowd. People
gathered fro m all parts of the station. We descende; and
walked in pairs down this avenue. ᴴats were raised. Women bowed.
 Someody even raised a little cheer. And a file of marines presented
arms. We bowed graciously from side to side; But we
did not smile. We believdd that native princes should be very
severe and dignified. Thus we marched with graet dig ity
to a car; and the officer again saluted; and we drove through the
streets to the pier; and then we entered the Admirals steam launch;
again the blue jackets stood at at ention; and then we steamed off
across the bay to the great ship that lay waiting us.

THE DREADNOUGHT HOAX

11

The
Dreadnought

arrival

W. W.
Fisher

Capt. Richmond

The Marines

There was the Dreadnought lying put in the bay. And as we
got nearer we heard strains of militray music. We saw a line of
marines dranw upon deck. We saw a grouop of officers in
full uniform drwn up at the gangway waiting us.
Horace Cole went first; then my brothe and th rest followed.
Adiral Sir William May bowed and saluted. We bowed.
But I could not look at the Admiral--indeed I hardly knew
what I did. For there facing me was my own cousin Willy Fisher;
He looked me full in the face; but he never recornised
me.Then I saw him loom at my brother. And as he looked I saw a
quuer startled expression come over his correct officers stare.
And he turned aside and said something to another officer who
stood by him. I couldnt catch what he said. For again I was
dismayed. The officer to whom he turned was xxx some one I
knew quite well. Captain Richmond. As fate would have it,
he was too was a friend of ours. What a hornets nest we had
plunged into! How could we possibly escape detection?
Meanwhile, my brother and Horace Cole were talking to the
Admiral. "Perhaps their His majesty would like to know that
the guard of honour is composed of marines; they are otwo kinds
and he went on to explain that omse of them were the red marines
and others the blue marines . .   My brother hesitated for a moment
and then he saidIt ll be rather difficult to e plain that in
A byssiian I'm afraid but I'll try." And he tried. What he said to
su was something like: Entaquoi, mahai, kustufani".
Now our first difficulty presented itself. Its very difficult
I found to look perfacetly blaok when you hear English pspoken;

12

Looking
Blank

Aeenqui [?]
Jorot [?] *go to*
the devil

The
Zanzibar
anthem.
The sailor
who cd
speak it.

The
tour.

and then to hshow great interest and intelligence when
you hear pure gibberish. But this of course was what we had to
do. And also we had to comment upon what we heard. So
after my brother said this I turned to Duncan ^{G}rant and muttered
what few words of Abyssinian i had learnt. They didnt sound very
convincing. And then I heard the Admiral say ; in his bluff
hearty voice; I must ask you to apolog se to his $_m$ajesty for
because we didnt play t e Abyssian national anthem.
We could only get ho d of the Zanzibar anthem.
And then my brother laughed; and said the Zanzibar anthem was
quite enough. And then he added, "I suppose you havent anynody
here who speaks Abyssinian?" That was a crticcal moment.
For suppose there was a sailor on board who knew Abyssinian our gibbeth
would be found out. The admiral laughed. And then he bethought himself
^{Y}es I believe there is one chap who speaks that language.
he paused as if he were going to send for him. Immensely to our
relief one of the leiutenants stepped forward and said that
he was ver sorry; but Jones or whatever his name was was on
eave that day. So we escaped that danger. Then the tour of the
battleship began. ^{T}he $_d$am ral again apologised. he said it was most
unfortunate. $_h$e had an anage ent-- the poor man had in fact as we
found out later planned a days golf on shore; he had given up
some hours of it to welcome us; but now he was determined to be
off. So he handed us over to his flag lieutenant, who was my cousin
and to his $_c$aptain; who w ^{c}atain richmond. They would show us
an thing we wished to se. An so with a pround bow to us all
and we responded he left us.

13

The tour

The the tour o the battleship began. They showed us the guns; they showed us the mess room; they showed us the mens quarters; they whoed us every sort of compass and telescope; and ways of doing this that and the other. And then they said; Now perhaps his ᴹajesty would like to xxlixx see our wireless equpiment. They were very proud of it. It was of course the newest and themost efficient kind. But in order to see this mechanica scientific marvel we had to climb up a kind of ladder onto one of the masts And a fresh breeze was blowing; and of course as we assembled in the crows nest or whatever it is called the wind blew harder. Then to my horror I felt my beard blwoing about. I began caressing it. No, it was quite firm. But tomy hrror I saw that ᴰuncan ᴳrants moustaches were waving wildly in the wind. I saw that one of them had pparted   om his lip. A space of pale skin showed underneath. nudged my b other. ᴴe looked and saw what was happening; and makinxxxxxxxx saying in arrher an agitated voice something like Histupani chew quota,,lef himaside into a dark corner. There he hastily dabbed the flying moustache into position. ᴴappily it stuck; and that danger was over.

The wind and umbrella.
A said he mentioned cold

Histupani

The bath-room.

We came down on deck again. Then the officers suggested that we should now visit the officers bath rooms. I suppose they were very proud of them. A horrid idea struck me. It came ovr me that this was a plot. I thought that theymeant to get us into the bath room; then they would turn on the water; and give us each a good ducking. After that, For I kept glancing at my cousins face. And I seemed to see that he was all the time glancing at my brother. ʸes ᴵ thought this is the plot--and ᴵ confess that ᴵ

14
held back rather modestly. However there was nothing for it.
We had to see the officers bath room. And we saw it. It was a very
nice bath room. no doubt. But all the time we were there I was
on tenterhooks. Were they going to turn on the water? Was I going
to be tipped up and t rown in? Nothing of th kind.
We were led out again. Then the officers became very hospitable.
In fact I suppose they had shown us everything; indeed I believe
we had seen far more than most visiors are shown. And now they

Drink. began to press all kinds of drinks upon us.They invited us to
come into the ward room and have a drink. Here was a problem.
Clarksons words returned to me. Any moisture wo ld be fatal to my
make up. How were we to get out of their offer?
My brother had a bright idea. he said It was awfull   ood of them;

A's dont eat. but in fact the Abyssinians never touched spiits of any kind.
That was a great blow to the officers. They were very sirry and
rather surprised to hear that we were so abste mous. But sure
they said, their Highnesses would take te_a? or coffee? or
soda water? Or No, said my brother the fact was that
the Abyssinas never touch food or drink of anyt kind until after sunst.
unless it was prepared in a special way.
It w   one of their religiousx habits. It was a
^Again the officers expressed surprise and regret.
And then an officer took my brother aisde and I heard him

The Salute asking whether the Emeoror would like it if a salute was fired
as he left the ship? It w_as obvious that firing a salute if
twenty one guns would mean a great deal of trouble. also some
expense. And by this time we had all of us begun to be

15

slightly ashamed of ourselves. The officers were so freindly, so charming so hospitable; and n w that we felt safe- or comparatively safe--- it seemed so easy to take them in; they were so simple and had taken us so entirely at our face value-- that we all felt we didnt want to give them ~~themtrouble~~

Emp didnt want one.

any more trouble than could be helped. "Certainly not" said my
My brother consulted the Emperor.
borther. The emperor tells me that he appr ciates your offer;
but would be glad to dispense with any further ceremeony.
The officer bowed. ¹ could s ee that he was g eatly relived.
The tour of the battleship was now over. Wesaw the marines the
blue and the red once more lined up along the deck.   Therewas the steam

Going back PW shows the Hawk

lauvh waiting us. Once more we bowed prodoundly. to our cousin
the flaf lieutenant and to our freind Captain richm nd. ᵀey saluted
with maginficent   And as I left the gangaway I looked at my cousin
standing there at the salute, and was very much tempted to
cry out as we used to cry out on April fools day We fool e we fool
ee we fool it cousin Willy; but instead I bow ade him a profound
bo ; and he gazed at me with the respect that was due from a naval
officer to a great ₑastern ᴾrince.

The same young officer who had met us at the station took
 s back tothe pier. His name was ₚeter Willoughby; and I am sorry
to say that he was killed very soon afterwards at the battle of ᴶutlad.
He was   There he sat beside Horace Cole pointing out
objects of interest. ₕe had perfect manners. ᴴe told us to look
the names of the healdnads; and the names of the other attleships.
Just over there he said pointing is H M. S Hawk.

16

And I thought how the officers on the Kawk were watching us through their spy glasses and chuckling at t e thought tht we had pulled the lef of the dreadnought. But o dly enough by this time I was rather on the side of the Dreadnought. I felt It had been on the whole so easy to score off them. And it seemed rarher a shame to be making a fool of this charming young man and very likely spoling

The order of the Star

his days work. But there qas no help for that now. And then just before we landed Horace Cole fu,bmlbled in his pocket and took out a little jewellers case. From this he extracted a glittering o ect--a little star set whith jewls which he had borrowed f orm Mr Clkson. It was a sham order. He presented this to Peter Willougby with a little speech.

"I am comanded by his Majesty he said to offer you the order of the Star of AEthiopia, by way of acknowledhing his Majesties gratitude for the courtesy you have shown him and the princes."

Refused

Peter Willougby blushed to the roots of his hair. He waved it aside. he stammered out, "Oh dear me sir its very good of you-- pleas express my gratitude to his majesty--but the fact is we₀re not allowed by the service rule to accept any orders from foreign power."

Cole lanked x expressed his regret; then he he explained it to the Emperor; the Emperor shook his head sadly. Cole pockted the Order of the Star of Athiopia. And we landed.

the car

There was the Sdmorals car waiting and again at the station there was the train; and our reserved first class carriage. We strode up the red carpet btween the barriers. And this time we carried

17

Abys
Emp's
Salute

tired
Hungry
Thirsty

No car

White
Gloves

ourselves like princes ind eeed. Cole showered coins upon the officlas. The people stared. A faint cheer was raised. And we lined up outside teh carriage door and bowed deeply, to the citizens of Weymouth. At last   the train moved. The ^{E}meror stood at the window and raised both hands to his forehead. And then we allsank back on the cushions in a state of complete exhaustion.

  I hadnt realised till that moment how tired I was--what a strain i had been.. how glad I was that it was over. I hadnt realised either how ravenous $_1$ was. My lips were parched. I could taste the piant on them. My dress was heavy. My wig made my head hot. Oh if we could oly take our things off and ave a meal! But that was impossible. It was then I suppose about five in the aftern oon. There was no restuarnt car n the train until we reached was it ^{S}windon? We had to wait for two hours before we had an thing to eat or drink. So th r we lay, dazed hungry, but in s a state of such relief that it was safely over. All the princes ^{1} think fell fast alssep.

At last the train pulled up. And a the re dining car was attached; and Cole went off to arrange a about a meal. ^{H}e had to arrange that it was served in our compartment; for if we ate in public the public would of course see that our dye melted as we drank. WA table was procured; the waiters laid the table. But then, to my horror, Vole who peristed in keeping up the farce till the last moment, told the waiters that it was quite out of the question for them to serve dinner unless they wore white gloves. ^{H}e said it wouo

18

Bought
Gloves

outrage the Emperors feelings--to take a plate from a man whose hands were bare. There was the soup steaming in the plates, but we werent allowed to eat it until those wretched men had dashed out into the town and bought white glvoes; and I believe the whole of that train was kept waiting several minute while they ran to a shop to get them. Yousee a hoax to Cole was a ~~workxofxart.xx~~ ^H~~exmixbdxhave~~ ^That shows you what a very serious bus ness ahoax wa to ^Horace Cole.

It was late when we reached home; and there was my old cook waiting for us. ButyI was so tired that and again she cried Oh ^Miss irginia what on earth--

Sophie
oh Miss
Bed

what on earth had Ibeen doing visiting a frend in devonshire
I ran up stairs threw off my clothes and j mped into bed.
~~Ixneverxaskedxher~~ and left her to think whatever she liked.
~~Nextxdayx~~ And next day ^I confessed what ₁ had done; and she said,

dressed as an
Abyssin

photo [?]

Now my brohte and I hoped that the whole affair was ended. Horace Cole it is true came round next mornin with a photographer; and the who e troupe lined up and was photographed. But we understood that this was merely by way of a private memento of the g eat hoax. We had avenged the honour of the ₕawk; and it was over. W ll we were counting without Horace Cole. Th~~exjokexwasxbyxxxxxxaxxxover.~~

D. Mirror

~~Xaxuxaxfarxtarxproxxkxxxxetxxxxxxxxxxxx~~ Two or three days later ^I was wa kinf down Oxford ₛtreet when ^I saw out ide a nespaper shop a ^Daily ^Mirror placard. There was the phtograoh of the Emperor of Abyssinia. on a placard. I bought a paper. ^The whole of the front page was full of the hox. It w called the ^Dreadnought ^Hoax. There was a long article upon it. It was called the most daring

19

hoax in history. Much to my relief I found that the reporter hadnot
given our names; but only Coles name. And when I looked at the
picture I foubted if any one would rcogise us. We didnt want to be

no recognised for we had sense enough to now tat if it got out
names we might be liable to some very unpleasant penalties.

I didnt want my Aun Mrs   sher to know. I didnt want ᵂilly ᶠisher
to know. And though ᵢ was not responsible for the forged telegram,
I was farid that if they found out who had sent it, that person--
a very innocent young man called ᶜastle-- would find himself

the H of in trouble. Nothing more happened for a day or two.
C. And then my brother ~~readxoutxinxthexTimes~~ reading the ᵀimes at bteak
fast exclaimed ᴳood ᴸord! ᵀheyre asking questions about us in the
House.   Some member of ᴾarliament had seen the ₔaily Mirror--
indeed the story had been in mall the paoers; and he got up and
asked whether his ᴹjesties government were aware that a party of

the irreposnieble and foolish people had dressed themselves up as
speaker Abyssinians and gone on board the ᴰreadnought. There were roars of
laughter. But the speaker went on to point out that it was a very
serious matter. ₕe said that it reflected upon the credit of the ₙavy.

spies ᴴe said thatit showed that anybody however foolish had only to send
a forged telegram and he would take in the ᴬdmiral of the Channel
ᶠleet. ᴴe said that we might have been ᴳerman spies. he said that
we had been shown secret isntruments. And he added that according to
 the papers we had held up the express train in ord er that a waiter
 might be sent out to b y white gloves. And he asked finally
that   steps sh ld be taken to deal with us.

That was rather unpleasant reading. And after consulting some of

[No pages 20, 21, 22. These three pages were published in Quentin Bell's 1972 biography, in appendix E, Vol I, 213-216. He writes, "Only three pages of erratic typescript have been found. These I give." Those pages fit logically and seamlessly in this manuscript, which is otherwise a full account.]

friends we were told that the best thing we could do was to go to Mr McKenna who was then First Lord of the Admiralty and make a clean breast of it. We were told by a friend of Mr McKenna's that if we took all the blame on ourselves they would not take any steps against the admiral or the other officers. The House of Commons would be told that we had apologised and there would be an end of it. So my brother

A. & D. go
To McKenna.

and Duncan Grant went to the Admiralty and were shown in to Mr McKenna. And there they had a very queer interview. They tried to explain that they didn't want to get the admiral into trouble; and Mr McKenna dismissed the idea that such foolish people could get so great a man into a scrape, and pointed out that one of them had committed a forgery and was liable to go to gaol. So they argued at loggerheads. The truth was I think that Mr McKenna was secretly a good deal amused, and liked the hoax, but didn't want it repeated. At any rate he treated them as if they were school boys, and told them not to do it again. But we heard afterwards that

Rules made.

one result of our visit had been that the regulations were tightened up; and that rules were made about telegrams that make it almost impossible now to repeat the joke. I am glad to think that I too have been of help to my country. With that interview with the First Lord of the Admiralty we hoped that the affair

W.W.s visit
on Sunday.

was over. But no-there was still the navy to reckon with. I was just getting out of bed on Sunday morning soon afterwards when there was a ring at the bell; and then I heard a man's voice downstairs. I seemed to recognise the voice. It was my cousins. It was Willy Fisher. And though I could [not] hear what he said I could tell that he was saying something very forcible. At last the voices ceased and my brother appeared. He was in his dressing gown. He looked very upset.

W.F.'s rage

And he told me that Willy Fisher had been in a towering rage; had said he had found out who we were. And he was horrified. Did we realise that all the little boys ran after Admiral May in the street calling out Bunga Bunga? Did we realise that we owed our lives to the British Navy? Did we realise that we were impertinent, idiotic? Did we realise that we ought to be whipped through the streets, did we realise that if we had been discovered we should have been stripped naked and thrown into the sea? And so on and so on. My brother throught he was going to whip a knife out of his sleeve and proceed to blows. But no, Willy Fisher explained that since my brother's mother was his own Aunt, the rules of the Navy forbade any actual physical punishment. Then he asked: 'I know who the others were; and

THE DREADNOUGHT HOAX

A. gives addresses. now you've got to tell me their addresses.' This my brother did. The next moment he realised his mistake. But it was too late. And Willy Fisher dashed out of the house brushing aside the hand which my brother-who was after all his first cousin-held out to him. We hadn't long to wait before we heard what happened next. Three naval officers were waiting outside in a taxi. They drove off to the address in Hampstead where Duncan Grant lived. Duncan Grant was just sitting down to breakfast with his father and mother. They sent word that a friend was outside and wished to speak to him. Duncan Grant got up and went down into the street. One of the young men tipped him up and flung him head foremost into [the taxi.] Mrs Grant, who was looking out of the window saw her son disappear head foremost and turned back in alarm. "What on earth are we to do" she asked her husband. "Someone's kidnapping Duncan." Major Grant who had been in the army himself merely smiled and said "I expect its his friends from the Dreadnought." Duncan Grant found that he was sitting on the floor at the feet of three large men who carried a bundle of canes. Duncan asked where they were taking him?

Officers call on D.

D.G. alone.

"You'll see plenty of Dreadnoughts where you're going" said Willy Fisher. At last they stopped somewhere in a lonely part of Hampstead Heath. They all got out. Duncan Grant stood there like a lamb. It was useless to fight. They were three against one. And this rather upset them. "I can't make this chap out" said one of the officers. He doesnt put up any fight. You can't cane a chap like that".

Won't fight.

My cousin however ordered them to proceed. He was too high in the service to lend a hand himself. And so, very reluctantly, one of the junior officers took a cane and gave Duncan Grant two ceremonial taps. Then they said the honour of the navy was avenged. There was Ducan Grant standing without a hat in his bedroom slippers. They at once conceived an affection for him and I am not surprised. They were really sorry for him. "You can't go home like that" they said. But Duncan Grant felt that he would much rather go home in the tube in his slippers than be driven back by the officers. And so he shuffled off; and the officers disappeared in their car.

23
Was that the end of it? I was beginning to hope it was.
For I had heard almost enough about the Dreadnought Hoax. ᴮut
it wasnt the end. ᵀhe sceret had leaked out. All our freinds
and relations had got wind of it. By every post letters poured in
upon us. We used to read them aloud to each other at breakfast.
And they were and go into raors of laughter.
Some were invitations from people we csracely knew.
ᴳreat adies implored us to come to their parties--and please
they added, do come dressed as Abyssininas. Then editors asked us to
write artciles; to give interviews to have our photographs published.
We could have made our firtunes that spring, if we had chsone.
ᴮut there was another side of it. Many of our freinds and

For Gods sake keep Virginias name out of it" an old cousin wrote. And another old cousin said that I h̶a̶d̶ she knew very well that I had only been led into the vulgar exploit because I had [not] found Christ. She begged me to find him instantly, & to help me sent me a small black volume & invited me to stay with her.

relations were furious. They said we had degraded our family name;
and were a disgrace to the   arents who had borne us.
ᴵ remember in particualr a letter from an old cousin,
ᴵ wish¹ had kept it. I can only say that she told me
that after this exhibition, which she said was in the worst of taste,
and showed thatᴵ was --oh all sorts of disagreeable things, she
must cease to have anything to do with me, unless
I apologised and swore never never to take part in such a hoax
again. Bu the same post however we got another letter.
 y w from the off cers of HM S ᴴawk. And it ran something like
this. "The Flag Lieutenant of the ᴴawk presents his compliments to
the Rpyal ᴾrinces of Abyysinia; and begs to i̶n̶f̶o̶r̶m̶ ̶t̶h̶e̶m̶ ̶t̶h̶a̶t̶
the o̶f̶f̶i̶c̶e̶r̶s̶ ̶m̶e̶s̶s̶ ̶x̶x̶x̶x̶x̶ ̶c̶o̶n̶g̶r̶a̶ ̶u̶l̶a̶t̶e̶s̶ ̶t̶h̶e̶m̶ ̶u̶p̶o̶n̶ ̶t̶h̶e̶ir
He wishes to congratylae them upon their courageous and
successful Hoax; and to inform them that their healths were
                    in the officers mess'
       drunk with full honours last night
I returned the book   &refused the invitation

[This final paragraph is transcribed from the papers in the Berg Collection of the New York Public Library (reel 12, M114 of the microfilm)]

24 at the Officers mess."

The
Real
Emp

There is only one thing to add. About a week or twilater the real Emperor of Abyssinia arrived in London. He complai that thex~~litxlexboy~~xx wherever he went the street boys ran after him calling out Bunga Bunga, and when he asked the first Lord of the admiralty whether he might visit the channel Fleet, Mr Mckenna replied that he regretted to inform his Majesty that it was quite impossible.

Notes to the Transcript

Peter Stansky's invaluable research on Bloomsbury and 1910 contextualizes these notes. His narrative gives a thorough overview of the hoax, and I reference some of his research when most germane to the lecture. See also S.P. Rosenbaum's excellent presentation, "Occasions." Rosenbaum's research is foundational to mine.

Page One

I wonder if nay of you   Woolf's audience is made up of the women of the Rodmell Women's Institute. The Women's Institute movement was begun in 1915 under the auspices of the Agricultural Organisation Society. The overview organization later became the Board of Agriculture, and by 1919 was "an independent, democratic organization, publishing its own monthly magazine, *Home and Country*. By 1925 it had a quarter of a million members" (Morgan 30). The specific Rodmell Women's Institute was founded in 1919, out of the Sussex Federation, which was formed in 1917 (see Rodmell), and it, like every village chapter, "operated fundamentally around a monthly meeting [which] consisted of the business, one or two talks or demonstrations, tea (known as the cement of the movement), and the entertainment half hour" (Morgan 31). (See Women's.)

an account of what he called the greatest hoax in history   Woolf refers, possibly, to the April 1, 1940 radio talk on Horace Cole: "Horace Cole—King of Jokers; A talk by Joseph Hone" ("Broadcasting"). Rosenbaum also cites this radio talk as the catalyst for Woolf's ("Occasions" 155).

the wireless version   The word "wireless" came into use in the late 1890s, with the wireless telegraph. By 1903, "wireless" also referred to wireless "telephony" (sound broadcasting), including radio broadcasts (*OED*).

Dreadnough[t]   The Dreadnought, H.M.S., was both a specific British battleship, launched in 1906, and a type of ship. It changed naval warfare because the Dreadnought had the largest range and superior weaponry. All existing ships were now "obsolete" and "a dreadnought-building war between Britain and Germany" ensued. By the beginning of World War I, Britain had nineteen and Germany thirteen of these types of ships ("Dreadnought HMS" 206). The dreadnoughts used turbine engines instead of steam engines and the majority of the guns used were 12-inch, replacing smaller armaments (Abbatiello). The *Dreadnought* was

THE DREADNOUGHT HOAX *Johnston* 33

the flagship of the Home Fleet 1907-1912, sunk the German submarine U-29 in 1915, and was taken for scrap metal in 1922 ("HMS Dreadnought").

Avyssinia Abyssinia is now known as Ethiopia. See also Stansky's note (253-4).

Horace Cole is underlined by hand in red ink.

Horace Cole William Horace de Vere Cole, 1881-1936, is now known in the history books as a prankster. He "was both conceited and lustful," states Richard Davenport-Hines, adding that *"Who's Who* excluded him after he filled in his recreation as 'f—g'."

neville Cgamberlain Arthur Neville Chamberlain (1869–1940). He did not begin his political career until after the Dreadnought Hoax; in 1911 he was elected to the Birmingham City Council. He became Prime Minister in 1937, resigning in 1940 when Germany invaded the Netherlands, Belgium, and France.

Annie Cole Anne de Vere Cole (1883-1967), the daughter of William Utting Cole (an army officer) and his wife, Mary de Vere.

she become the wife of a Prime Minister Anne de Vere Cole and Arthur Neville Chamberlain married in 1911, after the Dreadnought Hoax. He was forty-one; she was twenty-eight.

South [A]fr[i]can war The South African War, 1899-1902, was the British name for this war. It was also known as the Boer War and the Anglo-Boer War. Great Britain had annexed the Transvaal in 1877. In 1881, Britain gave the Transvaal self-government, and in 1884 ceased to hold special rights. By 1899, however, gold in the Transvaal was so lucrative that Britain created a pretext for invasion. The British insisted that voting rights be given to foreign temporary residents, and the Transvaal declared war. Fighting against 450,000 British troops, 88,000 Boer guerilla fighters defended with striking victories, especially at first. Negotiations ended the war (see Goldstein).

Page Two

a great ,any stories going the rounds about ᴴorace Cole   Richard Davenport-Hines recalls another hoax: "Once he was driving in a taxi with Shane Leslie and a dummy of a nude woman; as the taxi passed a policeman at Piccadilly he opened its door, banged the dummy's head on the road shouting 'ungrateful hussy!' and drove off at high speed." See Bell, "Introduction," for another of Horace Cole's elaborate jokes, that one involving a tape measure and two innocent bystanders.

my brohter   Adrian Stephen (1883-1948), Virginia (Stephen) Woolf's brother, was two years younger than she. Adrian Stephen was at Trinity 1902-1905.

who was then an undergraduate at ᶜambr idge   from 1902-1905. They played the Zanzibar Hoax in 1905, when he was studying for his exams.

They s[e]nt a wire to the ᴹayor of ᶜambridge   Algernon S. Campkin was Mayor of Cambridge 1904 to 1905. He was a pharmacist by trade; thus, Adrian Stephen, in his own version of the Dreadnought Hoax, refers to him as "a Cambridge tradesman (he kept a chemist's shop)," differentiating him as someone who could be hoaxed with impunity, as opposed to the Naval officers who were "'men of honour'" (29).

the Sultan of ᶻanzibar   Sayyid Ali bin Hamud Al-Busaid was the Sultan of Zanzibar from 1902 until he abdicated in 1911. In 1890, Zanzibar became a British Protectorate, and in 1911 the Sultan attended the Coronation of King George V. Zanzibar was made up of two islands off the coast of what was then Tanganyika. (They joined in 1964 to form the United Republic of Tanzania.)

sent down   expelled

Page Three

I was living with my brother then in London.   At 29 Fitzroy Square from 1907 to 1911.

My brother had come home from his chambers   Adrian Stephen studied law. Chambers are lawyers' offices, in the Temple area of London.

Page Four

The Hawk was a battleship oin the Channel Fleet. Probably Woolf refers to the HMS Hawke. The HMS Hawke was built in 1891. An armored cruiser, she was already, by the time of the Dreadnought, obsolete. She collided with RMS Olympic in 1911 under the command of Commander W.F. Blunt; it was judged she was not at fault. She was sunk by a U-boat in 1914, and Captain Williams, 26 officers, and 500 men died ("HMS Hawke"). (See also Rosenbaum "Occasions" 157-8).

the Em[p]erorr of Abyssinianwas in Europe Menelik II (1844-1913) was the Emperor of Abyssinia (now Ethiopia) from 1889 to 1913. He had a cerebral hemorrhage in 1906 and a stroke in 1909. His grandson, Lij Yasu, his heir, acted for him, with Taytu (Menelek's wife) as regent. It is, then, unclear who the "emperor" visiting England would have been, since Menelik II was incapacitated and Lij Yasu was not yet Emperor (see "Menelik" 279). See also Stansky's characterization (18 and 22).

Toulon France's principal naval base, with an arsenal. Toulon borders the Mediterranean Sea in southeastern France, across from Northwestern Africa. It is capital of Var département, Provence-Alpes-Côte d'Azur région.

Weymouth where the Fleet lay Weymouth is a port and seaside resort on the English Channel.

the Admirla of the ,fleet Since "Admiral" is also the title of any senior naval officer, and the Admiral has the interchangeable title of flag officer who commands a group of ships, Woolf must have been referencing Admiral Sir William May (see page 11 of Woolf's typescript).

Page Five

two of the conspirators had fubked it A typing error places the word between "fucked" (in general use in 1910) and "fubbed." The past tense of "fub" means "to cheat, impose upon, put off deceitfully" (*OED*). Ben Johnson used "fubb'd" in *The Alchemist*, defined by James T. Henke (using Hazelton Spencer's annotation) as "Cheated (Spencer), with glance at 'fucked'" (392).

[handwritten insertion (over the line): youll want to know how to swim]

another fre[ien]id of ours Duncan Grant happened to look in that night Duncan James Corrowr Grant (1885-1978) lived down the street at 21 Fitzroy Square. In 1911, he joined Virginia and Adrian (and Maynard Keynes and Leonard Woolf), sharing a house at 38 Brunswick Square (see Rosenbaum, *Bloomsbury*). Quentin Bell (revised by Frances Spalding), writes in *ODNB*, that "the turning point in Grant's career came in 1910, when he responded to the implications of a French post-impressionist exhibition which Roger Fry had mounted at the Grafton Galleries in London. He rid himself abruptly of all the pictorial conventions that had previously governed his art and experimented with an expressive handling of line, colour, and form."

Page Six

Clarksons the theatrical costumier in ᴳarrick ˢteert Willy Clarkson (1861-1934). Harry J. Greenwall records a version of the Dreadnought Hoax in his biography of Clarkson (36-39). (I thank Stuart Clarke for drawing this version to my attention.) Clarkson was a prominent wig-maker, costume designer, and make-up artist. He made wigs for the Royal family, and owned the Duchess Theatre. His first shop was on Wellington Street, and his second was on Wardour Street. Both shops were in Westminster, close to Garrick Street (see McLaren).

Horace cole was to be a young man from the F O The Foreign Office is the executive department that handles foreign affairs. Formed in 1782, the head of the Foreign Office was the Secretary of State for Foreign Affairs, the official agent of the crown in all communications between Great Britain and foreign powers.

We went to the ᶜharing ₵rsoss ᴿoad An area of London with many bookshops.

and bought a Swahili grammer Adrian Stephen, in his account of the hoax, gives the reasoning for learning Swahili as a language spoken in Africa: "He and I [Horace Cole and Adrian Stephen] went and lunched together, however, and spent our time largely in the attempt to teach me [Adrian] the Swahili language. Swahili is, I believe, spoken in some parts of East Africa. Whether it is spoken in Abyssinia or not I don't know, but we thought it might be as well for me to know a few phrases, and to that end we had bought a grammar from the Society for the Propagation of the Gospel. Of course, when the time came, I could hardly

THE DREADNOUGHT HOAX *Johnston* 37

remember two words, though some newspapers later described us as having talked 'fluent Abyssinian'" (33-4).

I remember telling my old cook   Sophie (or Sophy) Farrell had been the cook for the Stephen family at 22 Hyde Park Gate. She moved with the four Stephen children to Gordon Square in 1904, and again with Adrian and Virginia to 29 Fitzroy Square in 1907.

Page Seven

When we got to Paddington the porters and the-mil[k]men gaped   Paddington Station, established 1854, connects London with South Wales and Bristol. Stansky records that the train left from Paddington at 12:40 (41).

and the-mil[k]men gaped   "gaped" is underlined by hand.

Page Eight

Tony Buxton; the Emperor   Anthony Buxton (1881-1970), Trinity College Cambridge BA (1904), wrote *Fisherman Naturalist* (published in 1946) and *Travelling Naturalist* (published in 1948).

the Emperor   Yet, see the interesting inconsistencies presented by Peter Stansky (40). Stansky quotes Admiral Sir William May's report to the Admiralty, in which May states that Cole introduced Buxton as "Prince Makalen," a cousin of the Emperor, to Flag Commander Fisher. Was the character the "Emperor" or "Prince Makalen"? Was the group's story (even at the time) consistent? Possibly, Woolf simply followed, erroneously, her brother Adrian Stephen's 1936 account.

Guy ^{R}idley; Duncan Grant and myself. were princes   Guy Ridley (1885-1947) became a solicitor.

they had sent a forged telegram; just as we left Paddington   It ran thus; Please receive the Emp of A and suite and hos whtem all hopistality.   From "Please" through "hospitality" is underlined by hand in red ink.

This was signed ᴴardinge. Now Hradinge was the name of the for sec. Sir Edward Grey was the Foreign Secretary in 1910. Woolf must refer to Charles Hardinge (1858-1944), a diplomat who in 1910 was appointed governor-general of India in 1910 ("Henry"). From 1906 until this new appointment, he had been the Permanent Under-Secretary at the Foreign Office. Adrian Stephen, in his 1936 account, also states that "Hardinge" was the name signed (33).

Page Nine

Wiily ᶠisher is the Commander of the Dreadnought Sir William Wordsworth Fisher (1875-1937). His mother was Mary Louisa neé Jackson (an older sister of Julia Prinsep Stephen, Virginia Woolf's mother). He began his military career in 1888, became a Commander in 1906 (*Papers*), and became the flag commander in the Dreadnought in 1909 (Thursfield).

we were getting The phrase is underlined by hand in red ink.

Page Eleven

Perhaps their His majesty would like to know that the guard of honour is composed of marines; they are otwo kinds and he went on to explain that omse of them were the red marines and others the blue marines Possibly, the red and blue marines refer to the division in the British Naval Fleet. In 1620, the fleet was "formed into three squadrons with the admiral commanding the centre squadron, his ship flying red ensigns. The vice admiral in the van squadron flew white ensigns, and the rear admiral flew blue ensigns in his squadron" ("admiral").

"Perhaps their His majesty would like to know that the guard of honour is composed of marines; they are otwo kinds The phrase is underlined by hand in red ink.

Entaquoi, mahai, kustufani underlined by hand in red ink.

Page Twelve

then I heard the Admiral say   underlined by hand in blue ink

I must ask you to apolog se to his $_m$ajesty for because we didnt play t e Abyssian national anthem   underlined in red ink

So he handed us over to his flag lieutenant   The flag lieutenant is the junior officer who serves as the admiral's aide-de-camp.

his $_c$aptain; who w ^{c}atain richmond   Herbert William Richmond (1871-1946) served as Captain of the HMS Dreadnought 1909-1911. He was the son of the Slade Professor at Oxford University, Sir William Blake Richmond.

Page Thirteen

Now perhaps his ^{M}ajesty would like to ~~xxlixx~~ see our wireless equpiment. They were very proud of it. It was of course the newest and themost efficient kind. "The Times" reported in 1904 that "all the British warships, from the third-class cruisers up, are equipped with Marconi" ("'The Times'"). Wireless technology was known as "Marconi," since Guglielmo Marconi (1874-1937) was "the first to transmit radio signals to a mobile receiver on ships in the early 1900s" (Krishnamurthy 219).

The wind As Umbrella A said he mentioned cold   The handwritten side comments suggest that Woolf was taking notes from Adrian Stephen's account. Nowhere in the typed manuscript does she mention Adrian's umbrella, but Adrian Stephen mentions both umbrella and the cold: "I saw Duncan's moustache was beginning to peel off. A slight breeze had got up, and a little rain began to fall, so that I was terrified what might happen next. I did what I could with an umbrella, but there were five people to cover, and then I saw the obvious solution. I spoke to the captain of the heat of the Abyssinian climate and the chill of England, and he saw my point at once and took us below. For a moment or two I had to separate Duncan from the rest and dab hastily at his upper lip" (44-5).

Page Fourteen

a salute if twenty one guns   A Naval tradition to indicate honor. The custom began with warships showing peaceful intentions: they disarmed themselves by firing out to sea. By 1730, a twenty-one-gun salute was custom in the Royal Navy; it later came to indicate the highest honor.

Page Fifteen

His name was ₚeter Willoughby   Stansky reports that he was "P. R. H. D. Willoughby, a son of the Earl of Ancaster" (40).

the battle of ᴶutlad   The Battle of Jutland, May 31-June 1, 1916, a major battle between the British and Germans in the North Sea (the arm of the North Sea called Skagerrak), off the coast of Jutland, Denmark.

Page Sixteen

the Star of AEthiopia   The chivalric Order of the Star of Ethiopia was founded by Menelik in 1874 before he became Emperor. It consists of five classes: Knight Grand Cross, Grand Officer, Commander, Officer, and Member.

Page Seventeen

There was no restuarnt car n the train until we reached was it ᔆwindon   From Weymouth, the route is about 90 miles (145 kilometers) southeast to Swindon. From Swindon, the route would be about 80 miles (129 kilometers) east to London. Peter Stansky quotes a report made by Admiral May, who identified the train the party took as the 6 p.m. one (28).

Page Eighteen

Horace Cole it is true came round next mornin with a photographer; and the who e troupe lined up and was photographed [. . . .] There was the phtograoh of the Emperor of Abyssinia. on a placard.   The photograph is widely reproduced: see Curtis, Gilmore, Lehmann, Phillips, Stansky, Stephen, and Rosenbaum

(*Bloomsbury*). Another, with some of the participants seated, is reproduced in Bell, Reid, Stephen, and on the web, "Hoaxipedia."

It w called the ^Dreadnought ^Hoax. There was a long article upon it. The article appeared on Wednesday 16 February 1910. Alfred Harmsworth, Lord Northcliffe founded *The Daily Mirror* in 1903. It was the first halfpenny daily to print photographs, a practice that gave it the reputation for "tabloid journalism" (Ure). See Stansky's presentation of the articles written about the hoax at the time (32-35).

Page Nineteen

I didnt want my Aun Mrs sher to know. Mrs. Mary Fisher (1841-1916), mother of Willy Fisher, sister of Julia Stephen. In 1897, Virginia Stephen writes that she is "fearful of Aunt Mary" (Passionate Apprentice 130).

I was farid that if they found out who had sent it, that person--a very innocent young man called ^Castle Tudor Castle. See Stansky's narrative, in which he quotes the telegram and gives Castle's name and address, Tudor R. Castle of 33 Addison Road, Kensington (41).

Some member of ^Parliament had seen the _daily Mirror--indeed the story had been in mall the paoers; and he got up and asked whether his ^Mjesties government were aware that a party of irreposnieble and foolish people had dressed themselves up as Abyssinians and gone on board the ^Dreadnought. The MP was Captain William Vavasour Faber, Conservative MP in the House of Commons for Andover, Hampshire, 1906-1918. See the records for The House of Commons, Parliament, in *The Times*, Thursday, March 3, 1910, page 8, under "Abyssinians."

Pages Twenty to Twenty-Two

These three pages are missing from the Women's Library manuscript; the originals are transcribed by Quentin Bell in his biography of Virginia Woolf (Volume I, Appendix E, 213-216).

Page Twenty-Three

Great adies implored us to come to their parties—and please they added, do come dressed as Abyssininas. Yuko Ito connects the Dreadnought Hoax to costume parties of this time period.

another old cousin said that she knew very well that I had only been led into the vulgar exploit because I had [not] found Christ She begged me to find him instantly Stansky references the letter from the cousin, housed in the Berg Collection. The cousin, Dorothea Jane Stephen, wrote on 3 March 1910 (27 and 254, n.10). Stephen Barkway also gives an account of the letter, documenting Woolf's reply as well (24).

~~inform them that the officers mess xxxxx congra ulates them upon their~~ Woolf crossed through this material by hand, not by type.

Last Paragraph

Typescript from the Berg Collection, New York Public Library.

Works Cited

Abbatiello, John. "Dreadnought." *Encyclopedia of Modern Europe: Europe 1789-1914. Encyclopedia of the Age of Industry and Empire.* Eds. John Merriman and Jay Winter. Vol. 2. Detroit: Scribner's, 2006. 681-683. 5 vols.

"Abyssinians." *The Times.* Thursday, March 3, 1910. 8.

"admiral." *Encyclopedia Britannica* 2008. *Encyclopedia Britannica Online.* 19 Sept 2008. www.britannica.com

Barkway, Stephen. "The 'Dreadnought' Hoax: The Aftermath for 'Prince Sanganya' and 'His' Cousins." *Virginia Woolf Bulletin* 21 (2006): 20-27.

Bell, Quentin. "Grant, Duncan James Corrowr (1885–1978)." Rev. Frances Spalding. *Oxford Dictionary of National Biography.* Ed. H. C. G. Matthew and Brian Harrison. Oxford: OUP, 2004. 24 Oct. 2008 www.oxforddnb.com.

———. *Virginia Woolf: A Biography.* New York: Harcourt, 1972.

"Broadcasting." Arts and Entertainment. *The Times* [London] 1 Apr. 1940: 13.

Curtis, Anthony. *Virginia Woolf: Bloomsbury and Beyond.* London: Haus Publishing, 2006.

Davenport-Hines, Richard. "Cole, (William) Horace De Vere (1881–1936)." *Oxford Dictionary of National Biography.* Ed. H. C. G. Matthew and Brian Harrison. Oxford: Oxford UP, 2004. 26 Sept. 2008. www.oxforddnb.com.

"Dreadnought HMS." *The Oxford Companion to Twentieth-Century British Politics.* Ed. John Ramsden. Oxford: Oxford UP, 2002. 206.

Gilmore, Lois J. "Virginia Woolf, Bloomsbury, and the Primitive." Ed. Jeanette McVicker and Laura Davis. *Virginia Woolf and Communities.* New York, NY: Pace UP, 1999. 127-35.

Goldstein, Erik. *War and Peace Treaties: 1861-1991.* London: Routledge, 1992.

Greenwall, Harry J. *The Strange Life of Willy Clarkson: An Experiment in Biography.* London: John Long, 1936.

Henke, James T. *Courtesans and Cuckolds: A Glossary of Renaissance Dramatic Bawdy (Exclusive of Shakespeare).* New York: Garland, 1979.

"Henry Hardinge." *NNDB.* 1 May 2008. http://www.nndb.com/people/051/000101745/.

"HMS Dreadnought." *Navy Historical Center Home Page.* 4 October 2008. http://www.history.navy.mil/photos/sh-fornv/uk/uksh-d/drednt9.htm.

"HMS Hawke." 4 October 2008. http://www.battleships-cruisers.co.uk/hms_hawke.htm.

"Hoaxipedia." 2008. The Museum of Hoaxes. 19 September 2008. www.musuemofhoaxes.com/hoax/Hoaxipedia/Deadnought_hoax/.

Ito, Yuko. "The Exoticised Space in Virginia Woolf's Parties and the 'Dreadnought Hoax.'" *Chubu International Review* 2 (April 2007): 9-34.

Kennard, Jean E. "Power and Sexual Ambiguity: The 'Dreadnought' Hoax, *The Voyage Out, Mrs. Dalloway* and *Orlando*." *Journal of Modern Literature* 20.2 (1996): 149-164.

Krishnamurthy, Prashant. "Wireless Technology." *Computer Sciences*. Ed. Roger R. Flynn. *Vol. 2: Software and Hardware*. New York: Macmillan, 2002. 218-221.

Lee, Hermione. *Virginia Woolf*. New York: Knopf, 1997.

Lehmann, John. *Virginia Woolf and Her World*. New York: Harcourt, 1975.

McLaren, Angus. "Smoke and Mirrors: Willy Clarkson and the Role of Disguises in Inter-War England." *Journal of Social History* 40 (2007): 597-618.

"Menelik II." *Historical Dictionary of Ethiopia*. Eds. Thomas P. Ofcansky and David H. Shinn. Lanham, Maryland: The Scarecrow P, 2004. 279.

Morgan, Maggie. "The Women's Institute Movement—The Acceptable Face of Feminism." *This Working-Day World: Women's Lives and Culture(s) in Britain 1914-1945*. Ed. Sybil Oldfield. Philadelphia: Taylor and Francis, 1994. 29-39.

The Papers of Admiral Sir William Fisher. Ref Number GBR/0014 WWFI, Churchill Archives Centre. janus.lib.cam.ac.uk.

Pawlowski, Merry. "The Virginia Woolf and Vera Douie Letters: Woolf's Connections to the Women's Service Library." *Woolf Studies Annual* 8 (2002): 3-62.

Phillips, Kathy J. *Virginia Woolf Against Empire*. Knoxville: U of Tennessee P, 1994.

Reid, Panthea. "Virginia Woolf and the Prince of Abyssinia."*Biography* 22.3 (Summer 1999): 323-55.

Rodmell Women's Institute. 14 Aug 2008. http://www.rodmell.net/index.php?page=324.

Rosenbaum, S. P., ed. *The Bloomsbury Group: A Collection of Memoirs and Commentary*. Toronto: U of Toronto P, 1975.

———, ed. "The Dreadnought Hoax." *Platform*. 182-200.

———. "Occasions." *Platform*. 151-163.

———, ed. *The Platform of Time: Memoirs of Family and Friends*. 2nd Ed. London: Hesperus P, 2008.

Spencer, Hazelton, ed. *Elizabethan Plays*. Boston: Little, Brown, 1933.

Stansky, Peter. *On or About December 1910: Early Bloomsbury and its Intimate World*. Cambridge, MA: Harvard UP, 1996.

Stephen, Adrian. *The Dreadnought Hoax*. London: Hogarth P, 1936.

"'The Times' and Wireless Telegraphy." News. *The Times* [London] 15 June 1904: 4.

Thursfield, H.G. "Fisher, Sir William Wordsworth (1875-1937)," rev. Marc Brodie. *Oxford Dictionary of National Biography*. Oxford UP, 2004-08. www.oxforddnb.com.

Ure, Colin Seymour. "Northcliffe's Legacy." *Northcliffe's Legacy: Aspects of the British Popular Press, 1896-1996*. Eds. Peter Catterall, Colin Seymour Ure, and Adrian Smith. London: Macmillan P, 2000. 9-25.

Women's Institute Website. 10 July 2008. http://www.thewi.org.uk.

Woolf, Virginia. "The Dreadnought Hoax." 5FWI/H/45 The Women's Library, London Metropolitan University.

———. "The Dreadnought Hoax." Ed. Quentin Bell. *Virginia Woolf*. Appendix E. 213-216.

———. *A Passionate Apprentice: The Early Journals, 1897-1909*. Ed. Mitchell A. Leaska. New York: Harcourt, 1990.

———. Typescript, Last Page, Rodmell Lecture. The Henry W. and Albert A. Berg Collection of English and American Literature, The New York Public Library. Astor, Lenox and Tilden Foundations. Reel 12, M 114.

———. *A Writer's Diary*. (1954). New York: Harcourt, 2003.

A Translation of His Own: Borges and *A Room of One's Own*
Leah Leone

From 1935 to 1936, Victoria Ocampo published Jorge Luis Borges's translation of *A Room of One's Own* in four installments of her influential literary journal, *Sur*.[1] While *Mrs. Dalloway* had already appeared in translation in Spain in 1930, it is significant that Virginia Woolf's writing was introduced to Latin America in the form of a feminist essay. While Ocampo's involvement with Argentine women's movements is often described as brief and limited by her elite class alliance, her publication of *Un cuarto propio* (*A Room of One's Own*) and *Tres guineas* (*Three Guineas*, 1941) represented potentially important contributions to liberal feminist dialogue at a time when most Latin American women were without suffrage or full property rights.[2] In a study on *Sur*, John King states that Ocampo was able to use "'a publishing house of her own' to help combat some of the injustices revealed by Woolf's analyses." He adds, "on a purely literary level, Woolf was a consummate artist and Ocampo was lucky to find Borges as a translator" (81). Since he has become an internationally recognized author, Borges's name has undoubtedly promoted the sale of *Un cuarto propio*, and his translation of *Orlando*[3] (published by *Sur* in 1937), but a comparative analysis between the English and the Spanish texts suggests Ocampo's "luck" in employing Borges to disseminate a feminist message is most certainly up for debate. On both syntactic and semantic levels, the Spanish reveals translation practices that tone down, alter or even eliminate many of the most salient feminist elements of Woolf's essay.

In the following examination of Borges's problematic transposition of syntax and subversive translation of gender-related content in *A Room of One's Own*, I am not interested in a revisionist reading to denounce a translator in 1935 for not adhering to the standards of a feminist scholar in 2009. Rather, I seek to highlight the aspects of Borges's translation strategy that have created undermining or contradictory meanings in the text and to inquire about the consequences of those practices on *Un cuarto propio* and its legacy in the Spanish language. As the

---

[1] Issues 15-18.
[2] For more about the parallel forces of liberal and socialist feminism in the Southern Cone, see Asunción Lavrín, *Women, Feminism and Social Change in Argentina, Chile and Uruguay 1890-1940*. Lincoln: U of Nebraska Press, 1995.
[3] When Spain's widely read newspaper, *El País*, released its own edition of *Orlando* for a marketing promotion in 2002, the ad claimed, "The Spanish edition has deluxe translator: Jorge Luis Borges" (http://www.elpais.com/articulo/cultura/Orlando/Virginia/Woolf/elpepicul/20021003elpepicul_6/Tes).

product of a superb creative writer, Borges's translation is remarkable in many respects; indeed many of the practices with which I take issue are necessarily those of a skillful artist. The translation's ideological and aesthetic antagonism toward Woolf's English version, however, make it an unacceptable means for approaching her work. *A Room of One's Own,* as Susan Gubar states, "has become a classic—if not *the* touchstone text—in the history of feminism" (xxxvi); Spanish language readers of Borges's translation are excluded from many of the most innovative features that have rendered *A Room of One's Own* such an essential feminist text.

Since its full-length publication in 1936 by Ocampo's publishing house—also called Sur—the Borges translation has been reprinted numerous times, and remains the primary source through which Spanish language readers access *A Room of One's Own*. The 2003 reprint under Alianza Editorial of Madrid—one of the largest Spanish language publishers—is currently the most widely available edition, distributed both in Spain and the Americas. That same year, a feminist publishing house in Madrid, Horas y Horas, printed a new translation. The essay's translator, María-Milagros Rivera Garretas, claims that in the two previous translations available in Spain (by Borges and Laura Pujol), "the undifferentiated grammatical genders in English often do a dance of death with meaning [*sentido*]."[4] Rivera Garreta's concern is not a recent phenomenon: in 1993, two alternative translations of the text appeared in Latin America. The first was by Gerardo Gambolini, released in Buenos Aires through A-Z Editora. Another, by Edmundo Moure and Marisol Moreno was published in Santiago de Chile through Cuarto Propio Editorial—a feminist press—in an edition they claim is "based on a free adaptation" of Borges's translation (5). However, these retranslations may have more to do with the price of acquiring Borges's copyrighted work than with concern about his anti-feminist translation practices (Gambolini). Pujol's translation has been available since as early as 1967 through Seix Barral of Barcelona, under the title *Una habitación propia*. Despite the presence of alternative translations, the Alianza edition is by far the most affordable and available. Furthermore, as one of the world's foremost intellectuals and authors, Borges's name alone often sells the works he has translated.[5]

There is little documentation of *Un cuarto propio*'s immediate reception in Latin America.[6] King writes in general terms: "Ocampo disseminated Woolf's

---

[4] My translation; http://www.unapalabraotra.org/horasyhoras/cosecha.html

[5] This may especially be the case for Borges's translation of Faulkner's *The Wild Palms*, which is frequently mentioned as an important influence on Boom writers, but has received considerably less attention in English.

[6] In her study on the reception of Woolf in Spain, Laura Maria Lojo Rodríguez suggests that many of the Spanish translations produced by Sur had wider circulation in Spain than in Latin America, as a result of criticism by nationalist intellectuals who censured Sur's Eu-

work in Latin America at a very early date and thus helped to place on the agenda the problems of women in general...and women writers in particular" (81). Ocampo was a founding member of the women's advocacy group *Unión Argentina de Mujeres* (UAM), and worked as its president from 1936 to 1938, the same time she was publishing *Un cuarto propio*. It is therefore reasonable to expect the text to have circulated among UAM members. One might also deduce that the text was read and discussed among women associated with *Sur*, such as Silvina Ocampo, Norah Lange and María Rosa Oliver. While these seem safe assumptions, the manners in which *Un cuarto propio* actually contributed to Latin American women's movements of the 1930s and 1940s are yet to be established. Its influence on later generations of feminists, however, is quite clear. As Mónica Ayuso points out in her recent article, "Virginia Woolf in Mexico and Puerto Rico," Woolf's work was central to the formation of writers such as Rosario Castellanos and Rosario Ferré, who were leaders in the advancement of feminism in Mexico and Puerto Rico, respectively (1). Likewise, in her introduction to a Mexican edition (Colofón) of Borges's *Un cuarto propio*, Raquel Serur argues that "it would be impossible not to leave off names if we were to list all of the women writers who have nourished themselves with this text, both in terms of feminist thought and in the craft of writing of fiction" (18, my translation).

With regards to Ocampo personally, King argues that she took to heart Woolf's claim that women need money and a room of their own in order to write, and therefore used her journal as a forum and showcase for women writers (82). Woolf's essay influenced Ocampo's own writing as well; in 1937 she published an article in *Sur*, claiming: "My only ambition is to someday write, maybe well, maybe poorly, but as a woman.... [s]ince I understand that a woman cannot express her feelings and thoughts in a masculine style, just as she cannot speak with a man's voice" (12, my translation). [7]

Though she acknowledged her belief that women cannot express themselves as men do, Ocampo apparently did think it possible for men to express a woman's feelings and thoughts in translation. Borges may have seemed the perfect translator for Woolf's texts; he was an erudite writer and critic fluent in English and abreast of all of England's latest literary trends. Ocampo might even have found the two authors to have a significant amount in common, given their centrality to the modernist movements in their respective countries.[8] In addition to innovative

---

rocentric vision, the concentration of Spanish exiles working on the journal and Ocampo's own ties to the Spanish literary scene, particularly to Ortega y Gasset (240).

[7] "Woolf, Orlando y Cia." Issue 35 (1937). Based on a talk she had given at "Amigos del arte" in July 1937.

[8] It is interesting to note, however, that for *Al faro* (*To the Lighthouse*), published by Sur in 1938 and *Tres guineas* (*Three Guineas*) published in 1941, Ocampo did not employ Borges to translate, but two other men: Antonio Marichalar and Román J. Jimenez, respectively.

writing styles and revolutionary concepts of narrative time, the two authors share a tendency to include an unusually large number of external references, evidence of their vast literary repertoires. Each author's work also revealed contempt for the totalitarian regimes that proliferated across the globe during the first few decades of the twentieth century. Both writers belonged to elite intellectual circles at the center of the Spanish and English speaking worlds' literary avant-gardes, and both sustained themselves as authors by publishing literary criticism. In effect, within their intellectual and cultural spheres, Woolf and Borges held positions whose remarkable comparability merits further study.

The ideological and stylistic differences between the two, however, resulted in a translation of *A Room of One's Own* that bears problematic differences from the English. In an earlier article, "The Unlike[ly] Other: Borges and Woolf," Ayuso has pointed out that Borges was an improbable translator of Woolf's work because he had such great contempt for what he called "the psychological novel": one that emphasizes characters' thoughts, feelings and motives over plot.[9] Ayuso was also the first scholar to publish a critique of the sexist/gender normative tendencies in Borges's translations of *Orlando* and *A Room of One's Own*. In her assessment of his work she finds:

> When Borges translates literally and accurately, his voice is that of a purveyor of high culture responsible for transmitting, as transparently as he can, the ideas he received and so greatly admired. In this instance he positioned himself vis-à-vis Woolf's text almost as an absence. His presence is more clearly felt in the rendering of gender [in which] he adopts a critical masculine presence which sabotages the texts. (249)

In matters of overt acculturation of Woolf's work, Borges's intervention as a translator is fairly hard to see. However, in addition to the more visible manhandling of gender, Borges's rejection of the "psychological novel" is also

---

While Alberto Lázaro has found Marichalar to be an admirer of Woolf's work, it remains to be determined if this was a choice on the part of Ocampo or on the part of Borges (248-49). In her collaboration with the Buenos Aires publishing house Sudamericana, she also published *La señora Dalloway* (1939) in translation by Ernesto Palacio.

[9] Borges wrote in his introduction to Adolfo Bioy Casares' *The Invention of Morel*: "The typical psychological novel is formless. The Russians and their disciples have demonstrated, tediously, that no one is impossible: happy suicides, benevolent murderers, lovers who adore each other to the point of separation, informers who act out of fervor or humility.... In the end such complete freedom is tantamount to chaos. But the psychological novel would also be a 'realistic' novel, and have us forget that it is verbal artifice, for it uses each vain precision (or each languid obscurity) as new proof of verisimilitude" (243).

tangibly inscribed in his translations of Woolf, making the "absence" Ayuso notes particularly problematic. Sherry Simon argues that a feminist translation crucially affirms the translator's participation in the creation of meaning by drawing attention to her decision making process (29). Borges, by contrast, includes no footnotes, translator's note or theoretical discussion in either *Un cuarto propio* or *Orlando* to explain why, among other decisions, he chose actively to change the diegetic nature of Woolf's narrators in his translations.

In *La constelación del Sur*, a study on Sur's impact on Spanish language letters through its translation of foreign works, Patricia Willson finds physical evidence of Borges's well-known distaste for psychological narration in his translation of *Orlando:*

> By highlighting the intrusive nature of the narrator, Borges dismantles the syntactical structures often imposed by the notions "author" and "text," to create—within the English literary tradition—a new syntax which removes Virginia Woolf from the issue of psychological mimesis (154, my translation).

By breaking up run-on sentences, adding paragraph breaks and inserting colons, dashes and parentheses, Borges's translation of *Orlando* clearly marks the distinction between the narrator and the narrated action—covertly moving Woolf's narrative style from intradiegetic in English to extradiegetic in Spanish.[10] As we will see, the same narrative techniques Willson notes in *Orlando* characterize Borges's translation of *A Room* as well.

Transforming Woolf's "psychological" writing into a style of writing he found more artistically acceptable is a hallmark of Borges's translation aesthetic. Translation was a subject that intrigued the Argentine writer; translators, the act of translating and the reading of translated literature was a central theme in many of his critical and literary works. His non-fiction essays "Las dos maneras de traducir" ("The Two Ways to Translate," 1926), "Las versiones homéricas" ("The Homeric Versions," 1932) "Los traductores de las 1001 noches" ("The Translators of the 1001 Nights," 1935), and "Nota sobre el *Ulises* en español" ("Note regarding *Ulysses* in Spanish," 1946) demonstrate a clear and progressively developing theory regarding the art of literary translation. Laid out in detail in Efraín Kristal's *Invisible Work* and Sergio Waisman's *Borges and Translation*, his theory assumes that once a piece has been published, the intentions, rhetoric, personality, even the historical and cultural moment of the author cease to be of importance. The text belongs to the world of letters and will fulfill whatever function is required by the literary system in which it exists. Consequently, a translator is not bound by any

---

[10] For more on issues of gender in Borges's translation of *Orlando*, see Leah Leone, "La novela cautiva: Borges y la traducción de *Orlando.*" *Variaciones Borges* 25 (2008): 223-36; Mónica Ayuso, "The Unlike[ly] Other: Borges and Woolf."

ethic that obliges "fidelity" or "obedience" (two very problematic concepts in their own right[11]) to a text when translating. Rather, a translator should seek to fulfill the aesthetic potentialities of the source text, possibilities that existed but were not realized by the author. In his assessment of J.C. Madrus's translation of *The Thousand and One Nights* into French, for example, Borges praises the liberties the translator has taken with the text—finding them much more interesting than any notion of textual "fidelity": "his infidelity, his creative and felicitous infidelity, is what should concern us" ("Los traductores" 112, my translation).

If in Borges's opinion, "a translator should not be faithful to an imperfect text, but to a perfectable work" (Kristal 9), the "creative infidelities" this article will explore are, if not justifiable, at least consistent with his theoretical principles— what they say about what he found aesthetically pleasing is another story. His appropriation and re-working of texts in translation may even seem analogous to the practice of feminist translators like Susanne de Lotbinière-Harwood who "hijack" texts to make their translations explicitly feminist, bringing them in line with their own political aesthetic (von Flotow 78). A fundamental difference lies in the fact that feminist translators make themselves and their translation strategies visible in prefaces, footnotes and other paratext, while Borges's "invisible work" (to borrow a phrase from Kristal) may lead unwitting readers of *Un cuarto propio* to approach the text as if it were a mimetic copy of *A Room of One's Own*. Lawrence Venuti describes the "absence" noted by Ayuso as "fluent" translation strategy, which "produces the effect of transparency, whereby the translated text is taken to represent the foreign author's personality or intention or the essential meaning" of her text without the intervention of a third party (187). As a result of this "absence," Spanish language readers may engage with *Un cuarto propio* as if they were engaging with Woolf herself, free from the results of Borges's interpretative choices—which may or may not have been conscious acts of sabotage. As Venuti argues,

> the activity of the translator, and that of the foreign author as well, is shaped by social determinations of which they may or may not be aware, linguistic, literary and historical materials which constitute their texts and may very well be beyond their intentions. (196)

It is precisely because of this "provisionality of meaning"—the ubiquitous possibilities for (un)consciously determined interpretations—that feminist translators make their presence in the text visible (Simon 29). Their visibility paradoxically allows readers a clearer view by reminding them that the translated

---

[11] For more about the problematic conflation and positioning of women and translations as inherently inferior see Lori Chamberlain, "Gender and the Metaphorics of Translation." *Rethinking Translation*. Lawrence Venuti, ed. London: Routledge, 1992. 57-74.

text is a creative product that has moved beyond parameters of the language, culture and, in some cases, the ideology of the author.

Correspondingly, to Willson's observation of Borges's dismantling of Woolf's syntax, I would add a critical consideration of how his strategy affects the text's entire rhetorical structure. Much more than literary preferences are at play here. Borges not only subverted the "psychological" aspects of *A Room of One's Own* and *Orlando*, but inverted one of the text's most salient thematic expressions. Part of what makes Woolf's writing so innovative is her linking the syntax of her writings with her concept of a feminine experience of the physical world. In fact, Gilbert and Gubar argue that Virginia Woolf should be considered "the mother of all contemporary feminist linguistic theory" due precisely to the syntax and structures she employs (522).

A Room of One's Own is based on two papers Woolf read at the Arts Society at Newnham College, and the Odtaa at Girton College in the fall of 1928. Written in the form of a lecture, the text is marked by a sense of orality, as if it were given aloud. The essay is intimate, informal, and interacts with its audience. In beginning her lecture, Woolf advises the attendees at her talk that she will be unable "to hand you after an hour's discourse a nugget of pure truth to wrap up between the pages of your notebooks and keep on the mantel-piece forever" (4). Truth (meaning) is so elusive and so subjective, "one cannot hope to tell the truth. One can only show how one came to hold whatever opinion one does hold" (4). *A Room of One's Own* intends to communicate the opinions it holds not only through the semantic value of Woolf's words, but through the essay's syntax itself.

Julie Vandivere argues that Woolf's linguistic style functions as a rhetorical statement whose interpretation "requires close, careful scrutiny of how her irregular phraseology and her pairing and multiplying of subjects, verbs, tense, and moods challenge reality, subjectivity, and hegemony" (231). To ignore these aspects of the text is to miss how the themes of *A Room of One's Own* and the style in which it was written are mutually dependent; Woolf's intention of demonstrating the manner in which she has arrived at her own conclusions is the basis for the essay's linguistic construction. Consistent with Gilbert and Gubar's assertion, Christiane Bimberg suggests, "The gaps, jumps, interruptions, retrospectives, repetitions, narrative 'inconsistencies' etc. are accepted by her as necessary steps on the way to tentative conclusions (6). Indeed, the principal argument of Woolf's text is that, since they have had no room of their own—leading to countless interruptions—women throughout the centuries have faced serious obstacles in the creation of literature. The countless, often apparently arbitrary interruptions of the narration are Woolf's strategic textual evidence of her point. Borges's "editing" of *A Room of One's Own*'s narrative style blocks Spanish-language readers' access to Woolf's innovative mode of synthesis for her feminist arguments. Much of the narration's intentional arbitrariness, and consequently, its rhetorical function, were lost through Borges's impulse to make the translation more coherent.[12]

Consistent with what Willson noted in *Orlando*, in his translation of *A Room of One's Own*, Borges breaks long paragraphs into more digestible pieces without consideration of the textual effect they produce, and puts the narrator's unmarked interjections in parentheses or quotation. For example, in keeping with the text's tight correspondence between physical motion and the act of writing the narrator muses: "But why, I continued, moving on towards Headingley, have we stopped humming under our breath at luncheon parties?" (15). Borges puts an abrupt stop to the slightest meandering of the line and visibly marks a distinction between the narrated action and the narrator's thoughts: "¿Pero por qué, (proseguí yo, caminando hacia Headingley) hemos dejado de tarear *sotto voce* en los almuerzos y fiestas?" (17). (That Borges employs the Italian *sotto voce* to translate "under our breath" also alters the register of the passage.) In addition, Borges often highlights the narrator's significant points by restructuring the sentence, subordinating those arguments to the end of the sentence and prefacing them with a colon. "All this should be discussed and discovered; all this is part of the question of women and fiction" (77) becomes "Todo esto debe ser discutido y descubierto; todo esto es parte del problema: las mujeres y la novela" (70). (It is also noteworthy that Borges uses the word "problema" rather than the cognate "cuestión.")

There is a constant tendency on the part of Borges to "fix" the textual ramifications of Woolf's poetics of disjointedness and interruption. Mary Beton's explanation of her relief over no longer having to work since inheriting her aunt's fortune provides an excellent case in point:

> To begin with, always to be doing work that one did not wish to do, and to do it like a slave, flattering and fawning, not always necessarily perhaps, but it seemed necessary and the stakes were too great to run risks; and then the thought of that one gift which it was death to hide—a small one but dear to the possessor—perishing and with it myself, my soul—all this became like a rust eating away at the bloom

---

[12] The intended effect of the text's grammatical manipulation and meandering plot was not lost on Borges alone. In a 1928 review of *A Room of One's Own*, Woolf's literary rival Arnold Bennett critiques her "private notions about grammar" (258) and goes so far as to claim, "Virginia Woolf's thesis is not apparently important to her, since she talks about everything but the thesis. If her mind was not what it is I should accuse her of wholesale padding. This would be unjust. She is not guilty of padding. She is merely the victim of her extraordinary gift of fancy (not imagination). If I had to make one of those brilliant generalisations now so fashionable, defining the difference between men and women, I should say that whereas a woman cannot walk through a meadow in June without wandering all over the place to pick attractive blossoms, a man can. Virginia Woolf cannot resist the floral enticement" (259).

of the spring, destroying the tree at its heart. However, as I say, my aunt died... (37).

Woolf's syntax is unruly; her rambling interjections interrupt her own linear discourse. Borges was compelled to repair the broken syntax, the run-on sentences and arbitrary interjections—key parts of the text's rhetorical strategy.

> El hecho inicial de estar continuamente haciendo algo que a uno no le gusta y de hacerlo como un esclavo, con acompañamiento de lisonjas y adulaciones, quizás no imprescindibles, pero a mí me lo parecían y no quería correr ningún riesgo; y el pensamiento de aquel don solitario cuya ocultación comporta la muerte —un don pequeño pero caro a su poseedor— pereciendo y mi alma con él; todo eso era como una herrumbre devorando la frescura de la primavera, destruyendo el corazón del árbol. Sin embargo, como les estaba diciendo, murió mi tía... (35)[13]

Less disjointed and sporadic, Borges's text has smooth transitions, and clearly defined subjects. The first three fragments are subsumed into one, eliminating the jumpy sensation one derives from the English. The verbs "flattering" and "fawning" are turned into nouns which "accompany" the undesirable labor. In the second clause Borges avoids repeating terms by making the passive voice active, adding "me" where there was no object in the English text. The fact that the stakes were too high to avoid flattery, that Mary Beton had something to lose, is lost in Spanish, where she simply didn't want to "run the risk." Apart from the actual syntax of the passage, which exemplifies his translation strategy throughout the essay, Borges's choice for translating "slave" is also problematic. Despite the fact that a woman is narrating, he chooses "esclavo" rather than "esclava." By generalizing the term to the masculine, Borges reduces the force of her statement, negating her claim that women in particular have had to work like slaves. Similarly, Borges uses "poseedor" rather than the feminine "poseedora" when referring the possessor of the gift of writing. This neutralization or masculinization of undetermined or even specifically female referents characterizes Borges's translation from the very first page.

To further analyze Borges's grammatical shifts of gender I turn to *A Room of One's Own*'s famous opening line: "But, you may say, we asked you to speak

---

[13] Translated back:
> The initial fact of continually doing what one doesn't like and doing it like a slave, along with flattery and praise, perhaps not indispensable, but they seemed so to me and I didn't want to run any risk; and the thought of that solitary gift which is like death to hide—a small gift but valuable to its possessor—perishing and my soul with it; all of this was like a rust devouring the freshness of spring, destroying the heart of the tree. However, as I was telling you, my aunt died;...

about women and fiction—what has that got to do with a room of one's own?" (1). In Spanish, the first person plural "we" is a gendered pronoun: it is "nosotras" if the members of the group are all women and "nosotros" if the members are all male or if the group is mixed. The linguistic power of the masculine is such that even in a group of one hundred women and one man, the group would still refer to itself to as "nosotros." We know from Woolf's frequent interaction with her audience that it is entirely female. In Chapter Two, when discussing her research on women and poverty, she asks her audience, "Are you aware that you are, perhaps, the most discussed animal in the universe?" (26). And in Chapter Five she invokes Radclyffe Hall's recent obscenity trial, asking "Are there no men present? Do you promise me that behind that red curtain over there the figure of Sir Chartres Biron is not concealed?" (80). Despite their obvious absence from the text, Borges seems to find himself to be that single man added to the group who tips the linguistic scales. He translates: "Pero, dirán ustedes, *nosotros* le pedimos que hablara sobre las mujeres y la novela—¿qué tendrá eso que ver con un cuarto propio?" (7, my emphasis). In a more neutral approach, as Spanish verbs are synthetic, able to indicate the subject through the verb ending, Borges could have avoided any indication of the audience's gender by simply leaving off the term for *we*, "le pedimos que hablara..."

The very fact that *A Room of One's Own* deals primarily with issues of women and writing seems to come into conflict with Borges's own sense of narrative authority. Despite his tendency for self-effacement, he was often unforgiving in his criticism of other authors. In the Argentine periodical *El Hogar* of October 1936, Borges had the following to say about Virginia Woolf herself: "She is the daughter of Mr. Leslie Stephen, editor of the biographies of Swift, Jonson and Hobbes, books whose value lies in the clarity of their prose and the precision of their facts, and that they make little attempt at analysis and never any invention" ("Virginia Woolf" 122, my translation). This description was, of course, in satirical contrast with Woolf's fictional biography *Orlando*. In the same article, Borges obliquely questions the value and validity of Woolf's work because it was self-published by the Hogarth Press: "In 1912, Virginia Stephen married Mr. Leonard Woolf and the two acquired a press. They were attracted by typography, literature's occasionally traitorous accomplice, and they wrote and edited their own texts" (122-23, my translation). Skepticism about Woolf and women's writing in general appears to manifest itself in his translation through consistent subversion of their work and their intelligence, often in the form of subtle shifts in vocabulary.

When considering all of the new books being published by women, Woolf writes: "There are books on all sorts of subjects which a generation ago no woman could have touched" (78). In Spanish, however, it becomes not a question of women being allowed to write on a certain subject ("pudiera haber tocado" or "hubiera podido tocar"), but, rather, they were simply not motivated to write about traditionally non-feminine subjects—those that no woman "could have touched" become subjects that no woman "would have garnered the enthusiasm to take on": "Hay libros sobre todos los temas que ninguna mujer de la generación anterior se *hubiera animado a abordar*" (71, my emphasis). Woolf's allegory about Judith Shakespeare exemplifies her point that women were not permitted to write, despite their genuine interest or ability. As her miserable fate makes clear, contrary to the implications of the translation, she was indeed driven to write to the point of sacrificing her family and security.

Consistent with Borges's choice of terms, he also employs phrasing that transforms women from gifted to merely aspiring to write. When describing Judith Shakespeare's choice to abandon her home, Woolf indicates: "The force of her own gift alone drove her to it" (47). "Gift" refers to an innate quality, rather than one that entails labor to acquire. Yet instead of the word "don" which is the direct translation of "gift," Borges translated: "La fuerza de su *vocación* la impulsó" (44, my emphasis). "Vocation" implies a natural inclination, but not necessarily a successful fulfillment of that leaning. As is demonstrated above in his translation of Mary Beton's story about her inheritance, Borges does translate "gift" as "don" in other parts of the essay, suggesting this may have been a motivated decision on his part. He makes a similar decision on the next page: "yet," the narrator adds, "her genius was for fiction and lusted to feed abundantly upon the lives of men and women and the study of their ways" (48). Similar to "gift," "genius" refers to a quality one is born with, rather than a characteristic one must work for; it connotes a near-perfect ability to use one's gift. Borges once more divorces women writers from their natural talent: "Sin embargo, su *inclinación* era novelística y requería alimentarse infinitamente de vidas de hombres y de mujeres y del estudio de sus modos de ser" (44, my emphasis). Here, Judith's "genius for fiction" has been transformed to her "novelistic inclination," a choice of words which masks the crucial parallel of Woolf's argument: that Judith's talent was equal to that of her brother.

Borges's substitution of "fiction" for "novel" reinforces a notion Woolf seeks to dismantle with her essay—that women can only write novels. Woolf frequently employs the term "fiction" in her text; curiously, Borges never once uses the Spanish cognate, "ficción."[14] Rather, he uses "literature," "the novel," and even "fable." In his translation, the opening line of *Un cuarto propio* reads: "we asked you to speak about women and the novel" (7, my translation), instead of "women

[14] Coincidentally, his most famous compilation of short stories is called *Ficciones* (1944). While one may argue that the term "la ficción" might have seemed more awkward than "la novela," in one story from the anthology—"El jardín de senderos que se bifurcan"— Borges employs "las ficciones" as a generalized term with a connotation very much like that of Woolf (574 and 575).

and fiction" as it does in English. Problematically, the substitution of "novel" works directly against Woolf's famous claim that "a woman must have money and a room of her own if she is to write fiction."

Chapter Four of the essay is an inquiry into why almost all literature by women is written in the form of the novel. As women were forced to write without privacy in the common sitting-room, subject to frequent interruptions and often compelled to hide their work, Woolf finds, "it would be easier to write prose and fiction there than to write poetry or a play" (66). She also determines that having little legacy of their own, writers such as Jane Austen found "the novel alone was young enough to be soft in her hands" (76). But with a room of one's own, Woolf questions whether even the novel will remain "rightly shaped" for women's use. "No doubt we shall find her knocking that into shape for herself when she has the free use of her limbs; and providing some new vehicle, not necessarily in verse, for the poetry in her" (76). Consequently, when Borges translates, "para escribir *novelas*, una mujer debe tener dinero y un cuarto propio" he is specifically limiting women writers to the very form Woolf seeks to explode (7, my emphasis). One may concede that Woolf primarily uses the term "fiction" when talking about women and writing (as the theme of her talk indicates), rather than poetry or drama. Yet when we take into consideration her anticipation of a new genre for women writers that is both fictional and poetic, the specificity of Borges's "novela" still problematically limits Woolf's greater-encompassing "fiction."

In her own form of genre bending, Woolf deflates the importance of the author/narrator by using "one" instead of "I" and claiming, "call me Mary Beton, Mary Seton, Mary Carmichael or by any name you please—it is not a matter of any importance" (5). Reversing her strategy—perhaps to avoid a proliferation of feminine articles—Borges consistently translates "one" as "yo" (I) or "nosotros" (we, masculine). The anonymity of Woolf's line, "if by good luck there had been an ash-tray handy, if one had not knocked the ash out of the window in default… one would not have seen, presumably, a cat without a tail," is voided with Borges's imposition of the first person (11). Rather, Borges converts "one" into "I" and "me": "Si la casualidad *me* hubiera deparado un cenicero, si a falta de cenicero no hubiera tirado la ceniza por la ventana…*yo* verosímilmente no hubiera visto un gato sin cola" (14, my emphasis). In reference to facts, Woolf often opted for "one" rather than "I," perhaps to emphasize their objectivity. At the British Museum, for example, overcome by the proliferation of queries her research generated, she laments: "But one needed answers, not questions" (25). Yet in Spanish, it was she herself rather than people in general who needed answers: "Pero *yo* precisaba contestaciones, no preguntas" (25, my emphasis). Through her technique of using the third person, Woolf sought to avoid the problems of Mr. A's novel, in which "a shadow seemed to lie across the page. It was a straight dark bar...something like the letter 'I'" (98). Borges's translation strategy, however, revives the translator as that "I," casting his own shadow across the page. His insistence on grammatical normativization, whether conscious or unconscious have, quite like Mr. A, blocked our view of what lies behind them—in this case, an innovative style for undermining impositions of patriarchal authority.

While negating the exclusivity of first-person pronouns, Woolf did employ other means to assert her authority as both a writer and a critic. Despite her claim to have no university training, Woolf quotes or refers to numerous authors and journalists who have been writing in Europe from the sixteenth century on. At times her references are oblique, and only a well-educated reader would be able to pick them out, while at others she not only quotes an author but includes a footnote with the bibliographical information from which she is citing—most often when the author under scrutiny has a misogynist message that Woolf seeks to expose.

As will especially be noted in *Three Guineas*,[15] footnotes serve to establish the author's credibility by letting the reader know she is aware of and has read outside sources that contribute to the dialogue she is putting forth; they show her adeptness for the subject at hand. And most importantly, they provide her readers the references they may use to find this information for themselves, either to learn more about the matter or simply to see that she is indeed a credible author. Borges pilfers Woolf's (inter)textual authority by eliminating nine of her twelve footnotes in *Un cuarto propio*. It seems difficult to concede that this choice was for aesthetic reasons rather than through simple disregard of Woolf's authority, because he did include certain references (Boswell, Frazer and Davies), and when dealing with the poetry cited in *A Room*, Borges left it in English and included a translation of the poems specifically as footnotes.[16]

Woolf's extratextual reference was an additional way to "show how one came to hold whatever opinion she does hold" (4)—specifically, the feminist sentiment that women could function as authorities on a given subject. Feminism was a hotly debated concept in Britain at the time of *A Room*'s publication. A decade later, in Argentina, the situation was much the same. After decades of a strong feminist presence in the nation, a bill proposing women's suffrage finally passed the Chamber of Deputies and made it before the Senate in 1932. A growing backlash against feminism during the 1930s resulted in this historic bill being shelved, never making it to the floor for debate. In 1936—the year Victoria Ocampo published Borges's translation of *A Room*—proposals were made to reform the Civil Code

[15] See Vara Neverow and Merry Pawlowski. "Preliminary Bibliographic Guide to the Footnotes of *Three Guineas*." *Woolf Studies Annual* 3 (1997). 170-210.

[16] In the essay's first publication in the journal *Sur*, none of Woolf's notes appeared, nor were there any translations of the English language poetry. Spanish translations in the form of footnotes and three of Woolf's original citations were added for the publication as a book.

and rescind many of the rights women had already won. In addition to publishing the translation of *Un cuarto propio*, Lavrín notes that during this period, Ocampo made a "fleeting intervention in the feminist cause" with the publication of several articles denouncing various bills that proposed increased limitations to women's rights (283). While Borges, on the other hand, did not publish any commentary either for or against the feminist movement, his translation strategy for the very term "feminist" may be indicative of his position.

Mocking the threat men felt from feminism, Woolf describes how shocking they found women's disapproval:

> Does it explain my astonishment of the other day when Z, most humane, most modest of men, taking up some book by Rebecca West and reading a passage in it exclaimed "The arrant feminist! She says that men are snobs!" The exclamation, to me so surprising—for why was Miss West an arrant feminist for making a possibly true if uncomplimentary statement about the other sex? (35).

The word feminist has a qualifier, "arrant," which Woolf uses throughout the essay. In Borges's translation, the elimination of that qualifier gives the passage an entirely new connotation:

> ¿Sirve para explicar mi asombro del otro día cuando Z, el más comprensivo y modesto de los hombres, tomó un libro de Rebecca West y exclamó: '*¡Qué feminista!* ¡dice que todos los hombres son snobs¡' Esa exclamación sorprendente — ¿pues qué tenía *de feminista* Miss West al formular una declaración quizá verdadera, aunque algo descortés, sobre el otro sexo?" (33, my emphasis).

Rather than an "arrant feminist," Z says of Miss West: "What a feminist![17] She says all men are snobs!" while the narrator inquires, "what is so feminist about Miss West...?" In both versions, Z disparages feminists; without the qualifier, however, the irony of the remark is annulled. "Feminist" and the claim that all men are snobs become synonymous, and being feminist becomes inherently reprehensible. Later in the text, Woolf refers back to her comment, "Men, of course, are not snobs, I continued, carefully eschewing the 'arrant feminism' of Miss Rebecca West" (57). This time, however, Borges does provide a qualifier—though not exactly accurate: "Los hombres, por supuesto, no son snobs, proseguí, evitando cuidadosamente 'el feminismo *notorio*' de Miss Rebecca West" (53,

---

[17] An alternative translation of the Spanish "¡Qué feminista!" could also be "How feminist!"

my emphasis). While "arrant" refers specifically to Miss West, "notorious" also brings in the opinion of the public who unquestioningly censure feminism.

While his strategy appears to categorically define Borges's disapproval of feminism, many critics are quick to cite an interview with Oswaldo Ferrari in which Borges calls himself "feminista." In the same interview, he mentions his reluctance to translate Woolf, and, perhaps to distance himself from the text, alleges that his mother actually translated *A Room of One's Own* while he merely revised it. Since, he claims, he was already a feminist, convinced of the essay's message, the text was of little interest to him (Borges and Ferrari 12).[18] The diary of Borges's closest friend and collaborator, Adolfo Bioy Casares, provides another picture. Published posthumously in 2006, the immense volume details the writers' almost daily interaction. As late as 1968, Borges's opinion of women appears decidedly anti-feminist. Discussing among male friends the issue of women and Sir Thomas Browne's lamentation that human beings cannot procreate the way trees do, Borges stated "I don't believe that is where women's defect lies [their genitals]. It's in their brains." He added, "Samuel Johnson was right when he said that if a woman preached, one shouldn't praise her for doing it well, but for doing it at all, as one would for a dog who stands [sic] on his back legs" (Bioy Casares 1256, my translation). The irony will not escape a reader of *A Room of One's Own* that Woolf uses this very quote by Johnson to illustrate how women are not taken seriously as composers of music.

Borges's semantic choices such as "vocación" for a woman's "gift" and "inclinación" for her "genius" would appear to point toward a personal opinion that the problem with women did indeed lie with "their brains." It is of little surprise, then, that in the most telling case of mistranslation, Borges dispossesses the narrator of her most valuable possession, her power of thought. A famous line

---

[18] As a scholar, I do not put much credence into Borges's statements regarding his mother and translation; in his autobiographical essay he claims his mother not only translated Woolf but also other important authors whose translations are attributed to him, such as Faulkner and Melville. Yet later in the text he describes working on these same authors' translations during the weekends while he worked at the Biblioteca Nacional (*Ensayo autobiográfico* 14, 77). Borges similarly contradicts himself in a public interview with his English translator Thomas di Giovanni when he claims first that his mother did the translations while he revised them, and immediately reverses and says he did the translations while she revised them (Christ 407). Emir Rodríguez Monegal might come closest to truth when he writes: "A lapse in memory, a friendly hoax, a filial accolade? It is hard to say. Probably Mother helped him with those translations. She may have even done the first draft. But the Spanish style is so unmistakably Borgesian that it would have taken Mother years of hard labor to be able to imitate it" (293).

of the essay reads: "Lock up your libraries if you like; but there is no gate, no lock, no bolt that you can set upon the freedom of my mind" (75). This challenging cry is smoothed over, the authoritative "mind" is replaced by the airy and feminine "spirit": "Cierren sus bibliotecas si quieren; pero no hay puertas, ni cerradura, ni cerrojo que cierre la libertad de mi *espíritu*" (68, my emphasis). Borges's translation seems to be ushering the angel back into the house.

Even as Woolf satirizes the kind of peroration whose exhortations to be higher and more spiritual she will leave "to the other sex," Borges's choice in language blindly affirms the restrictive roles past which she is trying to push her audience. His translation of her declaration, "When I rummage in my own mind I find no noble sentiments about being companions and equals and influencing the world to higher ends" (109) again inscribes a transformation of Woolf's mind into her spirit: "Al revolver mi propio *espíritu* no encuentro el sentimiento noble de que todos [sic] somos compañeras e iguales y debemos encaminar el mundo a fines más altos" (98, my emphasis).

Unlike the many other occasions when Borges opts to masculinize terms of indeterminate gender, here he translates "companions" as "compañeras" rather than the general/masculine "compañeros." It is interesting that Borges includes the word "todos," as in "we are all companions and equals," when it wasn't present in the English, not least because the combination of male and female suffixes in reference to the same object, "tod*os* somos compañer*as*," is grammatically incorrect. It could potentially be used as a neologism to create gender ambiguity, but in other editions (UNAM Editorial) the phrase has been edited to read the specifically feminine "tod*as* somos compañer*as*" (194). Given Borges's tendency to eliminate gender ambiguity, this non-correspondence may likely be an error. Were it in recognition of the fact that "companions and equals" could refer to both women and men, all previous indications point to him choosing the male default. A possibility may be that Borges was trying to capture the universality of "all" but make it grammatically impossible for women and men to be companions and equals through the exclusivity of the feminine noun ending, "-as," whereby companionship and equality could exist only among women. In any case, upon arriving at the peroration, Borges seems finally to have realized that the audience being addressed is comprised solely of women; like the exclusive "compañeras," he translates Woolf's admonition to "be oneself" as "ser una misma," not "ser uno mismo." This was not enough, however, to make him go back and correct the first five chapters.

With the mind/spirit question, Borges could not have been mistranslating accidentally. On the contrary, he quite effectively manages to imprint his beliefs onto the text, as he makes a perfectly accurate translation of the term within the same chapter: "Still you may say that the mind should rise above such things"

(105). Here, "mind" becomes "intelligence": "Pueden sin embargo decir que la *inteligencia* debe sobreponerse a estas cosas" (94, my emphasis). It would seem that mind only becomes spirit when it is a woman who is speaking or being discussed. William Shakespeare, on the other hand, is allowed his own mind. But the fact that it is of "the androgynous, of the man-womanly mind" (97) appears to make the translator uncomfortable as well. Borges reduces the number of adjectives describing Shakespeare's mind to one: "inteligencia andrógina" (88). As I have written elsewhere (see n. 10), Borges has a tendency to eliminate gender ambiguity in a text by either assigning a subject a gender or by eliminating non-normative language altogether. One can only speculate about the reasons behind his translations' unyielding disapproval of feminism, of women writers and of gender ambiguity. It must be deceptively simple to entertain Woolf's suggestion that "possibly when the professor insisted a little too emphatically upon the inferiority of women, he was concerned not with their inferiority, but with his own superiority" (34)

Borges is correct in affirming that a text, once published, takes on a life of its own. As an English language text, *A Room of One's Own* has come under intense scrutiny by feminists. As Gubar writes in her introduction to the 2005 annotated edition of *A Room of One's Own*:

> while Woolf has been attacked as too angry in her caricaturing of men, she has concomitantly been chastened for being fearful of rage, put off by the all too justifiable rancor of her female predecessors. Similarly, she has been denounced both for inflating and for deflating women's cultural achievements. Although praised as quasi-Marxist in her materialism, she has been trounced for an elitism inculcated by her relatively privileged background. Heralded as an anti-imperialist, critical of England and Empire...she nevertheless has been taken to task as a racist, unconscious of her biases about third-world societies and people of color. (lviii)

These critiques, however, have been about a work that has been permitted to speak for itself. If, as Borges argues, texts are to be permitted to fulfill whatever function the reading public requires, his translation is not living up to its duty. *Un cuarto propio* is being read in Spanish as a feminist text, but much of what distinguishes it within the feminist canon is missing. To advance the important debates currently being generated by the essay, one must have access to a responsible representation of what the text actually says and the manner in which it was expressed in English.

Due to the limited availability of alternative Spanish translations of *A Room of One's Own*, my access has been exclusively to the Cuarto Propio edition by Moure and Moreno, and to personal correspondence with the A-Z edition's translator, Gambolini. Moure and Moreno have published no information about their choice to adapt Borges's translation, as opposed to creating their own, or about what they found problematic with his version. In their adaptation, I have found problems quite similar to those of the Borges translation: "nosotros" for "we" instead of "nosotras"; "novela" for "fiction" instead of "ficción"; "espíritu" for "mind" instead of "inteligencia" or "mente." Nor does the syntax change to more closely match the techniques employed by Woolf. And the text has eliminated all of Woolf's footnotes. Moure and Moreno appear to be more concerned with updating vocabulary for current usage than with "fixing" any mishandling of gender on the part of Borges. One hopes that other translations, particularly that by Horas y Horas, make a more responsible feminist rendering of *A Room of One's Own*, and that a feminist translation soon becomes widely available.

At the same time, part of Borges's translation's "life of its own" is the fact that it embodies a concrete act of anti-feminism. It is not an exaggeration to state that the damage already done by Borges's translation is incalculable. Yet despite his subversive intervention, the feminist message contained within *Un cuarto propio* has made its mark on generations of Spanish language readers. Translation has always called the role of the author/authority into question, but the curious position of Borges's translation as both a feminist and inherently anti-feminist work provides a unique case of textual resistance in action. Even as Borges sabotages the essay through edited syntax, semantic glass ceilings and blatant omissions, Woolf's authority as a leading feminist writer has somehow remained intact. The fact that a translator should be compelled to dismantle the feminist foundations of *A Room of One's Own* effectively functions as a meta-commentary on the same assertions Woolf seeks to prove with her essay. In his process of translation, Borges is demonstrating precisely the patriarchal obstacles outlined by Woolf that long kept women from producing literature. Viewed as such, Borges adds a potentially useful layer to Woolf's text. The Spanish language reader who is alerted to the embattled nature of *Un cuarto propio* would be in a position to benefit from the problems of his translation. Namely, an annotated edition of Borges's *Un cuarto propio* would be of immeasurable use; it could expose the translation's numerous subversions of Woolf's text and provide more appropriate/accurate phrasing, along with an explanation of how the Borges version is in conflict with the English. Readers would gain access both to the problematic aspects of Borges's decision-making process, as well as the feminist-oriented choices of the editor/translator who offers alternatives. Using the anti-feminist techniques of Borges's translation as a way to comment upon and advance the feminist message of the text itself would offer more than poetic justice. The visible demonstration of how language can function as a tool for both undermining and reclaiming feminist poetics and aesthetics would function as a testament to the power of Woolf's message in *A Room of One's Own*.

Works Cited

Ayuso, Mónica G. "The Unlike[ly] Other: Borges and Woolf." *Woolf Studies Annual* 10 (2004): 241-51.

———. "Virginia Woolf in Mexico and Puerto Rico." *Woolf Studies Annual* 14 (2008): 1-19.

Bennett, Arnold. "Queen of the High-Brows." *Virginia Woolf: The Critical Heritage*. Ed. Robin Majumdar and Allen McLaurin. London: Routledge, 1997. 258-60.

Bimberg, Christiane. "The Poetics of Conversation in Virginia Woolf's *A Room of One's Own*: Constructed Arbitrariness and Thoughtful Impressionism." *Connotations* 11.1 (2001): 1-28.

Bioy Casares, Adolfo. *Borges*. Ed. Daniel Martino. Barcelona: Destino, 2006.

Borges, Jorge Luis. "Adolfo Bioy Casares, The Invention of Morel." Trans. Suzanne Jill Levine. *Selected Non-Fictions*. Ed. Eliot Weinberger. New York: Penguin, 1999. 243-44.

———. "El jardín de senderos que se bifurcan."*Obras completas*. Vol. 1. Buenos Aires: Emecé, 2007. 567-77.

———. "The Superstitious Ethics of the Reader." Trans. Suzanne Jill Levine *Selected Non-Fictions*. Ed. Eliot Weinberger. New York: Penguin, 1999. 52-55.

———. *Un ensayo autobiográfico*. Barcelona: Galáxia Gutenberg, 1999.

———. "Virginia Woolf: una biografía sintética." *Ficcionario*. Ed. Emir Rodríguez Monegal. México D.F.: Fondo de Cultura Económica, 1981. 122-123.

———and Oswaldo Ferrari. *En diálogo II: edición definitiva*. Buenos Aires: Siglo XXI, 2005.

Christ, Ronald. "Borges at N.Y.U." *Prose for Borges*. Ed. Charles Newman and Mary Kinzie. Evanston: Northwestern UP, 1974. 396-411.

Gambolini, Gerardo. "Saludos y preguntas sobre *Un cuarto propio*." E-mail to the author. 22 Dec. 2008.

Gilbert, Sandra M. and Susan Gubar. "Sexual Linguistics: Gender, Language, Sexuality." *New Literary History*, 16.3 (1985). 515-43.

Gubar, Susan. "Introduction." Virginia Woolf, *A Room of One's Own*. Orlando: Harcourt Inc., 2005. xxxv-lxi.

King, John. *Sur: A Study of The Argentine Literary Journal and Its Role In The Development of a Culture*. New York: Cambridge UP, 1986.

Kristal, Efraín. *Invisible Work: Borges and Translation*. Nashville: Vanderbilt UP, 2002.

Lavrín, Asunción. *Women, Feminism, and Social Change in Argentina, Chile, and Uruguay, 1890-1940.* Lincoln: U of Nebraska P, 1998.

Lázaro, Alberto. "The Emerging Voice: A Review of Spanish Scholarship on Virginia Woolf." *The Reception of Virginia Woolf in Europe.* Eds. Mary Ann Caws and Nicola Luckhurst. London: Continuum, 2002. 247-262.

Lojo Rodríguez, Laura Maria. "'A gaping mouth but no words': Virginia Woolf Enters the Land of the Butterflies." *The Reception of Virginia Woolf in Europe.* Eds. Mary Ann Caws and Nicola Luckhurst. London: Continuum, 2002. 218-46.

Monegal, Emir Rodríguez. *Jorge Luis Borges, A Literary Biography.* New York: E.P. Dutton, 1978.

Morris, Adalaide. "First Persons Plural in Contemporary Feminist Fiction." *Tulsa Studies in Women's Literature* 11.1 (1992): 11-29.

Rodriquez Monegal, Emir. "Novedad y Anacronismo De Cien Años De Soledad." *Revista Nacional de Cultura* 185 (1968). 3-21.

Serur, Raquel. "La hermana de Shakespeare." Introduction to Virginia Woolf, *Un cuarto propio.* Jorge Luís Borges, Trans. México City: UNAM, 2006.

Simon, Sherry. *Gender in Translation: Cultural Identity and the Politics of Transmission.* London: Routledge, 1996.

Vandivere, Julie. "Waves and Fragments: Linguistic Construction as Subject Formation in Virginia Woolf." *Twentieth Century Literature* 42.2 (1996). 221-33.

Venuti, Lawrence. "Introduction." *Rethinking Translation: Discourse, Subjectivity, Ideology.* Ed. Lawrence Venuti. New York: Routledge, 1992. 1-17.

von Flotow, Louise. "Feminist Translation: Contexts, Practices and Theories." *TTR* 4.2 (1991). 69-84.

Waisman, Sergio Gabriel. *Borges and Translation: The Irreverence of the Periphery.* Lewisburg: Bucknell UP, 2005.

Willson, Patricia. *La constelación del Sur: traductores y traducciones en la literatura argentina del siglo XX.* Buenos Aires: Siglo XXI, 2005.

Woolf, Virginia. *A Room of One's Own.* Annotated and with an introduction by Susan Gubar. Orlando: Harcourt Inc., 2005.

———. *Un cuarto propio.* Jorge Luís Borges, Trans. México City: Colofón, 1986.

———. *Un cuarto propio.* Jorge Luís Borges, Trans. México City: UNAM, 2006.

———. *Un cuarto propio.* Trans. Eduardo Moure and Marisol Moreno. Santiago de Chile: Cuarto propio, 1993.

Animal Life and Human Sacrifice in Virginia Woolf's *Between the Acts*[1]

Vicki Tromanhauser

For the local villagers in *Between the Acts*, tormented by their dread of the coming war—"The doom of sudden death hanging over us" (70)—the annual pageant play and its depiction of scenes from English history offer a welcome relief from their present reality in June 1939. Like Mrs. Manresa and William Dodge, who are "lured off the high road by the very same instinct that caused the sheep and cows to desire propinquity," the villagers flock to the country house of Pointz Hall where the pageant is to be held (25). Having surveyed the grounds of Pointz Hall earlier that year, the pageant's director Miss La Trobe staked out the perfect site for her stage in a grassy terrace or "stretch of high ground" that "Nature had provided" (9). The natural stage drops off into a field where cows bellow and swallows dart between the trees, so that as the villagers take their seats on the lawn to watch their history play out, "The very cows joined in. Walloping, tail lashing, the reticence of nature was undone, and the barriers which should divide Man the Master from the Brute were dissolved" (109). In placing her theater outside, La Trobe shows the distinction between human mastery and animal nature to be illusory. Gazing past the actors onto grazing cows and darting swallows, the village audience loses its stretch of cultural "high ground" and encounters the prospect of humanity joining the herd.

In the face of imminent German invasion and cultural obsolescence, La Trobe's pageant, like the novel itself, confronts its audience with the question of how the human species understands its life and the limits of its qualitative difference from its animal neighbors. La Trobe's parodic production of England's past begins to tell against a concept of cultural identity as necessarily grounded in hierarchies of class, gender, and species: commoners are cast in the roles of monarchs and other prominent national figures; costume and style replace monumental events as markers of period; the Grand Ensemble and its homage to the imperial army are silently dropped; and the cows take their part in the choral song. For Woolf the coming war was not simply about geographical or national borders, but about the borders of the kind of life that is to be considered properly cultural, and thus inscribed within history's pageant, and the kind of life that must be purged, or even sacrificed, from its midst.

---

[1] I would like to thank Mark Hussey and the anonymous readers at *Woolf Studies Annual* for their encouragement and helpful comments on this article.

Between the Acts stands at the threshold of the demystification and exposure of sacrifice in the mass exterminations of the Second World War.[2] If the act of substitution at the root of the sacrificial transaction entails the exchange of an animal, such as the original scapegoat, for a human victim, Woolf's last novel asks: what happens to the culture that halts this sacrificial substitution and turns instead upon its own members? In his investigation of Western culture's conceptual and literary fascination with sacrifice from ancient Greece through the present, Derek Hughes traces the rite's symbolic power as the enactment of humanity's special place between gods and animals within the cosmic order. Yet Hughes's account of the sacrificial tradition underscores its fragility by exposing the contradiction upon which its ritual logic rests: "sacrifice...distinguishes man from the animal yet expresses itself in that which most closely unites them: the capacity for lethal violence" (Hughes 9).

Animal imagery has been a persistent focus of Woolf scholarship. In Harvena Richter's analysis of Woolf's symbolic modes, animal metaphors comprise a unique species for their metamorphic potential, offering the most vivid means of delivering the "shock content" of emotion and of capturing its instinctive and volatile nature (Richter 190-3). Yet Woolf's concern with animal life and the animality of human behavior extends beyond this imaginative strategy and, as Natania Rosenfeld has shown, became one of the principal means by which Woolf, like her husband Leonard, expressed her frustration with the political developments of the 1930s, from the failure of the League of Nations as an arbiter of peace to the rise of fascism in Europe and England's consequent rearmament (Rosenfeld 153-81). Naomi Black reminds us, however, that unlike Leonard Woolf and other members of the Bloomsbury group, Woolf did not see militarism and the warmongering spirit as "throwbacks to a less civilized era" or as a "reversion to savagery but instead a logical consequence of patriarchy" and thus as a "horrible progression" (Black 170). It is fitting, then, that, as Reginald Abbot has shown, Woolf's first feminist polemic, "The Plumage Bill" (1920) printed in *The Woman's Leader*, should be both occasioned and framed by animal advocacy. Even as her early essay maintains that the interests of women and animals are distinct, Abbott illustrates how Woolf's "ostensible subject" of the turn-of-the-century conservationist and bird preservation movements yields special insight into the economic and political inequities that women suffer within a male-dominated culture (Abbott 265).[3]

---

[2] Derek Hughes elaborates this paradigmatic shift in his final chapter, "Hitler and After" (240-74), in which he argues that the death camps of the Second World War superseded sacrificial ritual as the extreme form of human barbarity.

[3] Abbott (281-2) traces Woolf's interest in the bird preservation movement to the Victorian animal discourse that pervaded the Stephen household in her childhood and to the prevalence of both animals and animalized humans in the Bloomsbury circle, noting the group's penchant for adopting animal nicknames.

Moreover, this insight has a long and complex history with crucial implications for feminism. Carol J. Adams and Josephine Donovan have identified the way in which women's alleged kinship with the animal has historically provided the grounds for their exclusion from the full rights of political citizenship (1). Arguing for the necessity of feminist theory's engagement with the treatment of animals, Adams and Donovan demonstrate the interconnection of all forms of oppression and additionally hypothesize that the "male pattern of female subordination and degradation" may even derive from "the domination of animals by humans" (7). Richard Espley further connects the animalization of the female body in Woolf's writing with masculine anxiety about women's erotic desire. Identifying the prevalence of the London Zoo in her early fiction, like *Night and Day*, Espley has shown how this institution "at the heart of the patriarchal city" provides a "ready-made metaphor for woman as a primitive creature to be controlled, if gazed at admiringly" (23).

Due at least in part to the historical context in which Woolf wrote the novel, *Between the Acts* aims to shed light upon the "scaffolding in the background" against which civilized life defines itself and to illuminate the figures who function as its support, those unrecognized parts of ourselves that may in fact be at our very center (*MOB* 73). Woolf thus turns with special ferocity to the question of the end of humanity—that is, the extinction of the species as well as the limits that cultures use to define humanity. While the fascist state imagined itself as a machine for the production of an ideal human being, an Aryan master race, by supposedly paring away all traces of the animal, Woolf's novel—like the pageant play it depicts—attempts to reverse this lethal process by restoring to her readers a uniquely human awareness of their inherent animality. When Lucy Swithin looks up from the pages of Wells's *Outline of History*, she is unable to separate Wells's prehistoric "grunting monster" from the servant Grace who enters with her breakfast: "Naturally, she jumped, as Grace put the tray down and said: 'Good morning, Ma'am.' 'Batty,' Grace classed her, as she felt on her face the divided glance that was half meant for a beast in a swamp, half for a maid in a print frock and white apron" (8).[4] While Swithin's imagination seems to collude with eugenical ideologies that would associate higher classes with more evolved species, Swithin herself reading history on the verge of Nazi invasion resembles

---

[4] In the fictionalized accounts of prehistory that Lucy Swithin reads in "Outline of History," Woolf synthesizes H. G. Wells's *Outline of History* and G. M. Trevelyan's *History of England*, which she was reading in preparation for "Anon," a history of English literature that she was working on at the time of her death. For other echoes of Wells's history in *Between the Acts*, see Gillian Beer, "Virginia Woolf and Prehistory," esp. 21-22, 25, which traces Woolf's conception of the prehistorical throughout her novels. For Woolf's adaptation of Trevelyan, see Brenda R. Silver 356-435.

a mastodon contemplating the Ice Age, glimpsing the impending extinction of its kind. As though viewing her mistress's "divided glance" as a form of violation, Grace dismisses Swithin and her double vision as "Batty."

This spectacle of humanity's twinned image bears a close resemblance to one of Woolf's most haunting childhood memories, which she describes in "A Sketch of the Past," the memoir she was writing at the same time as *Between the Acts*. Following her revelation of having been sexually violated by her halfbrother Gerald Duckworth, Woolf recalls having "dreamt that I was looking in a glass when a horrible face—the face of an animal—suddenly showed over my shoulder. [...] Was I looking in the mirror one day when something in the background moved, and seemed to me alive? I cannot be sure. But I have always remembered the other face in the glass, whether it was a dream or a fact, and that it frightened me" (*MOB* 69). The looking glass of childhood trauma produces a shameful double vision, what Christine Froula has called Woolf's "Self-Portrait with/as Beast" (228). The indistinct and featureless face of the animal forms the obscure "background" against which Woolf is able to recognize the familiar contours of her own human face, at the same time that it captures the shameful apprehension of herself as animal to another, Gerald's dehumanizing touch provoking in her a "dumb" and "instinctive" feeling of repellence (*MOB* 69). Woolf's experience of abuse, staged in the shadowy periphery of the Victorian dining room, represents one of the private acts of violation that constitute England's domestic history and connects Woolf to "thousands of ancestresses in the past" who share both the traumatic experience of incest and an innate resistance to male assertions of dominance over the female body (*MOB* 69). Written during the German aerial bombardments, Woolf's childhood revelations of aggressive male sexuality provide an allegory of unspeakable political horrors, where the molested female body and invaded nation alike figure as abject animalized beings.

While Woolf composed *Between the Acts* she tracked Hitler's aggression in Europe, likening his territorial advances to a ravenous predator's pursuit of fresh quarry: "When the tiger, i.e. Hitler, has digested his dinner he will pounce again," and "All Europe in Hitler's keeping. What'll he gobble next?" (*D5* 132, 173). As Hitler stalked his prey, European diplomats seemed only too eager to appease him with repeated sacrifices, purportedly enduring smaller losses for the sake of preserving peace for the whole. During the Munich Crisis in the fall of 1938, Woolf witnessed Europe's democratic leaders' abandonment of Czechoslovakia to political death, ransoming their less powerful neighbor to stave off Hitler's predatory attack. When Czechoslovakia was forced by the Munich Agreement to cede the Sudetenland to Germany, Woolf echoed the general perception of the act's ritual staging, observing that for Chamberlain to preserve the peace "the

C[zecho] S[lovak]s will be sacrificed" and noting that Chamberlain's negotiated settlement with Hitler was equivalent to "serving C[zecho].S[lovakia]. on the altar & bidding it commit suicide" (*D5* 170, 173).

The social dynamics of communal and family life in twentieth-century Britain turn out to be no more highly evolved from the primitive rites of sacrifice than Chamberlain's concession of Czechoslovakia to Hitler in the Munich Agreement. As France and England search for political scapegoats they can offer up to Germany in lieu of themselves, the characters in *Between the Acts* hunt for personal scapegoats toward whom they can direct their private rage, silently asking, "Whom could they make responsible?" (115). Woolf's story of competitive struggle among cultures as among individuals not only pits predator against prey, but pits victims against each other, in a struggle that does not guarantee survival for any.

The novel presents a world in which even neighborly banter at the annual pageant can become an incitement to violence and other monstrous human acts. For the stockbroker Giles Oliver, who has read in the morning newspaper about the execution by firing squad of sixteen prisoners across the channel, "Words this afternoon ceased to lie flat in the sentence. They rose, became menacing and shook their fists at you" (30, 38). Woolf thereby raises the question: why do the villagers, in the midst of their fear of impending war, resort to animal instincts themselves? Old Bart Oliver's animal pantomime, which so terrifies his grandson, is all the more monstrous for Woolf's readers since the newspaper he holds over his nose in the shape of a beast's snout contains the stories of two additional acts of human brutality in the novel's present-day reality: the gang-rape of a young girl by a group of military guards at Whitehall and the French Prime Minister Daladier "pegging down the franc" as a desperate measure of economic appeasement for the benefit of his arming German neighbors (11). Beneath young George's traumatic discovery of his grandfather's animality lurks a more sinister lesson of enculturation for the reader, exposing the bestial acts of economic and sexual aggression that drive the supposedly civilized institutions of European patriarchy.[5]

Thinking back through the evolutionary anthropology of Walter Burkert, which derives the practice of human sacrifice from analogues in animal behavior, may illuminate the novel's preoccupation with humanity's de-evolution into the beast. Burkert likens human scapegoating rituals to the response of prey to the threat of predators, and he traces the origins of ritual sacrifice to the brute competition for survival in the animal kingdom, where the herd willingly offers

---

[5] In a persuasive reading of the novel as trauma narrative, both historical and sexual, Claire Kahane suggestively connects George's shock and the story of the girl's gang-rape with Woolf's account of her childhood sexual abuse by her half-brothers in "A Sketch of the Past."

up one of its members to the pursuing predator in order to secure safety, however temporary, for the rest.[6]

Burkert's theory of anxiety sacrifice, originating in the herd's panic in the face of a hungry carnivore, approximates René Girard's account of the scapegoat mechanism that he finds so pervasive in Western literature and myth, but for Burkert the selection of a surrogate victim is motivated by a direct biological threat to survival rather than by an abstract psychosocial complex of mimetic desire as construed by Girard.[7] It is not the act of killing, but of abandoning another to violence, that is constitutive of social being. While in *Three Guineas* Woolf provides a thorough analysis of the scapegoating mentality that underlies patriarchal authority within England's social and economic institutions, it is the anxiety of an outside menace that forms the more immediate concern of the characters in *Between the Acts*. The dominant force in Burkert's scapegoat rituals is not violence and aggression, but anxiety, and he argues that with this model in which all alike are persecuted "we are closer to the essence of sacrifice than with the sacralized feast" in which the group consolidates as collective persecutor (Burkert, "Problem" 173).

Burkert derives his conception of anxiety or aversion sacrifice (*apotropaia thyein*) from Jane Harrison's exegesis of apotropaic or aversion rites. Harrison, the feminist classicist and vegetarian whom Woolf greatly admired and immortalized as the great "J—H—" in *A Room of One's Own* (15), hypothesized that this species of aversion ritual comprises an earlier and more primitive stratum of Greek religion driven by superstition and motivated by the desire to avert danger. This cult of aversion and sending-away originally constituted the mainstay of Greek religious practice, connected not to the higher order of Olympian gods but to the lower chthonic order of divinity that included the vengeful Erinyes and underworld spirits. Its worshippers made offering and sacrifice to the gods not on the principle of *do ut des* ("I give that you may give") but that of *do ut abeas* ("I give that you may go, and keep away") (*Prolegomena* 7).[8] It is part of the

---

[6] Walter Burkert's theory of aversion sacrifice (*apotropaia thyein*), originating in the herd's fear of predatorial attack, is an alternative to his earlier hypothesis in *Homo Necans* (1972) that the sacrificial feast (*charisteria thyein*) derives from Paleolithic hunting as a way of atoning for the act of killing. These two accounts of sacrificial origins remain separate paradigms which Burkert does not attempt to synthesize; see "Discussion" 178. Burkert first adumbrated the later predator-prey model in *Structure and History* 71-2, and elaborated the theory in *Creation of the Sacred* 34-55.

[7] René Girard's theory of the scapegoat mechanism, first and most thoroughly developed in *Violence and the Sacred*, is nicely summarized by Girard in "Generative Scapegoating" 73-105.

[8] For a treatment of Woolf's engagement with Harrison's scholarship and the importance of

cruel calculus of the ritual to wish upon another the suffering or harm otherwise aimed at oneself; and thus, operating by what Burkert describes as the logic of *pars par toto*, or part for the whole, the panic-seized herd willingly abandons one of its members as ransom to hold the predator at bay: "The instinctive program seems to command: take another one, not me. This ancient program is still at work in humans, still fleeing from devouring dangers and still making sacrifices to assuage and triumph over anxiety" (Burkert, *Creation* 55). In ritual terms, the herd submits one of its members as a kind of gift offering to hold the predator off for a time, and it is this gift to the devouring enemy that Burkert maintains motivates sacrificial giving in the religious context. The anxiety sacrifice Burkert speaks of involves neither active killing nor collective violence. The victim is thus abandoned to death by a process of unnatural, or unholy, selection.

In *Between the Acts* the old widow Lucy Swithin, who hosts the village pageant, meditates on just this model of sacrificially enforced survival when she nurses a fantasy of "one-making" amidst the shrill auguries of war and social fracture:

> Sheep, cows, grass, trees, ourselves—all are one. [. . .] And thus—she was smiling benignly—the agony of the particular sheep, cow, or human being is necessary; and so—she was beaming seraphically at the gilt vane in the distance—we reach the conclusion that *all* is harmony, could we hear it. (104)

The imaginary unity Lucy Swithin entertains as would-be shepherd, piping her inaudible harmonies, turns human beings into herd animals, dispensable members of the greater flock. The pipe-dream here, filtered ironically through Swithin's wistful imagination, exhibits the very part-for-the-whole logic of Burkertian sacrifice and of appeasement that sanctions the "necessary" loss of the single victim for the sake of preserving a collective "we" that might outlast a Nazi invasion. Mapping Swithin's Christian piety onto the policy of appeasement, Woolf teasingly suggests the future of such illusions. The vision of unity Swithin presents conceals the grim horror of individual suffering, projecting a celestial paradise, or continuing European peace, that is founded upon the victim's "agony." Such a rite requires that one take the long view, and no sooner does the reader glimpse the violence beneath it than Woolf archly fixes Swithin's gaze upon the

---

her elaboration of pre-patriarchal mythologies for the novel, see Patricia Cramer 166-84. Moreover, Melba Cuddy-Keane 273-85 argues that the comedic form of *Between the Acts* embodies the communal art and leaderless choral dance that Harrison's scholarship envisioned.

"gilt vane in the distance." In the vain guilt that lurks beneath Lucy Swithin's "one-making," Woolf recalls the social mastery of Mrs. Ramsay in *To the Lighthouse*, turning the socially constitutive powers of the earlier heroine into the senile imaginings of an old woman radically out of touch with the world around her. And as the analogy instructs readers, the efforts of neither hostess can prevent the world wars that follow their momentary social triumphs and may even help to precipitate them. It is Woolf's ethical insistence in the novel not to lose sight of the suffering of the particular victim, be it sheep, cow, human being or nation.

Where Swithin entertains an escapist fantasy of holding the enemy at bay, her nephew Giles represents the other side of appeasement. As Woolf's title suggests, the dominant preoccupation of *Between the Acts* is inaction, what happens—or doesn't happen—in the intervals between events, whether on a local and personal or cultural scale, and, of course, between the twentieth century's two decisive historical "acts." Exhibiting the impatience with inaction that many British men felt on the eve of war, Giles responds militantly, mimicking the fascist forces that were stampeding their way through Europe and threatening to trample civilization under foot. Nature supplies Giles, who "had no command of metaphor" (34), with the figurative language he lacks when on the path to the barn he stumbles upon the hideous sight of a snake engorged with a toad it cannot swallow:

> There, crouched in the grass, curled in an olive green ring, was a snake. Dead? No, choked with a toad in its mouth. The snake was unable to swallow; the toad was unable to die. A spasm made the ribs contract; blood oozed. It was birth the wrong way round—a monstrous inversion. So raising his foot, he stamped on them. The mass crushed and slithered. The white canvas on his tennis shoes was bloodstained and sticky. But it was action. Action relieved him. He strode to the Barn, with blood on his shoes. (61)

Having just kicked a "flinty yellow stone" that is "edged as if cut by a savage for an arrow," Giles seems to have strolled out of the twentieth century and into the prehistoric past of arrow-shooting hunters described in his aunt's reading of Wells's history, thus coming in contact with what is ineradicably primitive in human nature as it asserts its will over its prey (61). In his story of human origins Wells contends that frogs and other amphibians offer us a glimpse into the wonders of evolution since they "still show in their life history all the stages in the process of this liberation" from the swamp, which the more advanced reptile conceals (Wells, *Outline* 1:24). Yet the novel exposes nature gone horribly wrong as Woolf's snake chokes on Wells's lesson in evolution and the idea that nature advances itself through self-selection. "Action" on the part of the aggressor here, as in Woolf's diary entry during the Munich Crisis, provokes only sickening relief. She could not help joining the celebration of the herd that had been spared, acknowledging her "extreme physical relief when peace seemed 24 hours longer. Some instinctive self preservation" (*D5* 178). And in doing so, she figuratively joins the predators feeding on the Czechoslovakian carcass: "we must have a bone to gnaw" (*D5* 178). As if the political fable is not lost upon him, Giles steps in to intervene but ends up behaving in the spirit of the predatory dictators so prevalent in Europe who take violent action in order to bring about their own relief (Rosenfeld 166-74): "Action relieved him." What proves remarkable about Woolf's fictional adaptation of such sacrificial politics in *Between the Acts* is her ability to meditate upon their destructive potential from the position of the predator. She thus prevents her audience from vindicating itself by righteously siding with the wronged victim against the vilified persecutor.

The history that Wells describes and that the novel dramatizes through La Trobe's pageant circles back upon itself like the "olive green ring." Nature has reached a fatal impasse where neither the predator nor its prey can survive, and both creatures become immobilized by the predator/prey dynamic that suggestively evokes the political paralysis engulfing Europe as diplomatic talks between nations broke down. For what motivates the fascist predator is not mere hunger, but a cruel gluttony that exceeds the need for sustenance, as W. H. Auden describes in his poem of the Second World War period, *The Age of Anxiety* (1944-46), "To hunt not from hunger but for hate's sake" (351). Through the image of the snake's engorgement of the toad, Woolf presses the fascist fantasy of the Corporate State to its terrifying conclusion: the social "mass" grotesquely embodied in the convulsing and bleeding flesh of the two creatures becoming one. Moreover, Woolf's snake provides a prescient image of Hitler's territorial greed as he would swallow the nations of Europe in his successive campaigns against the Rhineland, Austria, Czechoslovakia, Poland, England, and Russia— the last two proving the meal that would not go down. In this image, therefore, Woolf suggests the material effect of the more abstract harmony of all imagined by Swithin.

The engorged snake obstructing Giles's garden path provides an image of political, marital, and ontological impasse, which leads him to turn with a vengeance upon those figures who represent an embarrassment to his manly self-image. The violent action of crushing the beast thus becomes an extension of Giles's stone-kicking game, in which the other pageant guests become personal scapegoats onto whom he can deflect his inner rage: "The first kick was Manresa (lust). The second, Dodge (perversion). The third himself (coward)" (61). The novel ultimately suggests that diplomacy, whether on an international or domestic scale, between nations or lovers, is merely ritualized predation, in which each member of the herd casts about for another victim to offer up in its place. Giles prejudicially regards William Dodge's homosexuality as a "monstrous" form of coupling, yet William's sham marriage to a woman who bears a bastard son represents an inverse image of Giles's strained relations with his wife Isa and his implied infidelity with Mrs. Manresa in the greenhouse later that afternoon. Regarding William as a "half-breed" and a "snake in the grass," Giles projects upon him his own despised animal self (32, 46).

Giles targets the homosexual with the same sense of outraged humanity that causes one of the spectators, Mrs. Parker, to shrink from the leering and grimacing spectacle of Albert the "village idiot" and to observe to Giles,

> "Surely, Mr. Oliver, we're more civilized?"
> "*We?*" said Giles. "*We?*" He looked, once, at William. [. . .] It was a bit of luck—that he could despise him, not himself. (68)

In Mrs. Parker's calculations, Albert the "idiot" becomes the obscure background against which she measures her own humanity, the figure through whom she supports her claim to be "more civilized." In *Mrs. Dalloway* the despised and despising Doris Kilman, a character partially based upon the Christian eugenicist Jean Thomas, reaches a similar understanding as she identifies Clarissa with the repudiated part of herself, the concerns of the flesh she is unable to master: "But why wish to resemble her? Why? She despised Mrs. Dalloway from the bottom of her heart" (*MD* 125; see Childs 35). In La Trobe's pageant Albert takes his rightful place among the other actors, since, as William Dodge points out, "He's in the tradition" of village life and cannot be repressed (68). Mounting a soapbox at the play's end, the village rector sermonizes upon the meaning behind Miss La Trobe's casting of Albert: "He too, Mr. Streatfield appeared to be saying, is part of ourselves. But not a part we like to recognize, Mrs. Springett added silently..." (115). In the characters' shared horror of the figure in whom they see their own image distorted, Woolf exposes the instinctive program at work in producing and safeguarding what is properly human through the persecution of a scapegoat. The eugenical valence of Mrs. Parker's "we" is not lost upon Giles, who wishes to restrict her category still further according to a sacrificial balance in which the value of his own life is intensified to the degree that that of another is correspondingly reduced.[9]

In the same vein, Sir William Bradshaw's medical program in *Mrs. Dalloway* safeguards the nation's biological capital, preserving the strength and purity of

---

[9] Informed by Emmanuel Levinas's concept of the face-to-face encounter, David Eberly has examined this scene as an example of the characters' failure to recognize the ethical claim that the other, whether the homosexual William Dodge or Albert the idiot, makes upon the self ("Trauma and Audience" 214-15; see also "Talking It All Out" 131-2).

the English stock, according to a taxonomy of human life: that is, by dividing the population into different zones of life whose breeding should be regulated and unsocial impulses contained.[10] Bradshaw's biopolitical mandate represents a terrifying link in a chain of historical horrors that extends from nineteenth-century eugenics to the twentieth-century death camps. But in *Between the Acts* the utter banality of the villagers' eugenical thoughts, casually dropped in idle chitchat, nudges this self-protective fantasy one step closer to Hitler's Final Solution and its willing executioners.

What predatory aggression does on an individual level to its victims, invasion and conquest perform on a political level. If the human being is nothing more than what Aristotle called a political animal (*politikon zôon*), then the figure of the refugee becomes a harbinger of its demise. Stripped of their political identity as citizens, refugees become mere *zôon*, retaining only the bare life of the animal. During the pageant's interludes the Jewish refugee surfaces in the communal gossip as another disconcerting double: "And what about the Jews? The refugees...the Jews...People like ourselves, beginning life again..." (Woolf's ellipses, 74). The pauses that interrupt Woolf's text register the anxiety such a figure—and its likeness to "ourselves"—provoked as an anticipation of post-war or even post-invasion life. The refugee serves as the occasion to reflect upon what becomes of the person who outlives history's last act, the human life that survives the extinction of the species as a cultural, if not a biological, category.

The villagers' attempt to reckon with the special predicament of the refugee exposes a threshold figure whose exceptional position between natural and cultural life sheds light on the future of European political subjectivity. Having escaped certain death at the hands of predatory Hitler, the refugee foretells of a state in which all humans are reduced to huntable quarry. Perhaps more terrifying than the particular refugee was the exodus of refugees en masse who, appearing in ever greater numbers on British shores, testified to the fact that the exceptional political figure was rapidly becoming the rule. The gramophone that Miss La Trobe uses to prolong the emotion of her play and to preserve the integrity of her audience through the frequent intermissions ironically announces this political eventuality with its refrain, "*Dispersed are we.*" Isa, who is herself "the age of the century" (14), takes up history's burden and imaginatively joins the Jewish Diaspora, past and present,

---

[10] For the ubiquity of eugenical discourse in the early twentieth century and Woolf's likely sources for its ideology, see Childs 22-37; for an extended discussion of Bradshaw's biopolitics, see Childs 38-57. Roberto Esposito has recently described the communal mandate for self-protection in terms of an "immunitary paradigm," according to which a culture imagines it can inoculate itself against death by preemptively killing those deemed weak or degenerate; such a paradigm represents a lethal paradox that, Esposito explains, pushes the protection of life over into death (116, 98).

murmuring, "This is the burden that the past laid on me, last little donkey in the long caravanserai crossing the desert. 'Kneel down,' said the past. '[...] Rise up, donkey. Go your way till your heels blister and your hoofs crack'" (93).[11] In the face of imminent cultural dissolution, the artist proves unable to prevent her flock from scattering.

Under the threat of impending war as the future that is perpetually shadowing the characters' present, the prospect of a depopulated stage provokes the horror of cultural apocalypse and historical oblivion. In the midst of the mock Restoration comedy, La Trobe panics when her actors and gramophone simultaneously fail her and there is no sound to fill the void: "Beads of perspiration broke on her forehead. Illusion failed. 'This is death,' she murmured, 'death'" (84). As La Trobe's human drama founders, the pageant's repressed background asserts itself and the cows grazing in the fields just beyond the stage assume history's "burden":

> Then suddenly, as the illusion petered out, the cows took up the burden. One had lost her calf. In the very nick of time she lifted her great moon-eyed head and bellowed. All the great moon-eyed heads laid themselves back. From cow after cow came the same yearning bellow. The whole world was filled with dumb yearning. It was the primeval voice sounding loud in the ear of the present moment. Then the whole herd caught the infection. Lashing their tails, blobbed like pokers, they tossed their heads high, plunged and bellowed, as if Eros had planted his dart in their flanks and goaded them to fury. The cows annihilated the gap; bridged the distance; filled the emptiness and continued the emotion.
> Miss La Trobe waved her hand ecstatically at the cows.
> 'Thank Heaven!' she exclaimed. (84-5)

The herd's yearning bellow catches like an "infection," and gives voice more powerfully than the fascist dictator's bark to a shared worldly suffering that the human spectators, steeped in personal and cultural trauma, cannot adequately process or articulate. In this temporary union of cows, actors, and spectators, as Merry M. Pawlowski points out, La Trobe presents a feminine ideal of the leaderless group that counters masculinist theories of the necessity of an authoritative herdsman (Pawlowski 42-8). Moreover, through this sudden fellowship Woolf undercuts human confidence in its own difference, annihilating the gap between human rationality and linguistic facility, on the one hand, and the immediacy of animal sensation, on the other. Sounding in a "primeval

---

[11] Isa develops the refrain's implicit historical theme, privately humming: "Dispersed are we....All is over. The wave has broken. Left us stranded high and dry. Single, separate on the shingle" (59). For a sensitive treatment of Woolf's engagement with Freud's *Moses and Monotheism* (1934-38), and his suggestion of recent history's regression to a state of primitive disorder, see Abel 108-130.

voice" the naked agony of the common herd, the cows exhibit the spontaneity and raw emotional intensity that Jane Harrison attributed to the animal pantomimes and "beast dances" from which the ancient chorus evolved (*Ancient Art and Ritual* 45-6, 121-3).

Harking back to the totemistic cults of the Great Goddess that precede the anthropomorphic and patriarchal deities of Olympus, La Trobe's ritualist conspiracy with the "moon-eyed" mother cow joins humans and animals in a sympathy that elides distinctions of gender and species (Hussey 92-8). The cows' choral song complements the actors' performance, providing an ironic gloss on the Restoration comedy's exploration of human desire and on the collective psychology of the spectators themselves. Goaded like the actors in the play and the characters in the novel by "Eros" and "his dart," the cows exhibit an instinctive response to loss that underscores the pageant's comic plot of young lovers whose union is inhibited by their villainous elders as well as the novel's plot in which Isa privately endures the darts of love and hate in her estranged marriage to Giles (65).[12] In the midst of La Trobe's artistic triumph—a collaborative production that transcends species borders—the third-person narrator surfaces briefly to offer an arch interpolation of the animal world of pure sensation, translating the cows' "dumb yearning" into the highly artificial idiom of the Restoration comedy that frames this eruption of the wild. The narrator's facetious interjection, signaled rhetorically by "as if," reinstates the barriers between species, which the "primeval voice" of emotion otherwise effaces, by speaking in a symbolic register unavailable to the cows. Woolf points to the masking properties of language itself as a medium through which humans seek to conceal their fundamental kinship with the beast and marks the failure of such language—the signature expression of human difference—in the fact that words like "Heaven" cease to signify, since the providential hand behind this saving moment is none other than the author's.[13]

Following La Trobe's triumphant exclamation, Woolf reverses the anthropomorphizing strain of the preceding passage and abruptly assimilates the human to the bovine: "Suddenly the cows stopped; lowered their heads,

---

[12] In *Where there's a Will there's a Way*, Lady Harpy Harraden, for example, recalls a compliment paid to her by a former suitor, "*Cupid's dart—hah, hah! lighting his taper—tush—at my eyes... pooh!*" (77); Sir Spaniel Lilyliver, having been thrown over by the lovely Flavinda for a younger lover, complains, "*And she, making mock of me, points to my leg and cries 'Cupid's darts, Sir Spaniel, Cupid's darts'*" (87, 88); and Lady Harpy later pronounces the play's closing moral, "*The God of love is full of tricks; / Into the foot his dart he sticks*" (89). The characters' names speak to their hybrid natures, Sir "Spaniel" coyly referencing Woolf's extended fictional representation of animal consciousness in *Flush*, the autobiography of Elizabeth Barrett Browning's cocker spaniel.

[13] Dan Wylie has explored the ethical component of Woolf's anthropomorphic imagining in *Flush*, showing how Woolf's use of the third-person, omniscient narrative mode demonstrates the limits of empathy between human and animal worlds and thus provides "an enactment of an unbridgeable outside-ness" (122).

and began browsing. Simultaneously the audience lowered their heads and read their programmes" (85). Cows in the field and humans in the audience respond to their respective circumstances identically. Dropping all pretence of art's sublime powers, Woolf reduces La Trobe's ambitious aesthetic program to mere cattle feed. The Restoration play's dramatization of human treachery and broken alliances provides the overture to Giles's indulgence in animal lust, another dart that will goad his wife to fury. Opportunistically twisting the play's moral, *Where there's a Will there's a Way*, to suit his momentary impulses, Giles invites Mrs. Manresa for a rendezvous in the greenhouse and concedes his higher conscience to brute passion: "Damn the consequences" (89).

The ironic deflections of Woolf's modernist narratology open up a space for readers to meditate upon the problem of species and dominance. Just as the polyvocality of narrative discourse in Woolf's fiction challenges patriarchal authority by dismantling the idea of an omniscient and controlling narrator, Woolf's effacement of the narrator's voice in *Between the Acts* further deconstructs the human/animal divide by undermining the sense of mastery upon which such a distinction rests.[14] La Trobe's decision to replace the Grand Ensemble and its jingoistic celebration of imperial strength with a self-reflexive parade of mirrors at the end of her production represents the dramatic equivalent of the fictional experiment Woolf set for herself in *Between the Acts*, attempting to capture the collective choric voice in prose: "'I' rejected: 'We' substituted" (*D5*, 135). La Trobe's pageant boldly ends with its formal dissolution, returning the drama to its own purported origins in the ritual *sparagmos*, the sacrificial dismemberment of the Year Spirit or vegetation deity whose subsequent resurrection affirms the renewal of the natural world and the human tribe (Murray 64). The mirrors the actors hold up to the spectators present a vivid image of human community dismembered, or blasted into "orts, scraps, and fragments."

Between the Acts invokes the mythic accounts of cultural origins that so captivated the early twentieth-century imagination, yet Woolf depicts a world whose connection to its source material and the regenerating powers of its rituals has become so attenuated as to drain them of their symbolic value. Poetic fragments and literary allusions have become unmoored, dislocated from their sources, as have the bases for the ritual actions that magically produce cultural integrity and press the heterogeneous "we" into a singularity. Thus Lucy Swithin, weighed down by a cross pendant that declares her own conventional loyalties, is perpetually eluded in her quest for the source of human belief and expression:

[14] My consideration of the internal fluctuations registered in Woolf's narrative voice, and the political imperative behind her fiction's creation of a "polyphony of voices," has been helpfully informed by Kathy Mezei's discussion of free indirect discourse in *Mrs. Dalloway* (81) and by Jeanne Dubino's discussion of the carnivalesque and participatory dimensions of Woolf's language in "On Being Ill."

"What's the origin—the origin—of that?" (18). As the play reflects back upon its ritual origins, La Trobe's pageant—like Woolf's novel—opens up a space in which humanity might be released from myths of cultural formation that have outlived their use and free to reimagine or reinvent the basis for communal life: "Surely it was time someone invented a new plot" (128).

Even if Woolf never relinquished the biologically motivated aspects of human behavior and social formation, she explores the socially constructed aspects of gender and species identity through the novel's approximation of dramatic form. *Between the Acts* poses the problem of human identity in theatrical terms, rendering the anxiety over declaring oneself human a performance demanding an audience. The spectators' response to Reverend Streatfield's interpretive sermon adumbrates an ecological mode of thought that acknowledges human company with non-human others. It is in this sense that La Trobe's risk of staging the pageant in the open air, exposing both actors and audience to the natural elements, pays off. Reflecting on the play's meaning, one member of the audience muses, "To me at least it was indicated that we are members one of another. Each is part of the whole" (114). Another then speculates, following Streatfield's concluding speech, "I thought I perceived that nature takes her part. Dare we, I asked myself, limit life to ourselves?. . . (the swallows were sweeping round him. They seemed cognizant of his meaning. Then they swept out of sight)" (114). The spectator's suggestive expansion of the category of "life" to non-human animals beyond "ourselves" initiates a dialog that the swallows' cognizance of the rector's meaning implicitly continues, demonstrating what Stanley Cavell has called "companionable thinking." By reimagining human relations to animals not in the hierarchical terms of biological capacities, but in terms of a mutual exposure to the other, Cavell suggests that humans might respectfully acknowledge "the company we may keep with non-human animals" (122).

If, as I have argued, Lucy Swithin's dream of one-making exposes the escapist fantasy of appeasement, and Giles's stamping the toad-engorged snake mimics the fascist demand for militant action, then in another of the "unacted parts" that La Trobe's pageant stirs in her audience Isa offers herself up as a scapegoat to preserve the fragile edifice of civilization (92). In the prologue to the Restoration comedy, the figure of Reason, played by the villager Mabel Hopkins, magisterially declares civilization to have evolved beyond its war-making and sacrificial practices: *"At my behest, the warrior lays his shield aside; the heathen leaves the Altar steaming with unholy sacrifice"* (75). Yet Isa's fantasy of redeeming a suffering humanity through self-sacrifice suggests a more disturbing possibility that, far from eradicating war-making and heathen sacrifice from civilization as obsolete barbarisms, Enlightenment rationalism may instead promote such atrocities. Following the

Victorian drama within the pageant, La Trobe reproduces the spectators' pre-war anxiety by suspending dramatic action for ten minutes during which time she seeks to "expose them, as it were, to douche them, with present-time reality" (107). Nature appears to do her bidding when a shower of rain falls upon the audience's faces like the world's tears; her wish seems to compel the event like an act of sympathetic magic.

The prospect of the world's collective woe then prompts Isa to answer Swithin's call for sacrifice and instinctively to offer herself up as one of European civilization's "particular sheep" (104):

> "O that my life could here have ending," Isa murmured (taking care not to move her lips). Readily would she endow this voice with all her treasure if so be tears could be ended. [...] On the altar of the rain-soaked earth she laid down her sacrifice... (108)

Isa's overtly poeticized language is reminiscent of the tentative entries she scribbles in an account-book to hide them from her husband. Reciting bits of verse throughout the novel, as if shoring their fragments against her ruin, Isa expresses a longing to supply her life with the kind of shapely aesthetic coherence that at this moment La Trobe denies the pageant. Yet if, as Burkert reminds us, "After all, ritual killing is real killing" ("Problem" 153), Isa's imaginary self-sacrifice does not result in her actual death and remains in this sense an "unacted part" within the novel's drama. The conditionality of Isa's offering—"Readily *would* she endow this voice...*if* so be tears could be ended"—betrays her understanding of the futility of such a gesture, her faith in ritual's magic waning even as she invokes its fertile powers upon a "rain-soaked earth." This obsessive or melancholic attachment to the regenerative energies of a transcendental faith amounts to what Robert Pippin has called "a continuation of religion by other means."[15] Even as Woolf rescues her character from victimhood, Isa's unrealized sacrifice ruefully acknowledges the loss of the protections that such sacralized rituals offer to a human herd facing the prospect of its own extinction.

Woolf employs the liminal being of the animalized human in the novel to interrogate the collective categories of nation, race, and gender as well as the exclusions on which such categories are predicated. Insisting upon her status as an outsider within, she declared in *Three Guineas*, "as a woman, I have no country" (234). In her polemical writing, Woolf witnessed the particular

---

[15] Pippin 506. Isa's sacrificial impulse sounds the same doleful tone that Pippin identifies in the famous assertion of Nietzsche's madman in *The Gay Science* that "God is dead." Pippin (496-520) has thoroughly diagnosed this melancholic mood in European modernism, tracing the etiology of what he calls "the modern pathology" to the failure of the Enlightenment enterprise and its ideals.

vulnerability of the internal outsider to collective persecution as a *pharmakos*, a convenient political scapegoat who serves in moments of cultural crisis to deflect responsibility for the failings of the ruling class.[16] Yet if Woolf recognized in *Three Guineas* the extent to which sovereign power constitutes its authority in the act of excluding the life it deems sacred, *Between the Acts* explores the more sinister proposition that the sacred person under the totalitarian regimes of the 1930s and '40s is subject to a uniquely profane violence. What is important about this proposition is that it removes the sacral quality from the victim of sacrifice. This alarming prospect caused Woolf to revise the classical sacrificial paradigm, popularized by J. G. Frazer's *The Golden Bough* and Freud's *Totem and Taboo*, and to recognize the way in which the modern state destroys the sacred character of those it scapegoats.

The original function of sacrifice, early anthropologists maintained, was to establish humanity's unique position between the gods and the animals (Hughes 8-12). According to the new political realities of the 1930s and '40s, as Woolf realized, dehumanization becomes the basis for victimization. Citizenship and humanity become categories upheld by the repression of the denationalized and the animalized—negative categories produced in order to allow the positive categories to achieve definition. This repression might take many forms, but, even after the victim has been deprived of sacral status, sacrifice continues to figure as a system for delineating the place of the human. The totalitarian state, as Giorgio Agamben has shown, presses these oppositions to the point of collapse, transferring its human victims to the category of the animal and thus taking figurative "dehumanization" to a new level of literalness. Agamben's analysis of the cultural production of the human sets the scene for the spectacle of self-reflexivity at the end of the pageant, which strips away the appeasing fictions the characters have entertained about their own natural selection and the separation of the properly human life from the growing shadow of its degenerate, animalized other.

In this respect the victims of the concentration camp were executed neither as the exalted victims depicted by turn-of-the-century anthropology nor even as human citizens, but as mere "vermin," bare life denuded of national or cultural identity.[17] The person stripped of citizenship, referred to by Agamben as "a life lacking every political value," effectively collapses into the bare life of the animal (*Homo Sacer* 132). Illuminating like Woolf the threshold figures who prove the

---

[16] Christine Froula (259-84) offers an illuminating reading of sacrificial violence in *Three Guineas* that aligns Woolf's analysis of women's exclusion from England's social and political institutions with René Girard's scapegoat mechanism.

[17] James George Frazer's account of the dying god as a scapegoat is exemplary of the sacralization of the victim. See "The Scapegoat," Book 3 of *The Golden Bough* (1890), esp. 557, 588-9.

necessary condition for such an ontological hierarchy, Agamben identifies the special status of the *homo sacer*, the person who can be killed but not sacrificed, and shows that this exceptional figure of ancient Roman law was resurrected as the dominant political subject in the Nazi state. National Socialism insisted upon recodifying, and narrowing, the definition of what constituted a legitimate citizen of the German state, reaching its clearest articulation in the Nuremberg laws' designation of "citizenship in the Reich" for the "protection of German blood and honor" (qtd. Agamben, *Homo Sacer* 132). Exclusion from citizenship and denationalization formed the first stage in a process that would end with Hitler's Final Solution and the transportation of Jews, homosexuals, political dissidents, and other so-called extra-nationals (*Asocializen*, literally un-socials) to the extermination camps.[18]

According to Agamben's analysis, denationalization of people becomes a means of their dehumanization, which ultimately brings about their animalization. In his investigation of the relation between man and animal in Western thought, Agamben reminds us of the cultural origins of distinctions held to be natural. Returning to the zealous classifications of eighteenth-century science, he points to Linnaeus's inclusion of humans within the category of primates. A special irony adheres to the name *Homo sapiens* that Linnaeus assigns humans. What forms the taxonomic distinction between human and animal, what stands between people and primates, is not a substantive physiological difference but an imperative: the classical injunction to "know thyself." And he who doesn't recognize himself in the apes, Linnaeus's denomination would caution us, places himself among them. "*Homo sapiens*, then," as Agamben argues, "is neither a clearly defined species nor a substance; it is, rather, a machine or device for producing the recognition of the human" (*Open* 26). Agamben thus points to the artificiality of the very category of the human, which is itself a machine or device that is self-confirming.

Between the Acts turns our attention to the violence that is required to uphold this anthropocentric charade. When at the beginning of the novel Lucy Swithin looks up from the pages of her history to find Wells's primeval forest sprouting up in her bedroom, Agamben's "anthropological machine" starts to idle. In her experience of Wells, history reads like a catalog of obsolete worlds and extinct creatures "from whom presumably, she thought, jerking the window open, we descend" (8). With this violent jerk, Swithin (aptly nicknamed "Old Flimsy")

---

[18] Woolf was aware that should the Nazis prevail, her exceptional status as an outsider—a subversive artist and publisher—would land her, along with her Jewish husband Leonard, in one of Hitler's concentration camps. In the event of a German occupation, Woolf predicted "a German pro-Consul; Eng[li]sh Gov[ernment]t in Canada; we in concentration camps, or taking sleeping draughts" (*D5* 292, June 1940). She kept a lethal dose of morphine in her pocket for this eventuality (Cf. *D5* 297). A Nazi arrest list containing the names of both Leonard and Virginia Woolf ultimately substantiates her fears (Lee 718).

lifts the partition separating ostensibly civilized human beings from "barking monsters" (19, 8).

One of the pageant's final tableaux, in which the players carry bricks to rebuild the ruined wall of civilization and thus reinstate ontological distinctions, forms a fitting epilogue to the history La Trobe has been plotting while it harks back to the human origins evoked in Swithin's reading: "'Prehistoric man,' she read, 'half-human, half-ape, roused himself from his semi-crouching position and raised great stones'" (129). The anthropoid animal, the subhuman, is not a mysterious and remote ancestor crouching outside the drama of human history, but the well-kept secret of that history which has been chased out of hiding. As one spectator ruminates on the meaning of La Trobe's pageant, "Take the idiot. Did she mean, so to speak, something hidden, the unconscious as they call it? [. . .] It's true, there's a sense in which we all, I admit, are savages still" (118). At the close of the novel, in the summer twilight of peacetime, the old widow appropriately returns to this crouching figure, who becomes the protagonist of the post-war world Woolf would not live to witness.

The machine scratches to a halt when La Trobe's gramophone fails her, emitting only a "chuff, chuff, chuff" where music should play: "It was the noise a machine makes when something has gone wrong" (48). Having reached the end of history's pageant, "Present Time: Ourselves," La Trobe confronts her audience with its own imperiled humanity through a parade of self-reflection. Her actors emerge from the bushes holding mirrors that reflect back to the spectators their own images fragmented in bits and pieces, catching here a leg, there a face. In the pageant's astute and consummate irony, however, the people in the audience fail to recognize Linnaeus's self-conscious imperative. They squirm and shift in their seats, dodging the mirrors like the potential scapegoats of Burkert's herd, defensively protesting, "But she won't get me—no, not me. [...] Other people, perhaps" (106). All avert their faces from their reflections with the sole exception of Mrs. Manresa, who uses the mirror to apply her make-up and redden her lips as though to advertise her fertility and fitness to reproduce. The New Zealand-born woman who proudly owns she is "the wild child of nature," Mrs. Manresa is Linnaeus's *Homo ferus*, or *enfant sauvage*, the figure of the mute human being living on the fringes of Europe's villages (29). Lacking sufficient possession of her cultural heritage—she does not have her Shakespeare by heart as Bart flatteringly pretends—Manresa is the animal with a human face who reflects the characters' creatural selves.[19] "'Magnificent!'" old Bart Oliver says, applauding

---

[19] When her attempt at Hamlet's "To be or not to be" soliloquy trails off, Mrs. Manresa turns to Giles, the character least able to supply the wanted lines (35). For a discussion of the *Homo ferus* as Nature's "wild children," see Ruth Benedict, *Patterns of Culture* 12-13, a text which Woolf read "with pressure of suggestions" in July 1940 (*D5* 306); and more recently Agamben, *Open* 30-1.

her bravado for squarely facing her reflection: "Alone she preserved unashamed her identity, and faced without blinking herself" (110). In the reflected image of her unadorned face, Mrs. Manresa confronts the spectacle of her own bare life, her irreducible naked being. No sooner does she do so than she compulsively applies a cosmetic fix to conceal her animal self, a concealing that itself exaggerates her animal magnetism. It is likewise this specter of simple biological life that the audience faces in the figures deemed to be beneath its own humanity—be they Albert the "village idiot"; the homosexual "half-man" William Dodge (46); Jewish refugees; or the lesbian artist La Trobe, an "outcast" whom "Nature had somehow set apart from her kind" (125). Nature is called upon to corroborate the exclusion of those regarded as culturally unfit.

 La Trobe senses with growing unease that the strategies which both she and the other characters anxiously employ to forestall the end of human civilization instead hasten this eventuality. Exploring Woolf's modernist historiography, Stuart Christie interprets La Trobe as a female embodiment of Nietzsche's epigone, who, as a latecomer to the pageant of Western history, actively subverts its course and signals the demise of its nationalist and patriarchal imperative. Having set her stage on a natural terrace, La Trobe longs to reinstate the barrier between human and animal and admonishes herself, "If only she'd a backcloth to hang between the trees—to shut out the cows, swallows, present time!" (107). At the end of the novel the landscape of humanity's future appears indistinguishable from its prehistoric origins as the curtain rises upon a scene of domestic conflict where Giles and Isa, left alone together in a "night before roads were made," drop all pretense of civility and prepare to fight "as the dog fox fights with the vixen" (130, 129). Discovering the inescapability of the animal within the domain of the human, and conversely humanity's place in the animal's open field, *Between the Acts* ultimately leaves its readers in an interval, suspended between the animal and the human and belonging to neither.

 If *Between the Acts* attempts to effect a release from the anthropocentric mind, the novel simultaneously dramatizes the difficulty of relinquishing the type-casting of species or history. Woolf's posthumous fictional sketch entitled "Flying over London" offers a stunning vision of post-human England seen from an ascending airplane, which envisions the future that ominously looms over the characters in *Between the Acts*. The airplane's ascent becomes a metaphor for biological death and civilizational extinction, and she observes, "Perhaps the race was dead" ("Flying" 168). For "so inveterately anthropocentric is the mind," Woolf explains, that it needs to be shaken loose from its habituated values, freed from its mammalian flesh and the trappings of civilization with its divisions into nations and social classes ("Flying" 167). At the end of the essay, however, it turns out that "a defect of some sort in the machine" has prevented the plane's actual takeoff, and what Woolf has projected as the post-human future is in fact her readers' present grounded reality ("Flying" 172).

Likewise, pre-history and post-civilization coincide in the novel's closing vista: "The house had lost its shelter. [...] It was the night that dwellers in caves had watched from some high place among the rocks" (129-30). The trauma that induces this double vision is not simply a return to primitive forms of life, but instead marks a new origin. *Between the Acts* sketches a view of life after the fiction of human civilization is no longer sustainable, a view that shows that this very fiction is a consequence of bloodshed, sacrifice, and hierarchy. Woolf's elegy for England is, in effect, an elegy for specific ideas of civilization depicted in and around the pageant. Together, these ideas form a culture founded upon the hierarchies that scapegoating, elevating the masterful human over the sacrificeable animal, makes possible. The characters in the novel can no longer look to a transcendental idea of the human to provide "shelter" from the irreducible fact of their biological existence on the eve of a war that threatens its total destruction.

Works Cited

Abel, Elizabeth. *Virginia Woolf and the Fictions of Psychoanalysis*. Chicago: U of Chicago P, 1989.

Abbott, Reginald. "Birds Don't Sing in Greek: Virginia Woolf and "The Plumage Bill." In Adams and Donovan, eds. 263-86.

Adams, Carol J. and Josephine Donovan, eds. "Introduction." *Animals and Women: Feminist Theoretical Explorations*. Durham and London: Duke UP, 1995. 1-8.

Agamben, Giorgio. *Homo Sacer: Sovereign Power and Bare Life*. Trans. Daniel Heller-Roazen. Stanford: Stanford UP, 1998.

———. *The Open: Man and Animal*. Trans. Kevin Attell. Stanford: Stanford UP, 2004.

Auden, W. H. "The Age of Anxiety." *Collected Poems*. Ed. Edward Mendelson. New York: Random House, 1976. 343-409.

Beer, Gillian. "Virginia Woolf and Prehistory." *Virginia Woolf: The Common Ground*. Ann Arbor: U of Michigan P, 1996. 6-28.

Benedict, Ruth. *Patterns of Culture*. 1934. Boston: Houghton Mifflin, 1989.

Black, Naomi. *Virginia Woolf as Feminist*. Ithaca: Cornell UP, 2004.

Burkert, Walter. *Creation of the Sacred: Tracks of Biology in Early Religions*. Cambridge, MA: Harvard UP, 1996.

———. *Homo Necans: The Anthropology of Ancient Greek Sacrificial Ritual and Myth*. Trans. Peter Bing. Berkeley: U of California P, 1983.

———. "Discussion." *Violent Origins: Ritual Killing and Cultural*

Formation. Ed. Robert G. Hamerton-Kelly. Stanford: Stanford UP, 1987. 177-88.

———. "The Problem of Ritual Killing." *Violent Origins: Ritual Killing and Cultural Formation*. Ed. Robert G. Hamerton-Kelly. Stanford: Stanford UP, 1987. 149-76.

———. *Structure and History in Greek Mythology and Ritual*. Berkeley: U of California P, 1979.

Cavell, Stanley. "Companionable Thinking." In *Philosophy and Animal Life*. Ed. Cary Wolfe. New York: Columbia UP, 2008. 91-126.

Childs, Donald. *Modernism and Eugenics: Woolf, Eliot, Yeats, and the Culture of Degeneration*. Cambridge: Cambridge UP, 2001.

Cramer, Patricia. "Virginia Woolf's Matriarchal Family of Origins in *Between the Acts*." *Twentieth Century Literature* 39:2 (1993): 166-184.

Christie, Stuart. "Willing Epigone: Virginia Woolf's *Between the Acts* as Nietzschean Historiography." *Woolf Studies Annual* 8 (2002): 157-74.

Cuddy-Keane, Melba. "The Politics of Comic Modes in Virginia Woolf's *Between the Acts*." *PMLA* 105:2 (1990): 273-85.

Dubino, Jeanne. "On Illness as Carnival: The Body as Discovery in Virginia Woolf's 'On Being Ill' and Mikhail Bakhtin's *Rabelais and His World*." In *Virginia Woolf: Emerging Perspectives: Selected Papers from the Third Annual Conference on Virginia Woolf*. Eds. Mark Hussey and Vara Neverow. New York: Pace UP, 1994. 38-43.

Eberly, David. "Talking It All Out: Homosexual Disclosure in Woolf." In *Virginia Woolf: Themes and Variations: Selected Papers from the Second Annual Conference on Virginia Woolf*. Eds. Vara Neverow-Turk and Mark Hussey. New York: Pace UP, 1993. 128-34.

———. "Face-to-Face: Trauma and Audience in *Between the Acts*." In *Virginia Woolf and Trauma*. Eds. Suzette Henke and David Eberly. New York: Pace UP, 2007. 205-21.

Espley, Richard. "Courting Danger: Virginia Woolf, Sylvia Plath and Wooing at London Zoo." *Virginia Woolf Miscellany* 71 (Spring/Summer 2007): 23-4.

Esposito, Roberto. *Bíos: Biopolitics and Philosophy*. Trans. Timothy Campbell. Minneapolis: U of Minnesota P, 2008.

Frazer, James George. *The Golden Bough: A New Abridgement*. Ed. Robert Fraser. London: Oxford UP, 1994.

Froula, Christine. *Virginia Woolf and the Bloomsbury Avant-Garde: War, Civilization, Modernity*. New York: Columbia UP, 2005.

Girard, René. "Generative Scapegoating." *Violent Origins: Ritual Killing and Cultural Formation*. Ed. Robert G. Hamerton-Kelly. Stanford: Stanford UP, 1987. 73-105.

———. *Violence and the Sacred*. Trans. Patrick Gregory. Baltimore: Johns Hopkins UP, 1977.
Harrison, Jane Ellen. *Ancient Art and Ritual*. New York: Henry Holt. 1913.
———. *Prolegomena to the Study of Greek Religion*. 1903. Princeton: Princeton UP, 1991.
Hughes, Derek. *Culture and Sacrifice: Ritual Death in Literature and Opera*. Cambridge: Cambridge UP, 2007.
Hussey, Mark. "Reading and Ritual in Virginia Woolf's *Between the Acts*." *Anima* 15.2 (Spring 1989): 89-99.
Kahane, Claire. "Of Snakes, Toads, and Duckweed: Traumatic Acts and Historical Actions in *Between the Acts*." In *Virginia Woolf and Trauma*. Eds. Suzette Henke and David Eberly. New York: Pace UP, 2007. 223-46.
Lee, Hermione. *Virginia Woolf*. New York: Alfred A. Knopf, 1996.
Mezei, Kathy. "Who Is Speaking Here? Free Indirect Discourse, Gender, and Authority in *Emma, Howards End*, and *Mrs. Dalloway*." In *Feminist Narratology and British Women Writers*. Ed. Kathy Mezei. Chapel Hill: U of North Carolina P, 1996. 66-92.
Murray, Gilbert. *Euripides and His Age*. New York: Henry Holt, 1913.
Pawlowski, Merry M. "Toward a Feminist Theory of the State: Virginia Woolf and Wyndham Lewis on Art, Gender, and Politics." In *Virginia Woolf and Fascism: Resisting the Dictator's Seduction*. Ed. Merry M. Pawlowski. New York: Palgrave, 2001. 39-55.
Pippin, Robert B. "Nietzsche and the Melancholy of Modernity." *Social Research* 16:2 (1999): 496-520.
Richter, Harvena. *Virginia Woolf: The Inward Voyage*. Princeton: Princeton UP, 1970.
Rosenfeld, Natania. *Outsiders Together: Virginia Woolf and Leonard Woolf*. Princeton: Princeton UP, 2000.
Silver, Brenda R., ed. "'Anon' and 'The Reader': Virginia Woolf's Last Essays." *Twentieth Century Literature* 25:3-4 (1979): 356-435.
Wells, H. G. *The Outline of History*. 4 vols. 4th ed. New York: Review of Reviews Co., 1922.
Woolf, Virginia. *Between the Acts*. Ed. Stella McNichol. Intro. and notes by Gillian Beer. London: Penguin, 1992.
———. *The Diary of Virginia Woolf*. 5 vols. Eds. Anne Olivier Bell and Andrew McNeillie. New York: Harcourt, 1977-1984.
———. "Flying Over London." *Collected Essays*. Vol. 4. New York: Harcourt Brace, 1967. 167-72.

———. *Moments of Being*. 2nd ed. Ed. Jeanne Schulkind. New York: Harcourt Brace, 1985.

———. *Mrs. Dalloway*. Intro. and notes by Bonnie Kime Scott. New York: Harcourt Brace, 2005.

———. *A Room of One's Own* and *Three Guineas*. Ed. Michèle Barrett. London: Penguin, 1993.

Wylie, Dan. "The Anthropomorphic Ethic: Fiction and the Animal Mind in Virginia Woolf's *Flush* and Barbara Gowdy's *The White Bone*." *Interdisciplinary Studies in Literature and Environment* 9.2 (Summer 2002): 115-31.

Thinking Back Through Her Mothers: Judith Ortiz Cofer and Virginia Woolf
Jacqueline Doyle[1]

Judith Ortiz Cofer chose arguably the most famous line in *A Room of One's Own* for the epigraph to *Silent Dancing: A Partial Remembrance of a Puerto Rican Childhood*, her collection of stories, poems, and autobiographical essays: "A woman writing thinks back through her mothers" (*AROO* 97). In context, Woolf was writing of the importance of a female literary tradition for the woman writer.[2] Masterpieces are not "solitary births," as she remarks elsewhere in her lecture; they require preparation, foreground, and female models and mentors (65). The line has taken on a life of its own, however, and is often quoted in connection with the complex relations between biological mothers and daughters informing women's creativity, and also extended to the mother-daughter relations at the heart of many women's texts. Woolf postulated that future women writers would resurrect new literary forebears, create new forms, and write about new subjects. Mothers, both literal and literary, have become an abiding focus for women writers in the twentieth and twenty-first centuries.

In the preface and opening essays in *Silent Dancing*, Ortiz Cofer pays tribute to her Puerto Rican grandmother, mother, and aunts as oral storytellers,

---

[1] My thanks to the College of Letters, Arts, and Social Sciences at California State University, East Bay for a CLASS Faculty Fellows Award that aided me in the completion of this project.

[2] The first appearance of the line clearly refers to women's literary tradition: "they had no tradition behind them, or one so short and partial that it was of little help. For we think back through our mothers if we are women. It is useless to go to the great men writers for help ..." (76). The context is more ambiguous in her discussion of the androgynous "unity of the mind" necessary for great art, a state of mind more easily achieved by a man than a woman: "It [the mind] can think back through its fathers or through its mothers, as I have said that a woman writing thinks back through her mothers. Again if one is a woman one is often surprised by a sudden splitting off of consciousness, say in walking down Whitehall, when from being the natural inheritor of that civilisation, she becomes, on the contrary, alien and critical" (97). See London on the influence of the line as "model and inspiration for the recovery work of a new (female) literary history," countless works of feminist literary scholarship recuperating forgotten female authors, and anthologies such as *The Norton Anthology of Literature by Women* (16). Silver points out that *A Room of One's Own* has been central to battles over feminism and gender politics, as well as the literary canon. "It is no exaggeration to say that from the late 1960s on almost every work of feminist criticism and theory, at least in the United States, was more than likely to include a quotation from Woolf's essay in its epigraph, its introduction, and/or its text to support or authorize arguments of every conceivable persuasion" (215).

and to the centrality of her artistic foremother Woolf, whom she calls "my literary mentor for this project" (13). Despite a long history of ambivalence about Woolf's influence among many women writers of color in the U.S., Ortiz Cofer embraces Woolf's credo of female independence, woman-centered literary inspiration, and personal, poetic reclamation of memory in her autobiographical writings. She stresses the parallels rather than divergences between the mutable truths in Woolf's literary acts of memory, and the mutable stories in the ethnic women's oral tradition of her home culture. She also engages the problematics of embodiment and disembodiment in the female narrative voice central to *A Room of One's Own* and Woolf's autobiographical writings. Thinking back through her mothers, Ortiz Cofer explores the complex legacy of her maternal inheritances in her autobiographical collections *Silent Dancing* and *The Latin Deli*, evoking childhood "moments of being," and reshaping stories and memories of her later life and the lives of other Puerto Rican women, both on the island and the U.S. mainland. Commenting on Woolf's strong emotional ties to her mother (Woolf's earliest memory in "A Sketch of the Past"), her own ties to her mother and female relatives, and her essential relationship to Woolf, Ortiz Cofer suggests that "there is this invisible umbilical cord connecting us and in my case, it became a literary umbilical cord. I feel that the life of my imagination began with [them]" (Acosta-Bélen 93). Maternity becomes more than metaphor for the creative process and literary influence. In an implicit revision of Woolf's famous admonition to the female artist to kill the selflessly nurturing, mothering "Angel in the House" ("Professions" 285-86), Ortiz Cofer also thinks forward through her own daughter, comparing the "empowerment" she passes on to her to the "empowerment [that] ... the emerging artist needs to win for herself" (*Latin* 168). Like so many of Woolf's American successors, Ortiz Cofer figures female inheritance and legacy in both literal and literary terms.

I

Not all writers have assented to Jane Marcus's sweeping characterization of Woolf as the "mother of us all" (xiii). While American women writers of color have arguably drawn sustenance from Woolf's ideas, many have—openly or covertly—objected to her class, racial, and national biases. Alice Walker's well-known, extended homage to Woolf in "In Search of Our Mothers' Gardens" is as much a study in striking contrasts as in fruitful parallels. If Woolf tells us that a woman needs income and a room of her own in order to write, "what then," Walker asks, "are we to make of" a writer such as the eighteenth century poet and slave Phillis Wheatley, "who owned not even herself?" (235). Walker's interpolated substitutions within her extended quotations from *A Room of One's*

Own bristle with energy and outrage;[3] she pays tribute to Woolf's ideas even as she dramatically highlights the vast gulf between the artistic traditions and impediments to creativity of British women and African-American women:

> Virginia Woolf wrote further, speaking of course not of our Phillis, that "any woman born with a great gift in the sixteenth century [insert 'eighteenth century,' insert 'black woman,' insert 'born or made a slave'] would certainly have gone crazed, shot herself, or ended her days in some lonely cottage outside the village ... For it needs little skill and psychology to be sure that a highly gifted girl who had tried to use her gift for poetry would have been so thwarted and hindered by [...] contrary instincts [add 'chains, guns, the lash, the ownership of one's own body by someone else, submission to an alien religion'], that she must have lost her health and sanity to a certainty." (235, bracketed additions Walker's; *AROO* 49)

Walker pays homage to the artistry of her mother's garden, and finds evidence of thriving creativity among African American women, unimaginably "thwarted and hindered," in places that Woolf would surely overlook. Sandra Cisneros also thinks back through her mother, underlining Woolf's class bias when she notes that her poetic mentor Emily Dickinson had "a few essentials going for her," among them "a room of her own in a house of her own," and a female servant not unlike Cisneros' mother: "I wonder if Emily Dickinson's Irish housekeeper wrote poetry or if she ever had the secret desire to study and be anything besides a housekeeper. ... Maybe she was a woman like my mama" ("Notes" 75).

Encouraged by her mother, Cisneros' character Esperanza in *The House on Mango Street* seeks a Woolfian space where she can write:

> Not a flat. Not an apartment in back. Not a man's house. Not a daddy's. A house all my own. With my porch and my pillow, my pretty purple petunias. My books and my stories. My two shoes waiting beside the bed. Nobody to shake a stick at. Nobody's garbage to pick up after.
>
> Only a house quiet as snow, a space for myself to go, clean as paper before the poem. (108)[4]

---

[3] See London, Allan, and Fernald for perceptive discussions of the "double reading" required by Walker's insertions in this "re-fashioned double-voiced discourse" (London 26, Allan 132).
[4] For more on Cisneros' reconstruction of Woolf's *Room* in her *House*, see my article "More Room."

Maxine Hong Kingston also praises her mother's fierce independence, a woman who in China lived out every woman's daydream to have a room of one's own (61, 62). Jamaica Kincaid's Lucy follows her mother's advice when she seeks a room of her own, a bed of her own, books of her own, and achieves self-possession, if not happiness, in a "life of [her] own": "my mother had said to me many times: for my whole life I should make sure the roof over my head was my own; such a thing was important, especially if you were a woman" (143-44 , 161, 110).

Independence and ownership are crucially important to the descendant of slaves in a former British colony. Lucy thinks of her employer Mariah's family retainer Gus: "Do you not hate the way she says your name, as if she owns you?" (34). The word "own" occurs four times within the space of the two pages near the end of the novel where Lucy summarizes what she has achieved in her year in the U.S. (143-44). Alex Zwerdling points out that the repetition of "own" within Woolf's argument—"a room of one's own, an income of one's own, a mind and will of one's own, one's own work"—suggests "bourgeois" and not "working-class discourse," a clear "connection with ownership, with property and possession" (232). Lucy objects to her privileged employer Mariah's possession of people as well as things, and becomes tired of her lover Paul when "he got the idea he possessed me in a certain way" (*Lucy* 33-34, 155). Echoing Woolf's "own," she wrests ownership from the Mariahs and Pauls of the world to possess herself.

Kincaid would undoubtedly object to Woolf's construction of the female subject as white, British, and colonial in her comment in *A Room of One's Own* that "it is one of the great advantages of being a woman that one can pass even a very fine negress without wishing to make an Englishwoman of her" (50).[5] In this moment of self-congratulation on the white British woman's lack of imperialist instinct, Woolf unwittingly transforms the black woman into a sexual object of the presumably male gaze (with undertones of the slave on the auction block) when she says "even a *very fine* negress" (italics mine). She also constitutes the speaking subject—"a woman" and "one"—as European and exclusively white, excluding the negress from the "advantages of being a woman." Kincaid comments obliquely on Woolf's Eurocentrism and lack of world perspective when Lucy the au pair observes of wealthy Americans: "How luxurious, I thought, to have an empty room in your house, a room that nobody really needed. And isn't that what everyone in the world should have—more than was needed, one more room than you really need in your house?" (86-87). Trinh T. Minh-ha shares her global class-consciousness. While she agrees with the premise of *A Room of One's Own* that women's artistic productivity requires leisure, independence, persistence, and

---

[5] See also Cliff's postcolonial meditation on the imperial gaze and Woolf's dehumanization of the African head in *Orlando*.

working conditions "that do not require that writing be incessantly interrupted, deferred, denied, at any rate subordinated to family responsibilities," she also distances herself from "our reputed foresister Virginia Woolf" as well, pointing out that writing in a Third World context "is always practiced at the cost of other women's labor" (7).

Adrienne Rich, Tillie Olsen, and numerous contemporary American writers of color draw attention to other women's labor. If, in the peroration to *A Room of One's Own*, Woolf nodded to the "many other women who are not here tonight, for they are washing up the dishes and putting the children to bed" (113), she emphatically asserted elsewhere that it would not "be from the ranks of working-class women that the next great poet or novelist will be drawn" ("Memories" 147). Rich questions Woolf's myopia, conscious of women outside of her field of vision:

> Like Virginia Woolf, I am aware of the women who are not with us here because they are washing the dishes and looking after the children. Nearly fifty years after she spoke, that fact remains largely unchanged. And I am thinking also of women whom she left out of the picture altogether—women who are washing other people's dishes and caring for other people's children, not to mention women who went on the streets last night in order to feed their children. (38)

Both Walker and Olsen focus on women in the U.S. and across the world suffering the effects of slavery, diaspora, poverty, and illiteracy. Quoting Woolf's observation that "genius of a sort must have existed" among the working classes, as among women, Olsen appends the wry footnote, "Half of the working classes *are* women" (11; *AROO* 48-49).[6] Helena María Viramontes also draws attention to women unlikely to enjoy the privileges of rooms of their own: "Ideally, it would be bliss to manipulate the economic conditions of our lives and thus free our minds, our hands, to write. But there is no denying that this is a privilege limited to a certain sex, race, and class. The only bad thing about privilege, Virginia Woolf wrote (I'm paraphrasing from Tillie Olsen) was that not every one could have it" (292). While Olsen and Viramontes are nevertheless inspired by Woolf's

---

[6] Walker, the daughter of a sharecropper, also chooses this passage for one of her bracketed interpolations. Quoting Woolf's "Yet genius of a sort must have existed among women as it must have existed among the working class," she appends in brackets, "[Change this to 'slaves' and 'the wives and daughters of sharecroppers']" (239). Olsen implicitly appends and brackets the issue of class and creativity left unexplored in Woolf. In her "aftersection" to "Silences" in 1978, she laments, "No one has as yet written *A Room of One's Own* for writers, other than women, still marginal in literature. Nor do any bibliographies exist for writers whose origins and circumstances are marginal. Class remains the greatest unexamined factor" (146).

insights on the silencing of women, Gloria Anzaldúa is more impatient with *A Room of One's Own* and its utility for poor and working-class women: "Forget the room of one's own—write in the kitchen, lock yourself up in the bathroom. Write on the bus or the welfare line, on the job or during meals, between sleeping or waking" (170).

It is perhaps the uneven reception of Woolf's ideas that leads Ortiz Cofer to address the incongruity of her open admiration of Woolf. "People smile when I say that I consider her one of my literary mothers. After all, what does a Puerto Rican woman have to do with a wealthy Victorian English woman like Virginia Woolf?" (Ocasio 732). In an interview with Rafael Ocasio, she explains that when she was in college in the 1970s very few women writers were part of the curriculum. "Frankly, I had to use the models that I found" (732). Barbara Christian speculates that Toni Morrison turned to Woolf for similar reasons: in 1953, writing an MA thesis on William Faulkner and Virginia Woolf was "code" for writing on race and women; they would have been the only writers available to Morrison at the time for exploring these subjects (166). bell hooks recalls reading Woolf as a teenager, before she encountered African American writers. Like Walker and Cisneros she defines herself both with and against Woolf, who was an important early source of inspiration for her:

> At 13, I knew I wanted to write. Confident that this was my destiny, at 16 I read Virginia Woolf's *A Room of One's Own* and chose another guide. She was the sister-informant, sharing the secrets of what it would mean to be a woman and a writer, telling me what I would need. I never thought of Dickinson or Woolf as "white women." They entered the segregated world of my growing up as writers, and most importantly as women writers. Later I would learn the distance separating their experience from my own, the politics of race, sex, and class—still their work spoke to me. ("Zora" 244)

Ortiz Cofer also discovered Woolf before she began to read more widely in women's literature. In "In Search of My Mentors' Gardens," her tribute to Alice Walker and Flannery O'Connor, she looks back to her college years, a time, she says, when "I needed to write and I had no models of my own kind. In fact I remember only one woman's name coming up for serious discussion in my classes and that was Virginia Woolf" (*Woman* 95). Woolf was clearly more than a model by default, however. Elsewhere Ortiz Cofer refers to Woolf as the "only major woman writer I had heard 'speak' directly to me from the canon I was following in graduate school," although it was years later that she read *A Room of One's Own* and "thought back through my mothers ... my mothers through biology but also my literary mothers," naming Woolf first among them, along with "Mother

Morrison," "Sister Walker," her "southern muse" O'Connor, and contemporary Latin American and Latina writers (*Woman* 111-13).[7]

Woolf's influence on Ortiz Cofer is demonstrably indelible and thoroughgoing. Woolf "spoke" to her, from the emerging canon in the seventies, and as a pre-canonical feminist artist from the past. She addresses Woolf's ideas in the preface to *Silent Dancing*, in interview after interview, in her essays on writing, and in the classroom. Like Walker, Olsen, hooks, and others, she was inspired to apply *A Room of One's Own* to her own life:

> Virginia Woolf opened my eyes. Here was a woman who was defying her time by saying that a woman has to have a room of her own and an independent income to become a writer. If she is dependent on any man, if she doesn't have a place for herself, she will not write. She said that's why there are no female Shakespeares or Michelangelos, because we were not given the room and the space and the resources. And, as simple a truth as that was, I realized that, in order for me to fulfill my artistic ambitions, I had to keep working, I had to make my own money, I had to have control of my life. Although I am married and I have been a traditional mother in the sense that I have enjoyed that role, I also felt that I had to carve out a way for myself to write. So in my prologue to *Silent Dancing* I give credit to Virginia Woolf for having opened my eyes to the possibility of literary and artistic autonomy. ... I would like to be regarded as an artist on my own terms, and I found the model in Virginia Woolf. (Ocasio 732)

In a notable counterpoint to Anzaldúa, she writes of an assignment she introduced at the beginning of a writing workshop for working-class Latina women—"to write their version of Virginia Woolf's 'A Room of One's Own' to fit their individual lives"—first, by creating a private and relatively undisturbed "place to write for themselves," second, by "com[ing] up with a plan to make time to write every day," and third, by writing an essay about it (*Woman* 87). Despite the uproar of initial objections, the responses they brought to the following class meeting were creative and even ingenious. One single mother's "portable room" was a small handmade notebook in her back pocket that she took to the park and the grocery store; "she had even written [her] essay [for class] on her son's head while he leaned on her knees watching television" (*Woman* 88-89). The exercise became a "lesson," Ortiz Cofer says, about the "will to create," and even this small "act of claiming a bit of space and time for themselves was the beginning of something important for some of these women" (*Woman* 90).

---

[7] For discussions of Woolf's influence on Morrison and Walker, see Christian, Barrett, Harris-Williams, Williams, Allan, Courington, and Fernald.

While Anzaldúa suggests that women less privileged than Woolf abandon the requirement of a "room of one's own" and write in the kitchen, the bathroom, the welfare line, Ortiz Cofer and her students viewed the same solutions as a reinterpretation and extension of Woolf's principle. "The true artist," Ortiz Cofer concludes, "will use her creativity to find a way, to carve the time, to claim a kitchen table, a library carrel, if a room of her own is not possible. She will use subterfuge if necessary, write poems in her recipe book, give up sleeping time or social time, and write" (*Woman* 84-85). In her essay "5:00 a.m.: Writing as Ritual," Ortiz Cofer describes her own solution to the pressures and responsibilities of early motherhood, her undergraduate degree, her graduate degree, and part-time work, years when she was a "frustrated artist, waiting to have a room of my own and an independent income": she found a "room of my own" in the two hours at dawn before the household was up, a time of her own when she could write. "This apparently ordinary choice, to get up early and to work every day, forced me to come to terms with the discipline of art" (*Latin* 166, 167).

II

While Ortiz Cofer calls Woolf a "model" for the female artist and also "a model in all writing" (Ocasio 732, Bartkevicius 61), Woolf's influence is felt most centrally and crucially in Ortiz Cofer's conception and practice of autobiography. In the preface to *Silent Dancing* she discusses *Moments of Being* as the precedent for her poetic, semi-fictionalized explorations of her childhood: not a factual chronicle of events or "canned memories," as she puts it, but rather the evocation of pictures, "scenes," or "moments of being" at the very basis of her "creative imagination" (13, 12). Woolf "saw the past as a real place one could return to by following the tracks left by strong emotions," she observes, quoting directly from "A Sketch of the Past": "I feel that strong emotion must leave its trace; and it is only a question of discovering how we can get ourselves attached to it, so that we shall be able to live our lives through from the start" (*Silent* 13; *MOB* 67).

Ortiz Cofer evokes her childhood in Puerto Rico as a time when "I could still absorb joy through my pores," remembering the way the Island air "felt on my skin," and the "sensual joy" of the smells of her grandmother's kitchen (*Silent* 62, 61). "Moments of being" in early childhood for both writers are associated with almost preternaturally vivid sense impressions, a heightened apprehension of touch, sight, hearing, smell, and taste. Woolf recalls the soft sound of "the waves breaking, one, two, one, two, [the] splash of water on the beach," the light filtering through a billowing yellow blind with "purest ecstasy" (*MOB* 64-65). "I am hardly aware of myself," Woolf writes, "but only of the sensation. I am only the container of the feeling of ecstasy, of the feeling of rapture" (67). As Woolf's earliest memory begins in the lap of her mother, Ortiz Cofer opens *Silent Dancing* in her grandmother's Puerto Rican *casa*, in her womb-like room at the center of the house, "the place of our origin; the stage for our memories and dreams of Island life" (23). There the women of the family gather to tell stories, teaching Ortiz Cofer and her cousins "what it was like to be a woman, more specifically, a Puerto Rican woman" in Puerto Rico and *Los Nueva Yores*, the United States (14).

In a striking recuperation of Woolf, Ortiz Cofer thinks back through her grandmother and female relatives, and compares Woolf's mode of autobiographical storytelling to the oral tradition. If Walker famously argued in "In Search of Our Mothers' Gardens" that Woolf led ethnic women writers to "look high" when they should also have looked "low" to find the roots of their creativity, and celebrated her Southern mother's garden and the stories her mother passed on to her (239, 240), Ortiz Cofer combines high and low when she draws on the kinship between Woolf's written memoirs and her "unschooled" grandmother's oral tales.[8] What she learned from Woolf, she told Rafael Ocasio, is that "it's your childhood, and you reconstruct and re-create it any way that suits you, because memory is mostly fiction; each life is a series of recollections that is individual to that person" (732). She sees the oral tradition and her grandmother's *cuentos* in the same way. Her grandmother would tell a story, "claiming it was the absolute truth, the *la verdad*, but changing it every time to suit the occasion and the audience. She was teaching us that reality is relative, that we change it through our own interpretation" (Gordon).

Her grandmother's and aunts' *cuentos*—"morality and cautionary tales told by the women of our family for generations" (*Silent* 15)—are both by and about women. There are stories of women who are defeated by love, such as María la Loca, "the woman left at the altar," and stories of strong women who survive by their wits, such as María Sabida, "the woman who slept with one eye open" after foiling an attempted murder, whom her grandmother called "the prevailing woman," "always alert and never a victim" (*Silent* 76). Her Abuela tells her "an old, old story I heard when I was a little girl" of the witch's husband who learned not to pursue his wife on her nightly journeys (as her grandfather allowed her grandmother her own year of freedom when she needed it) (*Latin* 44). There is the tale of her grandmother Mamá, who in "More Room" decides that after five births and three miscarriages, she has undergone enough pregnancies, and has her husband build a new room onto the house and move into it. Because "her dreams

---

[8] Ortiz Cofer couples the two women as twin inspirations for her writing in a number of interviews (see, for example, Gordon, Ocasio 733, Kevane 116, Bartkevicius 61-62).

and her plans would have been permanently forgotten" with more children, she insists on her own space, her right to "own her nights," and the "right to own and control her body," to live "according to the dictates of one's own heart" (*Silent* 27, 26, 28). "More Room" in *Silent Dancing* is followed by the poem "Claims" on the same subject. In "Are You a Latina Writer?" Ortiz Cofer associates the poem directly with Woolf's line "A woman writing thinks back through her mothers," and discusses her grandmother together with the female writers—"all strong women"—who influenced her work (*Woman* 111-13).

Like Woolf in *Orlando*, Ortiz Cofer explores women's roles through cross-dressing, in her poem "The Changeling" (*Latin* 38), and through gender crossing, in the story her mother tells her of the boy in her Puerto Rican village who was raised as a girl through his teens, when he ran off with the mayor's daughter. Looking at the gentle old man Marina/Marino with his granddaughter, she says, "we now had a new place to begin our search for the meaning of the word *woman*" (*Silent* 160). Darker stories center on women, like Woolf's Judith Shakespeare, who are pregnant and abandoned. In "Silent Dancing," a female relative tells her of a cousin whose illegitimate pregnancy ended in an abortion and shameful return to Puerto Rico. Another illegitimate pregnancy across the street from her grandmother's house in Puerto Rico brings home the "potential for disaster" inherent in every young woman's body (*Silent* 140); after the girl, only a few months older than Ortiz Cofer, drops out of high school to run away with an older man who fails to marry her, she returns home "worn-out and spiritless" to bear a child at sixteen (140-41). At fifteen, Ortiz Cofer begins to discern the personal subtexts to the cautionary *cuentos* in the lives of the women who tell them, "their true feelings and frustrations in their marriages and in their narrowly circumscribed lives as women in Puerto Rico" (*Silent* 142).

Woolf suggested that there were new stories to be told in women's literature of the future—among them the stories of the servants below stairs, of the unremarked women on the street, of the shop girl behind the counter (*AROO* 88-90). "All these infinitely obscure lives remain to be recorded" (*AROO* 89). At the center of *The Latin Deli* is the shopkeeper Corazón, proprietress of the neighborhood bodega and confidante of all who buy groceries there. In the fictional stories in *The Latin Deli*, subtitled *Telling the Lives of Barrio Women*, Ortiz Cofer creates a microcosm of the neighborhood in the apartment complex "El Building," describing the residents' lives and hopes and fears, their jobs and their families and nostalgia for home. In the story "Nada," she shows the women of El Building rallying around the widowed Doña Ernestina, who eventually commits suicide after her son is killed in Vietnam. "Women help each other," the unnamed divorced housewife-narrator tells us (*Latin* 59). When Doña Ernestina dies they dress her in their own best clothing for the funeral—not unlike the trying on of other women's identities at the heart of Ortiz Cofer's hybrid autobiographical text.[9]

Like *Silent Dancing*, *The Latin Deli* includes multiple genres: poetry, fictional short stories, *cuento*s or tales, autobiographical creative nonfiction, more formal personal essays, character sketches, even letters by fictional characters. Almost all of the pieces are first-person narratives; a number of the fictional stories employ an alter ego "I" named Elena and other narrators much like those in the autobiographical pieces. At times the reader is several pages into a piece before the identity of the narrator is clear; many of the narrators remain nameless. The effect is to expand the autobiographical self in a startling achievement of the communal "I" narrator that Woolf establishes in *A Room of One's Own* and experiments with in her own fiction. "Anonymity runs in their blood," Woolf says of women (*AROO* 50). The collective narrator of *A Room of One's Own*—"I (call me Mary Beton, Mary Seton, Mary Carmichael or by any name you please—it is not a matter of any importance)"—reflects the even more fluid boundaries of identity in her novels (*AROO* 5). Tuzyline Jita Allan persuasively argues that the self-abnegating and depersonalized authorial presence that Woolf experimented with in her fiction and early essays lacks appeal for Walker and women writers of color, whose voices have already been discounted and effaced. Ortiz Cofer, however, develops a depersonalized or multi-personalized "I" narrator in *The Latin Deli* that expands her autobiographical presence to include a larger female and ethnic community. bell hooks describes the "relational self" of such autobiographical writing as a "coming together of many 'I's'": "We learned that the self existed in relation," hooks observes, "was dependent for its very being on the lives and experiences of everyone, the self not as signifier of one 'I' but the coming together of many 'I's, the self as embodying collective reality past and present, family and community" ("On Self-Recovery" 30-31). In *The Latin Deli* Ortiz Cofer achieves the collective autobiographical subject that she was moving toward in *Silent Dancing*. She credits Woolf as her inspiration. "Like her," she writes in the preface to *Silent Dancing*, "I wanted to try to connect myself to the threads of lives that have touched mine and at some point converged into the tapestry that is my memory of childhood" (13).

---

[9] In an interview Ortiz Cofer makes her autobiographical identifications even with the non-alter-ego characters explicit. Of the divorced housewife in El Building who narrates "Nada," she says: "'Nada' is a fictional work, I didn't know a woman to whom this happened and I didn't know a woman who was the narrator, but I knew many women to whom many of the things happened and I condensed it all and created a narrator that was me if I had stayed in the barrio. But not me since I did not stay in the barrio" (Bartkevicius 58).

III

Sidonie Smith opens her study on women's autobiography *Subjectivity, Identity, and the Body* with Woolf's well-known commentary in *A Room of One's Own* on the masculine "I," which looms in the foreground of the text, overshadows the page, and obscures the "landscape behind it" so that nothing can grow (Smith 1-2; *AROO* 100-01). Women, she argues, have "used autobiography as a means of 'talking back'" and destabilizing the universal subject of male writing. She describes the "I" of Woolf's own autobiographical writings as anonymous, "nomadic," "incorporative," and even "disembodied," ultimately an escape from "identity's body":

> Woolf's text reveals a nostalgia for the body before the cultural construction of identity (and the very real trauma of sexual abuse that testifies to the politics of gender) intrudes and partitions her off in identity's body. To escape the grotesque body, she imagines herself a disembodied spirit, the transparent eyeball. While the metaphor energizes certain aesthetic practices, such as the pursuit of narrative anonymity through which Woolf contests the cultural consolidation of male identity and strangulated individuality, it also sustains, through its contradictions, the troubled relationship between the autobiographical subject and the female body. (Smith 102)

Woolf recognized the relationship as problematic. In "Professions for Women" she marked out the female body as a central territory yet to be explored in her own writing—and also in writing by other women (288). In *A Room of One's Own* she imagined new literary forms in the future that would be "adapted" to the female body (78). Ortiz Cofer takes up Woolf's challenge to explore this uncharted territory and also takes on her ambivalence about the female body in "The Looking Glass Shame" in *Silent Dancing*, and in "The Story of My Body" in *The Latin Deli*, which extends her earlier meditation on shame, alienation, self-image, racism, and her changing body considerably further.

She borrows her title, "The Looking-Glass Shame," from a mirror scene in "A Sketch" where Woolf describes the shame she felt at the age of six or seven when she stole glances at her image in the entry-way looking-glass at Talland House. Woolf suggests that her "shame" and "guilt" went a "great deal deeper" than a "tomboy code," that they perhaps denoted a "streak of the puritan." "I must have been ashamed or afraid of my own body," she speculates (*MOB* 68). "At any rate," she concludes, and Ortiz Cofer uses this line as an epigraph to the essay, "the looking-glass shame has lasted all my life" (*MOB* 68; *Silent* 124). Woolf seems implicitly to contextualize her remarks on her alienation from her own body by following them with an account of being sexually molested by Gerald Duckworth, and then with a haunting description of a dream that she feels may be connected to the "incident of the looking-glass." Ortiz Cofer opens her essay by describing the dream and applying it to her own circumstances:

> In her memoir, *Moments of Being*, Virginia Woolf tells of a frightening dream she had as a young girl in which, as she looked at herself in the mirror, she saw something moving in the background: "... a horrible face—the face of an animal ..." over her shoulder. She never forgot that "other face in the glass" perhaps because it was both alien and familiar. It is not unusual for an adolescent to feel disconnected from her body—a stranger to herself and to her new developing needs—but I think that to a person living simultaneously in two cultures this phenomenon is intensified. (*Silent* 124, ellipses Ortiz Cofer's; *MOB* 69)

Woolf does not interpret her dream, which seems a striking eruption of the female Gothic that Claire Kahane delineates in "The Gothic Mirror," a moment of freakish disconnection when the maternal legacy of the female body is perceived as alien or other (343). Smith reads Woolf's dream as an abject identification of the female body with the lowly, the animal, and the grotesque. In contrast to the ecstatic "fluidity," "openness," and "permeability" associated with the bodily "moments of being" of childhood in Woolf's autobiography, "the figure in the mirror represents female selfhood shackled to the female body and engendered through specific social, cultural, and historical conditions" (91).

Ortiz Cofer devotes much of "The Looking Glass Shame" to her parents' anxieties and difficulties in the U.S., and to her unrequited crush on an older Italian-American boy. She does not explore the discomfort with her own body and only some of the debilitating "cultural schizophrenia" that the opening seems to promise. The essay, as a result, feels markedly incomplete. It is not until "The Story of My Body" in *The Latin Deli* that she confronts the alien "face in the glass," her deep-seated anxieties about her body in adolescence, and the cultural divisions and racism she experienced in the U.S. "Above all," Woolf counseled the female writer, " ... illumine your own soul with its profundities and its shallows, and its vanities and its generosities, and say what your beauty means to you or your plainness" (*AROO* 90). Ortiz Cofer describes her desire in adolescence to avoid mirrors, even to be invisible. Traumatized by scars from childhood chickenpox (not clearly visible to others) and anxiety about her looks, particularly her weight (she was called "Skinny Bones" on the playground), she shrinks from scrutiny, and perceives herself as a freak in a "circus" sideshow, "the woman without flesh" (*Latin* 140). Her anxieties about the scars on her face, "tiny cuts that looked as if a mad cat had plunged its claws deep into my skin" (135), and the lack of protective skin and fat on her bones—"I wanted flesh on my bones—a thick layer of it" (140)—are clearly projections of her deeper anxieties about threatening experiences of racial prejudice that bracket the essay:[10] an episode in her childhood, when she was denounced as a dirty Puerto Rican in a grocery store (a "moment ... frozen in my mind," she writes, "as if there were a photograph of it on file") and another in high school, when a boy retracted a prized invitation to a dance after his father forbade him to go with her (137-38). "Ted's father had shaken his head. No. Ted would not be taking me out. Ted's father had known Puerto Ricans in the army. He had lived in New York City ... and had seen how the spics lived. Like rats" (146). In both instances, her body image is contaminated by imagery of dirt and animality. The essay revolves around these two experiences of cultural trauma, and an unnerving cultural relativity surrounding looks, color, and size throughout her childhood. A "white girl" in Puerto Rico, she became a "brown girl" when she moved to New Jersey. Tall in Puerto Rico, she became short in the U.S. (grateful for the freakish midget Gladys in her new school, who replaced her at the center of class photos). A "pretty girl" in Puerto Rico, Ortiz Cofer suffered a reversal of body image and self-perception in the U.S. that she seems never to have fully overcome. She concludes the essay after college and marriage, when she appears to retreat from the story of her body altogether to concentrate on "brains" and "talent" and academic achievement as the "criteria for my sense of self-worth that I would concentrate on in my adult life" (146).

Smith suggests that Woolf's ambivalence about the female body occurs specifically in the "transition from the childhood of nondifferentiation to the young womanhood of overdetermined sexual identification," when she is definitively closed in the "prison house of gender" and Victorian gender roles (88, 89). In Ortiz Cofer's "Quinceañera" (the traditional rite of passage between childhood and womanhood) the adolescent female body is heavily policed, a "time bomb that might go off at any minute," a site of potential "devastation" because of the threat of unwelcome male attention and unwanted pregnancy (*Silent* 139, 140).[11] In her fifteenth year, the Puerto Rican women around her enforce gender expectations and restrictions and she suddenly feels "watched every minute" (139). In "The Story of My Body," the disturbing onset of puberty marks the point where Ortiz

---

[10] See Cheng's discussion of the "specter of racial melancholia" in immigrant literature, characterized by "obsession with the norm" and horrified fascination with the freakish (79), and also her analysis of the "discourse of hypochondria," where illness functions as a "parable for the narrator's psychical activities in the face of assimilation, activities that help to organize the self's response to intrasubjective threats in a racist and sexist world" (68). See also my article on "The Story of My Body" ("The Stories").

[11] See Springfield's discussion of "the body at center stage in the battle between individual desire and social convention" in *Silent Dancing*.

Cofer desires a kind of disembodiment. "Although I wanted to think of myself as 'intellectual,' my body was demanding that I notice it. I saw the little swelling around my once-flat nipples, the fine hairs growing in secret places; but my knees were still bigger than my thighs, and I always wore long- or half-sleeve blouses to hide my bony upper arms" (*Latin* 140). The division of the intellectual from the bodily presages the split in the essay's conclusion, when she seems to retreat from the body into the realm of the mind.

The tension at the close of "The Story of My Body" is not unlike the tension between Judith Shakespeare's gendered body (her thwarted female creativity and desires, and the death and devastation following her illegitimate pregnancy) and the disembodied, androgynous mind that Woolf admires and emulates. "Who shall measure the heat and violence of the poet's heart when caught and tangled in a woman's body?" she asks of Shakespeare's doomed sister (*AROO* 48). As Ellen Rosenman points out, Judith Shakespeare's painful experience of the female body is "submerged" and suppressed in Woolf's vision of androgyny, where the "mind has replaced the body" (275),[12] and in the metaphoric confusions of Woolf's closing vision of her immortality. "At the essay's end," Rosenman observes, "Judith Shakespeare's body is hardly a body at all; it is something which is 'put on' and 'laid down' like an article of clothing when her legacy is realized by other women writers, a spiritualized incarnation which has nothing to do with heat and violence" (276). The story of her body remains to be told.

IV

In "Professions for Women," Woolf defined the task for the woman writer as twofold: to kill the "Angel in the House," the selfless part of her that caters to the needs of others, and to "tell the truth about [her] own experiences as a body" (285-86, 288). She claimed that although she had succeeded in the first, she had not yet succeeded in the second. As a number of her successors have noted, the two

---

[12] Silver compellingly suggests that this is true in the popular iconography of Woolf as well: "But if Virginia Woolf often appears as a face, that face is nevertheless connected to a head and the head to a body, both of which prove equally threatening. As head, Virginia Woolf becomes emblematic of the mind or intellect, the intellectual (a 'talking head'), and hence a threat to the social and political division of genders that have excluded women from the public realm. But by virtue of her being a woman, her face and head can never be divorced from her body, that body that by weighing her down should ground her in the realm of the reproductive, the material, not the intellectual or transcendent. ... And if, as is the case with so many representations of Virginia Woolf, the body becomes so frail and fragile as to become ghostly, this too is frightening, carrying within it the taint of death. So does the nonreproductive body, whether the failure to reproduce is chosen or not" (85-86).

issues are not completely separate. Olsen redefines the "Angel in the House" in working class and maternal terms when she substitutes the "essential angel" who mops the floors, cooks the meals, and takes care of her children—an angel that she could hardly kill, since "there was no one else to do her work" (*Silences* 34, 38). And she further draws attention to the role of the mother when she says that she wouldn't want to kill the "caring part" of Woolf's angel in herself, even if she could (38). Ortiz Cofer enters this ongoing conversation among feminists in her essays "Taking the Macho" and "5:00 a.m.: Writing as Ritual." She acknowledges the pressures to become the "Angel in the House" and lose oneself (pressures that she and her grandmother resisted in different ways), describing herself as a woman whose "artistic drive often clashed with male macho" and "predetermined feminine role[s]," "a woman fiercely protective of her artistic and personal territory" (*Woman* 68, 66). In "5:00 a.m.," where she writes of achieving a "room of one's own" by claiming space in the early morning hours before the family began to stir, she mentions that she continues this practice even now that her daughter is grown. But she also suggests, as Olsen does, that the caring was part of her creativity. Looking back at the time spent raising her daughter, she says:

> ... I do not regret the endless hours of sitting in tiny chairs at the Rock-Ette Academy of Dance or of breathing the saturated air at the stables as I waited for her. She got out of her activities something like what I got out of getting up in the dark to work: the feeling that you are in control, in the saddle, on your toes. Empowerment is what the emerging artist needs to win for herself. (*Latin* 168)

The debate over motherhood and creativity is too long to summarize here. In a fertile consideration of the subject, Susan Suleiman sketches the broad themes: "opposition and integration, motherhood as obstacle or source of conflict and motherhood as link, as source of connection to work and world" (362). Olsen claimed that in the nineteenth and twentieth centuries, "until very recently almost all distinguished achievement has come from childless women," appending a list of thirty-three women, Woolf among them (31). Later in her 1972 essay she suggests that "more and more women writers in our century, primarily in the last two decades, are assuming as their right fullness of work *and* family life" (32). In a footnote she lists sixty-two writers, including Walker, who argues in her essay "*One* Child of One's Own" that women artists "should have children—*assuming this is of interest to them*—but only one" (*In Search* 363).

In "Taking the Macho," Ortiz Cofer observes that writing requires an element of macho; "you cannot be passive and *create*" (68). She cites Woolf on insanity as the outcome of frustrated silence, and on the dangers of becoming that "solicitous creature," the Angel in the House (68-69). Yet in "5:00 a.m.: Writing as Ritual," she also envisions mothering as consistent with and parallel to artistic creation. Ortiz Cofer thinks back through her mothers, literal and literary, and forward through her daughter in a sequence of poems in *Silent Dancing* and *The Latin Deli* addressed to her daughter Tanya. "To a Daughter I Cannot Console" suggests that worry over her daughter's experiences brings her closer to her own Puerto Rican mother, and revives memories of her adolescence; as her mother asks her "to remember the boy I had cried over for days./I could not for several minutes/recall that face" (*Latin* 163). In "Holly" and "Lessons of the Past" in *Silent Dancing* she resurrects memories of her own past as gifts for her daughter. She reads and writes the "forbidden book" of the body in a poem aptly entitled "Unspoken" in *The Latin Deli*. Despite the "covenant of silence" surrounding the pains of her daughter's changing adolescent body ("you wince in pain for the tender/swelling of new breasts"), she expresses her redemptive conviction that the "body/will find itself," and that her daughter, too, will experience the "pleasure of a lover's hands on skin," and an ecstatic "moment of being," that

> ... moment
> when a woman first feels
> a baby's mouth at her breast, opening her
> like the hand of God in Genesis, the moment
> when all that led to this seems right. (*Latin* 158)

Sandra Gilbert and Susan Gubar argue that the "emergence of the mother-writer" in late twentieth-century writing has effectively created a "new genre" in women's writing (378, 393). In poems addressed to their offspring, contemporary mother-writers look "backward and forward" (402), inhabiting the body in a way that male poets do not. "Certainly for contemporary women writers," they write, "the materiality of maternity no longer seems to undercut the supposed transcendence of fleshly imperatives necessary for or associated with literary authority":

> Since the 1950s women of letters have evidently achieved a new kind of solution to the mind/body problem: not a monolithic solution by any means and not one that we are prescribing, but one that seems historically unprecedented. (392)

Women have begun to tell the truths of their bodies in ways that Woolf anticipated but never fully imagined or achieved.

Woolf concluded *A Room of One's Own* with a vision of women writers of the future putting on the body of Shakespeare's silenced sister to give birth to her poetry: "Drawing her life from the lives of the unknown who were her forerunners, as her brother did before her, she will be born" (114). Ortiz Cofer draws on the mother-daughter relations at the center of Woolf's work, Woolf's theories of creativity and female achievement, her fascination with the female body and literary embodiment, her vividly recollected "moments of being" and conception of memoir to produce new literary forms in a new historical moment and socio-economic and cultural context. As concerned with her "literary legacy" as with her "literary heritage" (Harris-Williams 33), Woolf would undoubtedly have been pleased to imagine that her words would bear fruit in Ortiz Cofer's writings, and among so many different writers in the twentieth and twenty-first centuries, who would think back through their mothers and feel the tug of what Ortiz Cofer describes as the "invisible umbilical cord" connecting her to her British modernist foremother (Acosta-Bélen 93).

Works Cited

Acosta-Bélen, Edna. "A MELUS Interview: Judith Ortiz Cofer." *MELUS* 18.3 (1993): 83-97.

Allan, Tuzyline Jita. "A Voice of One's Own: Implications of Impersonality in the Essays of Virginia Woolf and Alice Walker." *The Politics of the Essay: Feminist Perspectives*. Ed. Ruth-Ellen Boetcher Joeres and Elizabeth Mittman. Bloomington: Indiana UP, 1993. 131-47.

Anzaldúa, Gloria. "Speaking in Tongues: A Letter to Third World Women Writers." *This Bridge Called My Back: Writings by Radical Women of Color*. Ed. Cherríe Moraga and Gloria Anzaldúa. Watertown, MA: Persephone P, 1981. 165-74.

Barrett, Eileen. "Septimus and Shadrack: Woolf and Morrison Envision the Madness of War." Hussey and Neverow. 26-32.

Bartkevicius, Jocelyn. "An Interview with Judith Ortiz Cofer." *Speaking of the Short Story: Interviews with Contemporary Writers*. Ed. Farhat Iftekharuddin, Mary Rohrberger, and Maurice Lee. Jackson: U of Mississippi P, 1997. 57-74.

Cheng, Anne Anlin. *The Melancholy of Race: Psychoanalysis, Assimilation, and Hidden Grief*. New York: Oxford UP, 2001

Christian, Barbara. "Layered Rhythms: Virginia Woolf and Toni Morrison." Hussey and Neverow. 164-77.

Cisneros, Sandra. *The House on Mango Street*. New York: Random House, Vintage, 1984, rev. 1989, 1991.

———. "Notes to a Young(er) Writer." *The Americas Review* 15 (1987): 74-76.

Cliff, Michelle. "Virginia Woolf and the Imperial Gaze: A Glance Askance." Hussey and Neverow. 91-102.

Courington, Chella. "Virginia Woolf and Alice Walker: Family as Metaphor in the Personal Essay." Hussey and Neverow. 239-45.

Doyle, Jacqueline. "More Room of Her Own: Sandra Cisneros' *The House on Mango Street*." *MELUS* 19.4 (1994): 5-35.

———. "The Stories Her Body Tells: Judith Ortiz Cofer's 'The Story of My Body,'" *a/b: Auto/Biography Studies* 22.1 (2007): 46-65.

Fernald, Anne. "A Room, A Child, A Mind of One's Own: Virginia Woolf, Alice Walker and Feminist Personal Criticism." Hussey and Neverow. 245-51.

Garner, Shirley Nelson, Claire Kahane, and Madelon Sprengnether, eds. *The (M)other Tongue: Essays in Feminist Psychoanalytic Interpretation.* Ithaca: Cornell UP; 1985.

Gilbert, Sandra M. and Susan Gubar. *No Man's Land: The Place of the Woman Writer in the Twentieth Century, Volume 3, Letters from the Front.* New Haven: Yale UP, 1994.

Gordon, Stephanie. "An Interview with Judith Ortiz Cofer. *AWP Chronicle* (1997): 1-9. Judith Ortiz Cofer Home Page. 21 Jun 2005. <http://www.english.uga.edu/~jcofer/gordoninterview.html>

Harris-Williams, Ann. "Woolf and Toni Morrison: Moments from the Critical Dialogue." Hussey and Neverow. 32-37.

hooks, bell. "On Self-Recovery." *Talking Back: Thinking Feminist, Thinking Black.* Boston: South End P, 1989. 28-34.

———. "Zora Neale Hurston: A Subversive Reading." *Moving Beyond Boundaries. Volume 2: Black Women's Diasporas.* Ed. Carole Boyce Davies. New York: New York UP, 1995. 244-55.

Hussey, Mark and Vara Neverow, eds. *Virginia Woolf: Emerging Perspectives. Selected Papers from the Third Annual Conference on Virginia Woolf.* New York: Pace UP, 1994.

Kahane, Claire. "The Gothic Mirror." Garner, Kahane, and Sprengnether. 334-51.

Kevane, Bridget. "The Poetic Truth: An Interview with Judith Ortiz Cofer." *Latina Self-Portraits: Interviews with Contemporary Women Writers.* Ed. Bridget Kevane and Juanita Heredia. Albuquerque: U of New Mexico P, 2000. 109-23.

Kincaid, Jamaica. *Lucy.* New York: Penguin Books, Plume, 1990, 1991.

Kingston, Maxine Hong. *The Woman Warrior: Memoirs of a Girlhood Among Ghosts.* New York: Random House, Vintage, 1976, 1989.

London, Bette. "Guerrilla in Petticoats or Sans-Culotte? Virginia Woolf and the Future of Feminist Criticism." *diacritics* 21.2-3 (1991): 11-29.

Marcus, Jane. "Introduction." *New Feminist Essays on Virginia Woolf.* Ed. Jane Marcus. Lincoln: U of Nebraska P, 1981. xiii-xx.

Ocasio, Rafael. "The Infinite Variety of the Puerto Rican Reality: An Interview with Judith Ortiz Cofer." *Callaloo* 17.3 (1994): 730-42.
Olsen, Tillie. *Silences*. New York: Dell, 1989.
Ortiz Cofer, Judith. *The Latin Deli: Telling the Lives of Barrio Women.* New York: W.W. Norton, 1999.
———. *Silent Dancing: A Partial Remembrance of a Puerto Rican Childhood.* Houston: Arte Público P, 1990.
———. *Woman in Front of the Sun: On Becoming a Writer.* Athens: U of Georgia P, 2000.
Rich, Adrienne. "When We Dead Awaken: Writing as Re-Vision." *On Lies, Secrets, and Silence: Selected Prose 1966-1978.* New York: W.W. Norton, 1979. 33-49.
Rosenman, Ellen. "Writing the Body of Virginia Woolf." Hussey and Neverow. 272-77.
Silver, Brenda R. *Virginia Woolf Icon.* Chicago: U of Chicago P, 1999.
Smith, Sidonie. *Subjectivity, Identity, and the Body: Women's Autobiographical Practices in the Twentieth Century.* Bloomington: Indiana UP, 1993.
Springfield, Consuelo López. "Stories of a Chameleon: Judith Ortiz Cofer's 'Moments of Being.'" *a/b: Auto/Biography Studies* 18.1 (2003): 105-16.
Suleiman, Susan Rubin. "Writing and Motherhood." Garner, Kahane, and Sprengnether. 352-77.
Trinh, T. Minh-ha. *Woman, Native, Other: Writing Postcoloniality and Feminism.* Bloomington: Indiana UP, 1989.
Viramontes, Helena María. "'Nopalitos': The Making of Fiction." *Making Face, Making Soul, Haciendo Caras: Creative and Critical Perspectives by Feminists of Color.* Ed. Gloria Anzaldúa. San Francisco: Aunt Lute Books, 1990. 291-94.
Walker, Alice. *In Search of Our Mothers' Gardens.* New York: Harvest/HBJ, 1983.
Williams, Lisa. *The Artist as Outsider in the Novels of Toni Morrison and Virginia Woolf.* Westport: Greenwood P, 2000.
Woolf, Virginia. "Memories of a Working Women's Guild." *Collected Essays.* Vol. 4. New York: Harcourt, Brace, and World, 1967. 134-48.
———. *Moments of Being.* Ed. Jeanne Schulkind. New York: Harcourt, 1976, 2d. ed, 1985.
———. "Professions for Women." *Collected Essays.* Vol. 2. New York: Harcourt, Brace, and World, 1967. 284-89.

———. *A Room of One's Own.* New York: Harcourt Brace Jovanovich, Harvest, 1929, 1989.
Zwerdling, Alex. *Virginia Woolf and the Real World.* Berkeley: U of California P, 1986.

"Success in Circuit Lies": Editing the War in *Mrs. Dalloway*
Jane Lilienfeld

"Tell all the truth/But Tell it Slant/Success in Circuit lies," cautions a poem by Emily Dickinson (Johnson 506-07). Dickinson died in 1882, the year of Virginia Woolf's birth; in 1934, Woolf gave Elizabeth Bowen a copy of the *Complete Poems of Emily Dickinson* (*L5* 309). Did Woolf speculate as to their similarities? Both writers faced similar circumstances: entrapment in father-centered families, unattainable and absent mothers, social class position vitiated by familial and cultural attitudes, and, in each of their cases, illness that was questioned by others, who doubted causation as well as the illness itself.[1] Each writer used numerous personae; each writer had a searing wit; neither writer, as some feminist literary critics have asserted, believed or enacted the heterosexual romance myth (Rich 157-8, Bennett 84).

Hence, a famous line in the Emily Dickinson poem numbered 1129 by Thomas H. Johnson may be pertinent to Virginia Woolf: "Tell all the Truth but tell it slant/Success in Circuit Lies." The wry wit, the subtle pun, and the bold assertiveness of its imperative mark this line as being that of Emily Dickinson. In light of this comparison, such an assertion serves well as the starting point for my essay, which examines the representation of the conflagration of a world war in a novel that does not seem to focus on war.

This essay argues that although Virginia Woolf knew a great deal about World War I, in fact, she decided against an explicit discourse of the Great War in *Mrs. Dalloway*. First, Woolf refused to insert the "self" into the text (*D2* 20). Second, Woolf abhorred political detritus emerging into what she considered to be literary art ("The Artist and Politics" 226-7). One may argue these two points and the results of them if one acknowledges that which many scholars have documented. Basing their views on the work of Jane Marcus, numerous scholars have argued that Woolf censored her pre-publication drafts (Marcus 53). If this is the case, one question that naturally arises is whether World War I is more fully represented in the many texts that precede the published versions of *Mrs. Dalloway*? In order to investigate the representation of warfare in the pre-publication texts, which of the numerous early versions might a scholar investigate?

As Mark Hussey has argued, the complex origins of *Mrs. Dalloway* incorporate Woolf's reading and translating of Greek tragedies (172-3) and her setting *The Waste Land* in type for the Hogarth Press (*A to Z* 172). Further, Woolf

---

[1] Hermione Lee trivializes the incestuous attacks on Woolf by using the term "sexual interference" (124). See also Bennett 15-17.

wrote a short story cycle about Mrs. Dalloway's acquaintances, her husband's political connections, the preparations for her party, and various guests' embodied appearance in the mind of the self and other (Prose viii-ix). Earlier and less likeable characters named Clarissa and Richard Dalloway in *The Voyage Out* also must be noted, although they differ markedly from their counterparts in the novel.

Just as there are earlier versions of the central characters, there are several drafts of the novel itself. Three and one half notebooks of holographs are in the Berg Collection of the New York Public Library. There are also three holograph notebooks at the British Museum (Hoffman). There are also two proofs, one for the first American and another for the first British edition (Shields). Woolf sent the third extant proof to Jacques Raverat shortly before his death (Wright; Wussow xx).

These abundant drafts of parts and drafts of the whole of that which became the published texts of *Mrs. Dalloway* exemplify what Donald Reiman and Brenda Silver term "versioning," the co-existence of numerous forms of a narrative, of which no one text can claim to be definitive (Silver 13-14). No matter how one approaches the motivating question of this paper, most scholars would admit that interpretation depends on textuality. In order to examine the representation of the war in earlier forms of the novel and in one published text, I will rely on a comparison of Helen Wussow's transcription of the three holograph notebooks in the British Museum and the British Library to the first Harcourt Brace edition of *Mrs. Dalloway* published in the United States in 1925, and subsequently used as the basis for American paperback editions.

However, the very instability of the text under consideration indicates that no one analysis can be definitive. Thus, whichever edition of *Mrs. Dalloway* the reader delves into, the text(s) convey(s) the view that the griefs of World War I are necessarily traumatic (Showalter 168, 172). The aftershock of that war strikes many when they see what Neil Hanson in his recent book, *Unknown Soldiers*, terms "[t]he bald statistics of the Great War . . . ."

These statistics each mark a life lost: "9 million soldiers dead or missing, 21 million maimed or wounded" (Hanson xiv). In the trenches, "some 7,000 British men and officers were killed and wounded daily, just as a matter of course. 'Wastage' the Staff called it" (Fussell 41).

The widespread insistence in Britain and the Continent on decent burials for those killed in war arose because survivors knew that thousands had been thrust without sufficient religious ceremony into shallow graves that soon exposed bodies to be eaten by rats and dogs (Hanson 55). Because the war involved civilians and the home front had been bombed (Levenback, "Civilian" 80-82), few so-called civilians may have felt safe in Britain, and food shortages had affected those on the Continent. There were few in Western Europe whose lives had not been altered by the War.

"History," notes Claire Kahane, "[. . .] can be thought of as the history of traumatic events [. . .] historical change and movement [occur] through the disruption of the ordinary flow of time, through the inherent violence of the extraordinary act which ruptures sheer being" (223). Thus, as Kahane argues, a society as well as a person can experience war trauma. Indeed, in many studies of trauma, that war can affect a society as a whole is now well established (van der Kolk, et al. 3). Karen DeMeester's recent essay substantiates the argument that the culture depicted within the world of *Mrs. Dalloway* is in traumatic shock after World War I ("Obstacles" 77-8).

Thus it is not surprising that, although not constantly mentioned, World War I is pervasive in the transcription by Wussow of the British Museum typescript and holograph, "The Hours."

Further, one may confidently assert that Virginia Woolf had a more exact knowledge of conditions at the French front than the Harcourt edition of *Mrs. Dalloway* may directly represent. During the war, Virginia Woolf knew more about it than did many British civilians. Many British families, who depended on their sons' letters for both information and emotional sustenance, did not receive the full text of those letters, for soldiers' letters home were heavily censored. Additionally, popular journalism was jingoistic and propagandized, thus reinforcing the limiting effects on knowledge of letters home to families (Levenback, *Great*, 56, 98, 102-4).

Leonard Woolf was a source of information that others would not have had about the war. The marriage of Leonard and Virginia Woolf depended on a vigorous and many-faceted life of ideas, and their exchange of views was a vibrant aspect of both their creative lives (Spater and Parsons 62). Therefore, it is not amiss to note that Leonard Woolf's activities as a Socialist activist and journalist during the war years gave him access to the extensive masculine network of war discourse, formal and informal, extending beyond the pacifists who gathered at Garsington and Charleston.

For example, in 1915, three years after his love affair with Vanessa Bell, Roger Fry, a Quaker pacifist, visited the front on a fact-finding mission. Fry's observations appeared in September 1915 in *War and Peace*, a journal edited by, among others, Leonard Woolf (see appendix). It seems probable that Fry and Leonard Woolf would have discussed the specifics and results of trench warfare (Fry 183-4).

Norman Angell was a man typical of how extensive and layered were the networks created by Leonard Woolf. Angell, the founding editor of *War and Peace*, was a then well-known pacifist in pre-World War I Britain. Angell identified himself (in the third person) thus in his autobiography: "Angell [. . .] was one of the earliest advocates of the League of Nations and one of its severest critics"

(207). Angell remarks that he worked at Dunkirk as a stretcher bearer, for he sought to "join one of the Quaker Ambulances [units] that were forming and get work at the front in that way" (190). Angell's purposes overlapped though were not entirely congruent with aspects of Roger Fry's Quaker pacifism and Leonard Woolf's anti-militaristic work.[2]

Additionally, Virginia Woolf had strong connections to soldiers who fought in the war. She reviewed in the *Times Literary Supplement* an early volume of war poems by Siegfried Sassoon (Showalter 192). In 1924, when she was writing *Mrs. Dalloway*, Woolf met Sassoon at Garsington, and later invited him for lunch (Showalter 192). It seems likely that they discussed the war and its aftermath. Mentored by Robert Graves (Wilson 238-9, 297-9) and a mentor thence to Wilfred Owen (Showalter 180-1), Sassoon's novels and memoirs render the daily experience of trench warfare in terms of what Paul Fussell calls "sardonic pastoral" (166), a viewpoint that metaphorically structures *Mrs. Dalloway*.

An entry in what the editor asserts is Leonard Woolf's handwriting in Woolf's *Diary* for May 1, 1918 uses the phrase "never-endians" (146), so common was the sense that the war would drag on into soldiers' old age.[3] Many civilians were apprehensive, for the enemy bombed the British coastal areas. From 1915 until better defenses were established in late 1917, the Germans flew 103 bombardment missions over London and southern Britain ("War in the Air").[4]

After her recovery in 1915 through 1918, Woolf herself scanned the skies over Asheham Downs and over London, just as surely as British soldiers scanned the sky above their trenches—and for the same reason: would the enemy bomb? Reviewing Woolf's published *Diary* entries from 1915 through 1918, I counted thirty-two notations of cloud, color, mist, rain or fog. Typical is Woolf's entry of July 18, 1918: "The Germans are not succeeding this time, & the weather is windy, hot, violently wet & sunny all in turn [sic]. We are once more getting safe through the moon" (170).

Therefore, it is clear that Jane Marcus's assertion might be true: Woolf "disembowelled" her inchoate ideas, even in the process of crafting the earliest drafts of her novels (Marcus 53). In this case, Woolf deleted direct statements about World War I when turning the segments of holographs and subsequent typescript corrections of such holographs into the published novel.

For example, Woolf begins the first scene in the Wussow transcription of the three holograph notebooks of "The Hours" with a visit by "weedy boys" to

[2] For slightly different contextualizations, see Glendinning 189-90 and 200.
[3] See Fussell 55; Blunden, Sassoon, and Graves shared this view.
[4] At some point between 1915 and his death in 1916, 2nd Lt. William Ratcliffe recorded that clouds were transformed into "aeroplane" detritus (Fussell 55). Levenback discusses Woolf's response to the dread of being bombed from the air in her essay "Civilian," 84-87.

the Cenotaph monument to the war dead (Wussow 4-5, 11-12). The published edition of the novel subsumes the marching boys into Peter Walsh's self-satisfied observations at Kew Gardens (*MD* 54-5), some fifty-four pages into the book. Fortunately, Woolf retained the word "weedy" in both Wussow and the published editions, thus reminding readers of the metaphors of death, dismemberment, and the grasses grown on fertile graves that course through that version of the novel (Bradshaw, "Vanished").

Others of Woolf's textual choices have attracted commentary, too. For example, David Bradshaw examines the very heart of some of Woolf's most serious excisions: "[I]t was in the trenches," Septimus explains to his doctor, that "my friend Evans was killed at Verny Ridge" (Wussow 138). Woolf's handwriting is notoriously difficult to read (Goldman), giving the varied editors room to maneuver in their interpretations. As Bradshaw notes, a name that Wussow transcribes as "Verney Ridge" ("Virginia" 496), Levenback states as "Virney Ridge" ("Virginia" 496).

Differing from the two variants noted by Wussow and Levenback, is Bradshaw's interpretation of Woolf's handwriting. Bradshaw interprets the "er" or "ir" as an "m," concluding that in the holograph Virginia Woolf alludes to "Vimy Ridge" ("Virginia" 496). If in fact Bradshaw's reading is accurate, then one should pause to consider as serious such a near-allusion to the infamous battle of Vimy Ridge of 1915—part of the Artois/Champagne Campaign—that extended over several months, in which the losses were "appalling": "The Germans lost six hundred thousand, the French lost one million, two hundred, and the British lost two hundred seventy-nine thousand troops" (Dupuy and Dupuy 1039).

If it were Vimy Ridge to which Woolf referred, then recently published surviving letters from Alec Reader, one of the British soldiers who fought there, recount the horrors of many days of fighting. His battalion had set out with one hundred twenty soldiers and returned with only seventeen alive after almost eighteen hours of continuous battle (Hanson 52). Alec Reader witnessed men blown to bits, drowned in mud, lost to friendly fire (Hanson 56).

Not only did Woolf delete allusion to any battle scene from the published edition, she moved both Evans and Septimus later in the war to the Italian front, and she kept Evans alive until almost the close of the war. Why? Grace Radin suggests that in *The Years* often Woolf would "soften" political specificity or "place [events] in a broader context" to "make them more palatable and persuasive" to the reader (4). It seems that is the case here. To keep both men creditably alive, Woolf had to remove them from specific entrenched battlefields. Extending their service to the war's end would strengthen their intense attachment, add to the poignancy of Evans' loss right before the armistice and make creditable Septimus's designation as a war hero.

Nor is this the only excision of specific war references. One sentence in the Wussow transcription, for example, suggests how Woolf might have presented the impact of the war on the Dalloway family so very differently than the final version of the novel suggests. This discarded variant occurs within Elizabeth Dalloway's comparison of Miss Kilman to her parents. "And [Miss Kilman] made Elizabeth realize all sorts of things [. . .] she had another point of view. [. . .] Her father and mother always thought the English were right. There were wounded soldiers about the house all day long" (Wussow 219).

This is very different than, for example, Clarissa's infamous query, "was it the Armenians or the Albanians" (*MD* 129), excoriated by Trudi Tate (154-7). The presence of the wounded in their bustling, servant-filled, orderly household would implicate both Dalloways in an extensive civilian contribution to the war effort and would directly represent the war's impact on civilian life. Wounded soldiers taken in, comforted and whose care was apparently paid for by the Dalloways, would suggest a depth of patriotism that one could imagine in Richard, but for which there is little evidence in the Clarissa who herself admits that she "lacked [. . .] something central which permeated" (*MD* 32). Woolf deleted the above paragraph in Wussow from the published edition.

These two examples must suffice to stand for the many that space does not permit investigating. Since it is now clear that Woolf intended the war to interpenetrate each sentence of the novel, then, if not by explicit statement, how did Woolf manage to achieve her narrative goal?

Woolf's aesthetic preferences that novels banish "the damned egotistical self" (*D2* 14) and not stoop to propaganda suggest two reasons why Woolf chose narrative indirection (Radin 6-7). But perhaps, too, the experience of trauma could be another motivating factor for a method in which allusion and imagery direct the reader (Eberly 208-9, 211), not the omniscient author of nineteenth century fiction.

Numerous feminist North American academic critics over the past forty years have forged the theoretical underpinning of my comparison of the depiction of World War I in Wussow's transcription of the three holograph notebooks of "The Hours" and the published edition of *Mrs. Dalloway*. Woolf replaced omniscient narration by a flexible polyvocality, part of which consists of a narrative of imagery that accrues more meaning with each deployment. Feminist critics have argued that what Harvena Richter identified in 1974 as "symbol clusters" (207) may be read as a series of allusions, which, traced to their sources, reveal more than a character's personal unconscious or "the collective unconscious" (Marcus 36-56).

In *Woolf Against Empire*, Kathy Phillips interprets allusions throughout Woolf's major novels in political, postcolonial terms. In two articles about the goddess, Evelyn Haller views allusions through Woolf's thorough knowledge of women's history ("Isis," "Anti-Madonna"). Extensive narratives of lesbian love flourish via metaphor in *Jacob's Room* and *The Years,* argue Vara Neverow and Patricia Cramer (Neverow, "Goddess"; Cramer). These are only some of the substantial interpretations by numerous Woolf scholars that analyze how continuous narratives of metaphor create indirect feminist, political and critical commentaries.

Thus metaphorical indirection (or, as Dickinson called it, "truth in circuit") enabled Woolf to make the Great War ever present in *Mrs. Dalloway* without recourse to sentimentality or to political harangues.

In 1922, in what is Appendix Two of Wussow's transcription, Woolf explicitly paralleled the author with her fiction: "S[eptimus's] character [. . .] Had been in the war. [*sic*] or founded on me?" (Wussow 418) Thus "Woolf connected the shell-shocked war veteran with [the women diagnosed as Woolf had been] through their common enemy, the nerve specialists" explained Elaine Showalter (192). The doubling of Clarissa Dalloway with Septimus Warren Smith is one of the major means that Woolf used to soften points more explicitly depicted in "The Hours" manuscript (Radin 4).

Imagery of trenches, sky, time itself form what many critics term the novel's elegiac pastoral elements (Bagley; Froula 88; Erica Johnson; Zeiss). As one would expect, flowers occur in profusion in both manuscript and published book. One haunting example is the ruined garden where Peter proposes to Clarissa in almost exactly the same words in both manuscript and published text (*MD* 68; Wussow 40). Similarly, Septimus proposed to Rezia in her family's backyard garden, which, ironically, is mostly concrete (*MD* 93). Under the tutelage of Miss Isabel Pole, Septimus imagines the war in terms of a Shakespearean idyll, as did so many. In the manuscript he was one of the first to volunteer (*MD* 93) "[to enter] In the dark soil, which no gardener turns with his trowel" (Wussow 106), that is, the graveyard of the front.

Certainly, it is true that at the troops' arrival, the French battlefields looked, smelled, and sounded Edenic. Larks and nightingales sang and soared. Cultivated gardens burgeoned. Streams flowed clear. Poppies, wild flowers, and roses bloomed amidst the grasses (Fussell 134, 166-9). Returning infantryman Stephen Hewett recalled, for instance, "the nightingales in the warm darkness by a [. . .] weedy river," and marching "in some pretty village full of shady trees" (qtd. in Fussell 326-7).

Thus, on page 8 of *Mrs. Dalloway*, Clarissa thinks that "she [is] part [. . .] of the trees at home [. . .] [which] lifted her on their branches as she had seen the trees lift the mist [. . .]" (*MD* 8). Similarly, Siegfried Sassoon's autobiographical novel, *Memoirs of an Infantry Officer*, recalls that "[o]n wet days [. . .] the trees a mile away were like ash-gray smoke rising from the naked ridges [. . .]" (qtd. in

Fussell 136). Edmund Blunden, too, saw "[t]he white mist [. . .] [flow with] slow, cold currents above the pale grass" (36). Ironically, this mist could be "lingering pockets of [poison] gas" that each side directed into one another's trenches (Fussell 49). Like mist, the stench of death hovered over this once-Edenic setting: "you could smell the [trenches] miles before you could see [them]" (Fussell 49).

Read through these narratives, Septimus's visions resonate with the voices of other soldiers. They, too, experienced the beauty turned grotesque, as once "noble" trees became "ghostly gallows" (Blunden 79, 117). Septimus's belief that "leaves were alive, trees were alive. And the leaves were connected by millions of fibres with his own body" (*MD* 22) appears in David Jones's memory of "wounded men and wounded trees" (qtd. in Fussell 145). Sky, clouds, time, trenches and a ravaged pastoral, unite soldier Septimus and civilian Clarissa. An inexorable link ties imagery of the battlefield to civilian life after the war.

To explore this assertion, I will now examine three major tropes of *Mrs. Dalloway* and of the many texts consequent on World War I, allusions to time, to the sky, and to the trenches.

Time

As Paul Fussell notes, British soldiers either literate or orally schooled in the great British poetic tradition, read the landscape of the trenches in which they found themselves literally entombed, through an oral and written tradition of a British landscape turned from earth into language by centuries of poets (115, 161-3, 231-5).

It is a critical truism that this book, first named "The Hours," dramatizes the ravages of time (DiBattista 30-33; Samuels). It should be remembered, however, that the novel's narrative of metaphoric time forwards soldiers' harrowing sense of time into post-war civilian daily life.

The daily procession of the sun and moon across the sky, observed by thousands of soldiers trapped in trenches, ironically conveyed stasis, for many believed the Great War would last forever (Fussell 71-74, 162-7). As the stalemate dragged on, time itself became the soldiers' enemy. Clarissa's persistent sense of time's brutality, as do so many of her feelings, encodes in it sentiments from the trenches. For instance, Clarissa "fear[ing] time itself, and read[ing] on Lady Bruton's face, as if it had been a dial cut in impassive stone [. . .] how year by year her share was sliced" might allude to the rat-gnawed faces of the war dead moldering side by side with those living in the trenches (*MD* 31; Fussell 49).

Smashing the clock face, the Great War transformed British poetic tradition (Fussell 52). In the trenches, dawn suggested not love, life, or hope as in poetry, but death. In the dawn all soldiers formed in ranks to "stand to." "Standing to," soldiers stood poised on the first rung of the ladders which they would climb, if under morning siege, to storm across "no man's land" to attack the Germans lodged in their trenches (Fussell 51-2). For centuries poets had used dusk to suggest the ebbing of life into death. But dusk in the trenches signaled relief, a respite from enemy shellfire. Night became time to repair the wire and regroup to make ready for the next day's attack (Fussell 47).[5]

Sky Imagery

Frequently, the sky imagery of postwar London presents both Septimus and Clarissa with a means of making meaning in a world both fear is meaningless (*MD* 83-4, 95). As does Clarissa, soldiers crouched in their trenches used the sky as a means of orienting themselves, finding in it beauty, stability, and permanence (Fussell 51-64). Fussell states that:

> To be in the trenches was to experience an unreal, unforgettable enclosure and constraint, as well as a sense of being unoriented and lost. One saw two things only: the walls of the unlocalized, undifferentiated earth and the sky above (51).

Repeatedly, soldiers' letters home, their memoirs, their poems depict the skies, the cloud formations, the constant interplay of shape, color, movement as inseparable from their daily experience of war (Fussell 162-9).

Returning to her party, having undergone through her empathic imagination Septimus's suicide from the after-effects of shell shock, Clarissa is astonished by the sky outside the window:

> It held, foolish as the idea was, something of her own in it, this country sky, this sky above Westminster. She parted the curtains, she looked [. . .] [at] the sky. It will be a solemn sky, turning away its cheek in beauty. But there it was—ashen pale, raced over quickly by tapering vast clouds. It was new to her. The wind must have risen [. . .] (*MD* 282-3).

Woolf's deft besmirching of the sky goddess's (DiBattista 30-1) deathly pale loveliness interrogates the classical male equation of the female with the natural while simultaneously alluding to the *Book of Common Prayer*'s burial service, the

---

[5] The novel's up and down rhythm, frequently noted by critics (DiBattista 24-28), may be read as an echo of the rhythm that structured soldiers' lives, just as it did the lives of those firing at them. Often, the narrative's rising and falling rhythm is crystallized in military metaphor. The airplane advertising Glaxo dives as if to drop a bomb, and the disturbance in the atmosphere that supersensitive Septimus experiences "falls like shells" (*MD* 20), reminding readers that aerial bombardment threatened civilians and soldiers alike.

incantation of "ashes to ashes and dust to dust." The allusions echo the haunting history of British pastoral elegy, through which, as Lisa Low argues, Woolf transformed Miltonic tropes for feminist purposes (235-9). The overarching sky connects the lost Septimus, the soldiers in the trenches, Clarissa's past life (*MD* 8) with the cloudy future. Nor can readers ignore the unstable pronoun reference, "it," which marks the dehumanization of war, Septimus's objectification by his doctors, and the hidden selves of Clarissa and Septimus. For floating pronouns loosened from their reference point in Woolf's writings gather meanings with each recurrence. "It" reminds readers that Septimus had shouted "I'll give it you" (*MD* 162) as he jumped to his death, a phrase critics suggest may be both a curse and his gift of a shared life to Clarissa.[6] The London sky outside the window is indeed a "new sky," as Clarissa calls it, for to survivors of World War I the skyscape suggests the view from the trenches.

Trench Warfare

Earlier I noted that Woolf's understanding of trench warfare was based on diverse and accurate sources. Not surprisingly, Woolf seems to have had metaphors of the trench system in mind as she described her narrative method in this book of World War I, a "tunnelling" back through the "caverns" of the past" (*D2* 272).[7] Obsessed all his life by the war, Blunden compared memory itself to "a trench system, with main stems and lesser branches [. . .]" (qtd. in Fussell 184).

The trenches in which soldiers hunkered down gave an ironic illusion of safety. Trenches recur in the repeated image of the hollowed-out-space in a watery world,[8] as, for example, is the little room where Clarissa repairs her party dress and speaks with Peter on his return from India (DiBattista 24-29; *MD* 41).

Clarissa's withdrawal to her attic bedroom echoes the soldiers' retreat to their trenches, suggesting death as well as rest (*MD* 32). Seemingly haunted by Marvell, the clinging sheet stretched tight is an allusion, not just to preserved virginity, but to a shroud (Fussell 165). The candle burned down close to its

end suggests not only ebbing life, but recalls an iconic experience recorded in many soldiers' memoirs of stolen moments to read by candle light in the trenches. Like the soldiers, Clarissa, huddled with "Baron Marbot's [war] *Memoirs*," seeks

---

[6] Clarissa received his gift at her party, which was itself "an offering" (*MD* 131). See also Eileen Barrett's analysis of Septimus's reaction to trench warfare (27).
[7] Many soldiers envisioned the trench system as an endless maze (Fussell 313). In December 1914, one British major wrote to his wife, "the trenches are a labyrinth. I have already lost myself repeatedly [. . .] you can't get out of them [. . .]" (Fussell 163).
[8] British trenches were poorly constructed and were often waterlogged. One's feet rarely dried if one lived in these for any length of time (Fussell 43-45).

escape in reading (*MD* 33).⁹ Indeed, argues Fussell, "Sassoon speaks for the whole British Expeditionary Force when he says, 'I didn't want to die—not before I'd finished *The Return of the Native* anyhow'" (163-4).

The line "narrower and narrower would her bed be" (*MD* 31) is usually interpreted as Clarissa's traumatized risk-aversion to sexual penetration, but, as well, the image suggests the war's trenches (Fussell 47-64). What were the trenches' dimensions? "[T]here was no standard trench system" (Keegan 176); "[t]he first shelter [might be] an existing ditch or field drain,"(177), for "trenches had to be *narrow* enough to present a difficult target [. . .]" (Keegan 176, italics mine).

Trenches frequently became graves. In a vision found only in the published edition, not in Wussow's transcription of "The Hours," an image forms in Richard's mind as he hurries from lunch with Lady Bruton and Hugh to present Clarissa with a love token. These are at first "blood red tulips" in the manuscript that in mid-scene (Wussow 175, 187) become roses, a flower that grew profusely on the battlefields of France (Fussell 243):

> Really, it was a miracle thinking of the War, and thousands of poor chaps, with all their lives before them, shovelled together, already half forgotten, it was a miracle. (*MD* 125)

According to Hanson's *Unknown Soldiers*, Richard's summary is accurate:

> Bones, body parts and whole corpses were even used as building materials [. . .][Fortifying "ditches"]. [Y]ellowing skulls, arms, legs could be seen packed tight into the dank, black soil . . . . [. . .]. A doorway into the underground bunker [. . .] might be propped by corpses [. . .] to give increased protection to those inside. (Hanson 87)

As the imagery insists, World War I is a shared trauma that unites both Clarissa and Septimus. Intertwined pastoral imagery recalling the savagery of trench warfare undergirds the oft-noted traumatic symptoms displayed by both (DeMeester; Henke, "Virginia"; Lilienfeld). Both witnessed the violent deaths

---

⁹ Dannell Jones was kind enough to share with me the section of her dissertation that identifies Baron Marbot as a leading commander of the Napoleonic wars. His memoir includes the attack on and retreat from Russia. Jones speculates that Woolf used candlelight anachronistically, for the house of a Member of Parliament in 1923 would have had electricity, even up in the attic. The candle and the baron both recall a time when war was fought for honor, in hand to hand combat, not with the hideous implements that killed thousands daily.

of those they loved: Septimus, of his commanding officer, Evans, Clarissa of her sister Sylvia (*MD* 84; Abel 33-4; van der Kolk 175-7). Both are risk averse and both startle easily. Fear motivates their marriages. Septimus becomes numbed, unable to grieve, feel or love. Clarissa acknowledges that she "lacks" warmth and physical passion (*MD* 32). Rezia's hat making (*MD* 94-5) and Richard's rustling the *Times* (*MD* 202*)* enable Septimus and Clarissa to find shelter with protectors.

But five years after the war's end, his wife's protection is insufficient to keep Septimus alive. The published version presents sketchily what Wussow's transcription of "The Hours" elaborates. Clarissa resents the sudden death of Septimus Warren Smith as it interrupts her party. She feels that the Bradshaws "dispersed" Septimus's suicide "as a trinket[. . .] <jingled> among their chains" (Wussow 388). This may not indicate her shallowness but rather allude to her risk-aversion to any emotional interruption that might lead to a painful sense of destabilization. The war has not left her, though she may repeat the self-soothing phrase, "but it was over, thank Heaven—over. It was June. The King and Queen were at the Palace" (*MD* 3). In contrast, Richard immediately accosts the Prime Minister to gain his support for a pending bill to address the delayed effects of shell shock (Wussow 383). Richard's compassion resonates, while what may appear to be Clarissa's selfishness is clearly an aspect of her traumatized private self.

"I'll give it you," yells Septimus as he flings himself on the spikes of Mrs. Filmer's iron railings. The published version truncates the lengthier statement flashed from Septimus into Clarissa's mind. Septimus's death figures the war dead: impaled on the fence, he visually refers back to the soldiers speared by the barbed wire of the battlefield (Briggs 137; Wussow 366; *MD* 260). The published edition of Septimus's vision of Evans is relevant here: the returned Evans of persistent memory has "no blood" or "wounds" (*MD* 75). That Evans's wholeness startles Septimus hints that Septimus witnessed dismemberment. This suggests but does not reproduce the dismembered bodies of the war dead, ubiquitous in survivors' visual memories (Blunden 57), a sight absent, too, from Wussow's transcription of *The Hours*.[10] Embodying the "macerated" (*MD* 72) bodies of the dead, Septimus expiates the crime of his survival and Evans's death, as does Clarissa.

In the published edition, Woolf cropped the language Septimus gave to Clarissa but extended the literally sensational. For, withdrawing for a moment from her party to regain her composure, Clarissa instead enters into the bodily dismemberment consequent on Septimus's death. That which Septimus might have experienced as he flung himself to his death, Clarissa experiences: "Up

---

[10] Trudi Tate restores the title of one of Dorothy Sayers's mystery stories to seriousness of purpose: "Vile Bodies" alludes to "[the] two sights [. . .] figured repeatedly in the soldiers' narratives of the Great War: corpses and bodies in pieces" (64).

had flashed the ground through him, blundering, bruising went the rusty spikes. There he lay with a thud, thud, thud, and a suffocation of blackness" (*MD* 200). Clarissa's body bears Septimus's physical pain (*MD* 26). The result is to insistently double the protagonists, but to mute what Septimus himself had earlier termed his messianic anti-war message (DiBattista 61-3; *MD* 25-6, 72).

Is the emotional connection between Septimus and Clarissa convincing to the reader? Would it have been more so if Woolf had hewn more closely to the manuscript version? Determined not to be betrayed by self-referentiality, Woolf muffled what she had faced in 1922, where, to quote Roger Poole, she formed Septimus as "a cogent symbol of what was really wrong with her" in the early years of World War I (Poole 185-6). Christine Froula reminds readers that Septimus's name, the number seven, is autobiographical; the writer was the seventh child of Julia Stephen (94).

However, in revising for publication the material transcribed by Wussow, Virginia Woolf deleted direct representation of her thorough knowledge of The Great War. What she rendered explicitly in the notebooks of "The Hours" became in the published text not so much expunged as implied. This she achieved by creating continuous and powerful metaphors conveying the pervasive social trauma of World War I.

Appendix: A Visit to France[11]
By Roger Fry

    Even after so many months of European war it requires a constant control over one's thoughts to believe in it entirely and completely. European war is in fact so fantastic, so improbable, it fits so well the rhetoric of the historical style, that we reject as soon as possible from our minds this alien material. It takes on perpetually a legendary character. The legend, it is true, is more boring than any medieval rigmarole, but it persists, in spite of all the poignant evidence to the contrary, in maintaining its legendary character.

    The journey to Paris is contrived, it is true, so as to exhibit the reality of war by the imposition of innumerable discomforts and inconveniences, but the war spirit is here felt only as an exaggeration of the methods and habits of our celebrated southern railway companies. But France, in wartime is, except just near to the fighting line, but little distinguishable from France at peace. The evidences of the war are mainly negative. There is less business, less light, less gaiety, less interest. The whole life of the community is carried on on a lower level. There is less of all that makes the life of a town like Paris stimulating and valuable to the whole world. There is, however, a kind of fixed determination or fatalistic endurance of the whole hideous reality, and a quiet confidence that whatever can be done is being done. In part this is due to a complete and universal belief in Joffre. This is a surprising trait in the French, who usually speak of all authorities with ironical cynicism and scepticism. In short, the French are taking the war with a dignity which is altogether lacking on this side of the Channel. Here, as we all know, wartime has brought a curious feverish excitability of temperament. In many places one would think that it was fête day. Here we are met at all turns by violent appeals to our sentiments or by threats and menaces from the screamers and hooters of the Yellow Press. There is a general atmosphere of ferocious Bank Holiday. This may be in part due to the sudden circulation of so much money in the families of the lower and lower middle classes. In France, with its conscriptionist army with a sou a day for each soldier, there is, of course, a general restriction of spending power. In any case French life is carried on with a dignity and sobriety which make the contrast on returning to England humiliating. One feels that under no circumstances would the French tolerate the fatuous sentimentality of the poster which exhibits a domineering lodging-house keeper driving her feeble-minded son to the Front.

---

[11] My thanks to Michael Currier of Widener Library and Marcia Deihl of Tozzer Library for their help with access to the Periodicals Collection at Widener Library, Harvard University, Cambridge, MA, where I found Roger Fry's essay.

Paris is, of course, under martial law, but the consequences of this do not obtrude themselves on the ordinary visitor. It is different, however, when one once gets within the military zone. There it becomes impossible to enter or leave a railway station without a permit, or indeed to circulate from one village to another without a safe conduct, which must be signed by the mayor and viséd by the military authorities. Under these circumstances the countryside is almost deserted. In the whole district of the Marne battlefield one scarcely sees a country cart or a motor-car unless it be either a military car rushing to or from Headquarters or one of the many cars used by the Quakers who have been for many months assisting the distressed peasants and villagers. It was in connection with their work that I was enabled to visit the whole of this district, and in assisting in their investigations I got some idea of the conditions and feelings of the countryside. In hundreds of villages the destruction has been immense, and often, as far as one could judge, entirely wanton.

The peasant proprietors crept back to their homes as soon as the tide of invasion withdrew to the Aisne, and there they still were, either living in cellars or, when these too had crumbled, finding lodgings in the nearest available commune. This was often ten or more kilometres away, and the extra labour involved in coming and going to cultivate the land caused great suffering. But the tenacity and courage of these peasants was admirable. To them the idea of leaving land fallow is the *gran refiuto*. They would tell one of communes farther up country, nearer the fighting line, where indeed this last and utter demoralization had overtaken the population; where they had given up work and lived as best they could on the army provisions which the Government allows to invaded districts. But they spoke of this with a kind of horror as of some unheard-of sin. With this amazing devotion to the soil there goes, unfortunately, an avarice and jealousy which sometimes makes the life of these small communes rather ugly and sordid, and strangely enough the common disaster which had overwhelmed them did not seem to have evoked a [184] common effort. Rather, the more powerful proprietors saw a chance of squeezing out the weaker under the stress of the new conditions. Above all, anything like a common action, any mutual aid in the matter of sowing and reaping, seemed almost unthinkable. It is impossible to tell by the general appearance of these peasant proprietors whether they are rich or poor—all wear the same clothes and none look as prosperous as they generally are. One found that every one of them had possessed a set of the most modern American or English agricultural machines, though of course most of these had been destroyed in the general conflagration.

Just those conditions which one finds so admirable in French country life are aggravations of the disaster which they have suffered by the German invasion. In England, alas! our peasantry is only too well accustomed to charity, and its organisation by the landowner and parson. Under such a calamity they would certainly look to "their betters" to organise all manner of relief, and one might be certain they would not look in vain. But in a French country commune, where every family owns its land, its implements and its cattle, charity is unknown, there is no one above them but the Government, no one to look after them but the Prefect acting through the Mayor. And their action, as the peasants knew, was hindered by all the creaking incompetence of bureaucracy. I think that in most places the Government authorities have worked with zeal and goodwill, but their aid was slow in coming and the need was pressing and immediate, so that the rapid and efficient organisation of the War Victims relief by the Society of Friends in England has probably saved many districts from something like famine in the approaching winter.

I know nothing of the feelings of politicians or of the governing classes, but conversations with innumerable peasant proprietors, with soldiers and small bourgeois leave in my mind no doubt that the mass of the French people is intensely pacifist in sentiment. It is not only that there is no idea of glory or of the splendour of war in their minds, but, however bitterly they hate the "dirty Boches," they recognise the futility of any policy of revenge. With what sounds to us like pedantry, a simple peasant will tell you that war is an "anachronism in our century," and over and over again comes the phrase, "C'est trop bête, la guerre."

Therein, I think, lies the great importance of French pacifism. Its condemnation of war is not merely a pious horror at the cruelty of this "bloody murder," it is a profound intellectual contempt for war as a means of settling international disputes and international rivalries.

Now and again, of course, when some peculiarly atrocious piece of calculated cruelty by the German invaders was being discussed, the revenge motive would come in. On one occasion an indiscretion on my part brought me to the unfavourable notice of the military authorities, and I spent some time under the care of the military gendarmes in a very much improvised prison in a nearly ruined town. Inevitably we discussed the war, and though I was at the time suspect I found no difficulty in stating my views freely. One of the gendarmes began about the necessity for executing on the Germans all and more than all that they had inflicted on the French, but instantly he was taken to task by his companions. They too hated the Germans, but they knew the futility of hatred, the folly of revenge. What they wanted was to end all this, to make quite sure that it would not happen again, and they saw clearly that revenge would merely be the beginning of another cycle of iniquity.

It is this widespread intellectual perception of the folly of revenge as a means of attaining the end that seems to me such a hopeful sign for the future, if only the people gets the power to express itself. It is not for nothing that Voltaire is still one of the most popular and widely read authors in France. If only the Philosophical Dictionary could be made to replace the history of the Jews in all elementary schools!

Certainly I believe this reasoned pacifist sentiment is common among the troops at the Front. In confirmation of this I will quote from a letter written by a French soldier who has fought since the beginning of the war in one of the most obstinately contested parts of the whole line. It shows that those who expose themselves daily to every kind of danger and misery manage to keep a truer and saner view than the majority of those who face the enemy from the journalist's desk.

"This war, in spite of all that is asserted, draws to its end. That is a fact of which one has a very clear intuition and apprehension when one is at the Front. The idea of a winter campaign can only be envisaged by those who are not at the war. Here (in the trenches) it seems too paradoxical to everyone. If diplomacy doesn't put an end to the war, the war will congeal like a sauce that one simply cannot keep boiling; and that in both camps.

"As to the results of the war, one must hope that they will be *none* for anybody—that is to say, without advantages for anyone, so that this costly lesson may be still more demonstrative. And if after that there does not arise a general European conscience strong enough to condemn war for ever, if the war, *that other war* which we shall wage, does not come off, one must despair of everything; for what an opportunity! I wish I were in it already."

War and Peace (September 1915): 183-184.

Works Cited

Angell, Norman. *After All: The Autobiography of Norman Angell.* London: Hamish Hamilton, 1951.

Bagley, Melissa. "Nature and the Nation in *Mrs. Dalloway.*" *Woolf Studies Annual* 14 (2008): 35-52.

Barrett, Eileen. "Septimus and Shadrack: Woolf and Morrison Envision the Madness of War." *Virginia Woolf: Emerging Perspectives. Selected Papers from the Third Annual Conference on Virginia Woolf.* Ed. Mark Hussey and Vara Neverow. New York: Pace UP, 1994. 26-32.

Bennett, Paula. *My Life a Loaded Gun: Dickinson, Plath, Rich & Female Creativity.* Urbana: U of Illinois P, 1990.

Blunden, Edmund. *Undertones of War.* London: Collins, 1928.

Bradshaw, David. "Vanished Like Leaves: The Military, Elegy, and Italy in *Mrs. Dalloway.*" *Woolf Studies Annual* 8 (2002): 107-126.

———. "Virginia Woolf and Vimy Ridge: An Interesting Cancellation in 'The Hours' Manuscript." *Times Literary Supplement* (December 2002): 496-8.

Briggs, Julia. *Virginia Woolf: An Inner life.* Orlando, FL: Harcourt, 2005.

Cramer, Patricia. "Pearls and the Porpoise: *The Years*—a Lesbian Memoir." *Virginia Woolf: Lesbian Readings.* Eds. Eileen Barrett and Patricia Cramer. New York: New York UP, 1997. 222-240.

DiBattista, Maria. *Virginia Woolf's Major Novels: The Fables of Anon.* New Haven: Yale UP, 1980.

DeMeester, Karen. "Trauma and Recovery in Virginia Woolf's *Mrs. Dalloway.*" *Modern Fiction Studies* 44.3 (1988). 649-673.

———. "Trauma, Post-Traumatic Stress Disorder and Obstacles to Recovery in *Mrs. Dalloway.*" Henke and Eberly. 77-94.

DeSalvo, Louise. *Melymbrosia: An Early Version of* The Voyage Out. New York: New York Public Library, 1982.

Dupuy, R. Ernest and Trevor N. Dupuy, eds. *The Harper Encyclopedia of Military History, From 3500 B.C. to the Present.* 4th ed. New York: Harper Collins, 1973.

Eberly, David. "Face to Face: Trauma and Audience in *Between the Acts.*" Henke and Eberly. 205-222.

Froula, Christine. *Virginia Woolf and the Bloomsbury Avant Garde: War, Civilization, Modernity.* New York: Columbia UP, 2005.

Fry, Roger. "A Visit to France." *War and Peace* 2.24 (September 1915): 183-4.

Fussell, Paul. *The Great War and Modern Memory.* London: Oxford UP, 1975.

Glendinning, Victoria. *Leonard Woolf: A Biography*. New York: Free Press, 2006.
Goldman, Jane. "Who is Mr. Ramsay? Where is the Lighthouse? The Politics and Pragmatics of Scholarly Annotation." Woolf Editing/Editing Woolf. 18th Annual Conference on Virginia Woolf. Denver CO. 20 June 2008.
Graham, J. W. *Virginia Woolf: The Waves, The Two Holograph Drafts*. Toronto: U of Toronto P, 1976.
Hanson, Neil. *Unknown Soldiers: The Story of the Missing of the First World War*. NY: Knopf, 2008.
Haller, Evelyn. "Isis Unveiled: Virginia Woolf's Use of Egyptian Myth." *Virginia Woolf: A Feminist Slant*. Ed. Jane Marcus. U of Nebraska P, 1983. 109-31.
———. "The Anti-Madonna in the Work and Thought of Virginia Woolf." *Virginia Woolf: Centennial Essays*. Eds. Elaine Ginsburg and Laura Gottlieb. Troy, NY: Whitston, 1993. 93-109.
Henke, Suzette. "Virginia Woolf and Post-Traumatic Subjectivity." *Virginia Woolf: Turning the Centuries. Selected Papers from the Ninth Annual Conference on Virginia Woolf*. Eds. Ann Ardis and Bonnie Kime Scott. New York: Pace UP, 2000. 147-152.
Henke, Suzette and David Eberly, with the assistance of Jane Lilienfeld, eds. *Virginia Woolf and Trauma: Embodied Texts*. Eds. New York: Pace UP, 2007.
Hoffman, Charles. "From Short Story to Novel: The Manuscript Revisions of Virginia Woolf's *Mrs. Dalloway*." *Modern Fiction Studies* 14.2 (Summer 1968): 171-186.
Hussey, Mark. *Virginia Woolf: A to Z*. New York: Oxford UP, 1995.
Johnson, Erica L. "Writing the Land: The Geography of National Identity in *Orlando*." *Woolf in the Real World: Selected Papers from the Thirteenth Annual Conference on Virginia Woolf*. Ed. Karen V. Kukil. Clemson: Clemson U Digital P, 2005. 105-9.
Johnson, Thomas H., ed. *The Complete Poems of Emily Dickinson*. Boston: Little Brown, 1960.
Jones, Danell. *"From the threshold of the private house": Women, War, and Culture in Virginia Woolf's Novels of the Twenties*. Diss. Columbia University, 1993.
Kahane, Claire. "Of Snakes, Toads, And Duckweed: Traumatic Acts and Historical Actions in *Between the Acts*." Henke and Eberly. 223-246.
Keegan, John. *The First World War*. New York: Random House/Vintage, 2000.
Lee, Hermione. *Virginia Woolf*. New York: Knopf, 1997.

Levenback, Karen. *Virginia Woolf and the Great War*. Syracuse, NY: Syracuse UP, 1999.

———. "Virginia Woolf and the Great War: Civilian Bombing and Strategic Bombing." *Re: Reading, Re: Writing, Re: Teaching Virginia Woolf. Selected Papers from the Fourth Annual Conference on Virginia Woolf*. Eds. Eileen Barrett and Patricia Cramer. New York: Pace UP, 1995. 80-87.

Lilienfeld, Jane. "Accident, Incident, and Meaning: Traces of Trauma in Virginia Woolf's Narrativity." *Virginia Woolf: Turning the Centuries. Selected Papers from the Ninth Annual Conference on Virginia Woolf*. Eds. Ann Ardis and Bonnie Kime Scott. New York: Pace UP, 2000. 153-58.

Low, Lisa. "Feminist Elegy/Feminist Prophecy: *Lycidas*, *The Waves*, Kristeva, Cixous." *Virginia Woolf and Literary History*. Part I. Eds. Jane Lilienfeld, Jeffrey Oxford and Lisa Low. *Woolf Studies Annual* 9 (2003): 221-242.

Marcus, Jane. *Virginia Woolf and the Languages of Patriarchy*. Bloomington: Indiana UP, 1987.

Neverow, Vara. "The Return of the Great Goddess: Immortal Virginity, Sexual Autonomy and Lesbian Possibility in *Jacob's Room*." *Virginia Woolf and Literary History*. Part II. Eds. Jane Lilienfeld, Jeffrey Oxford and Lisa Low. *Woolf Studies Annual* 10 (2004): 203-231.

Phillips, Kathy. *Virginia Woolf Against Empire*. Knoxville: U of Tennessee P, 1994.

Poole, Roger. "'We All Put Up With You, Virginia': Irreceivable Wisdom About War." *Virginia Woolf and War: Fiction, Reality, and Myth*. Ed. Mark Hussey. New York: Syracuse UP, 1991. 79-100.

Prose, Francine, ed. *The* Mrs. Dalloway *Reader*. New York: Harcourt, 2001.

Radin, Grace. *Virginia Woolf's* The Years. *The Evolution of a Novel*. Knoxville: U of Tennessee P, 1981.

Rich, Adrienne. *On Lies, Secrets, and Silence: Selected Prose, 1966-1978*. New York: Norton, 1979.

Richter, Harvena. *Virginia Woolf: The Inward Voyage*. Princeton: Princeton UP, 1970.

Samuels, Marilyn S. "The Symbolic Function of the Sun in *Mrs. Dalloway*." *Modern Fiction Studies* 18.3 (Autumn 1972): 387-401.

Shields, E. F. "The American Edition of *Mrs. Dalloway*." *Studies in Bibliography* 27 (1974): 158-175.

Showalter, Elaine. *The Female Malady: Women, Madness, and English Culture, 1830-1980*. New York, Penguin, 1980.

Silver, Brenda. *Virginia Woolf Icon*. Chicago: U of Chicago P, 1999.

Spater, George and Ian Parsons. *A Marriage of True Minds: An Intimate Portrait of Leonard and Virginia Woolf*. New York: Harcourt Brace Jovanovich, 1977.

Tate, Trudi. *Modernism, History, and the First World War.* Manchester: Manchester UP, 1998.

Van der Kolk, Bessell, Alexander C. McFarlane, and Lars Weisaeth, eds. *Traumatic Stress: The Effects of Overwhelming Experience on Mind, Body, and Society.* New York: Guilford P, 1996.

War in the Air: Bombing Raids on Britain. 14 Dec. 2005. Spartacus Educational Schoolnet. Jan. 2006. http://www.spartacus.schoolnet.co.uk FWWairwar.htm.

Wilson, Jean Moorcroft. *Siegfried Sassoon: The Journey from the Trenches. A Biography (1918-1967).* London: Duckworth, 2002.

Wright, Glenn P. "The Raverat Proofs of *Mrs. Dalloway.*" *Studies in Bibliography* 39 (1986): 242-261.

Woolf, Virginia. "The Artist and Politics." *The Moment and Other Essays.* New York: Harcourt Brace Jovanovich, 1948. 225-9.

———. *The Diary of Virginia Woolf. Volume Two: 1920-1924.* Ed. Anne Olivier Bell. New York: Harcourt, Brace, Jovanovich, 1978.

———. *Mrs. Dalloway.* San Diego: Harcourt, Brace & Company, 1981.

Wussow, Helen, ed. *"The Hours," The British Museum Manuscript of Virginia Woolf's* Mrs. Dalloway. New York: Pace UP, 1996.

Zeiss, McKenzie L. "The Pastoral Legacy of the Garden: (Anti) Pastoral Images and National Identity in Virginia Woolf and Vita Sackville-West." *Woolf in the Real World: Selected Papers from the Thirteenth Annual Conference on Virginia Woolf.* Ed. Karen V. Kukil. Clemson, SC: Clemson U Digital Press, 2005. 100-04.

"Virginia Woolf's 'The Cinema': Sneak Previews of the Holograph Pre-Texts through Post-Publication Revisions"

Leslie Kathleen Hankins

> It then occurred to me that the very manuscript itself which Lamb had looked at was only only a few hundred yards away, so that one could follow Lamb's footsteps across the quadrangle to that famous library where the treasure is kept
> (*AROO* 7-8).

> Manuscripts have something new to tell us: it is high time we learned to make them speak.
> (Louis Hay, "History or Genesis?" 207)

> All is hubble-bubble, swarm, and chaos. We are peering over the edge of a cauldron in which fragments of all shapes and savours seem to simmer; now and again some vast form heaves itself up, and seems about to haul itself out of chaos.
> (Woolf, "The Cinema," *Nation & Athenaeum* 381)

In *A Room of One's Own*, Virginia Woolf's narrator anticipates entering a famous library to research the manuscripts of Milton and Thackeray, a venture that, as we know, ends on a sour note; she is shut out of the library by a patriarchal guardian angel and retreats cursing the famous library. This essay, in a different century, in a different country, enters a different famous library to consult the treasures there—manuscripts of Virginia Woolf this time—and to study and celebrate, rather than curse. Reversing the trajectory of Woolf's outsider narrator and entering the library, yet honoring Woolf's vision of an Outsiders' Society, researchers delight in sharing archival treasures with those who remain outside. Unlike the student in the British Museum whom Woolf both envies and mocks in *A Room*, we do not want a nugget of pure gold to hoard, but wish to point to a vein of gold that warrants further mining. Or, perhaps even that image is too static, for what we find in the archive is more akin to Woolf's bubbling cauldron in the dynamic simmering of which each beholder sees unique and mutable insights. As *Orlando* reminds us that manuscripts are not dead ("The manuscript which reposed above her heart began shuffling and beating as if it were a living thing"[*O* 200]), scholars—such as Christine Froula and Edward Bishop—remind us that Woolf's published texts can be renewed as we bring them into a relationship with their pre-texts. The adventurous spirit of scholarship that "seeks, rather, to undo these same texts and to suspend their interpretations" (Jenny 19) welcomes us into Woolf's rich pre-texts about cinema in order to create a space for interplay among all the orts and fragments, from unpublished to published, from thoughts written or between the lines or crossed through, that are part of the stimulating study of Woolf and film.

"That famous library where the treasure is kept": A Woolf Scholar at the Berg

Scholars in recent decades have brought critical attention to the published versions of "The Cinema" (Hankins; Humm; Trotter; Marcus); the time is now ripe to extend our collective scholarly scope by beginning to peruse the inviting pre-texts of that essay, holograph fragments and drafts which are fascinating to read on their own, but which also provide valuable insights about Woolf's arguments and aesthetics. In a famous library, the Henry W. and Albert A. Berg Collection of English and American Literature at the New York Public Library, seeking the holograph drafts of Woolf's "The Cinema," we encounter generous, welcoming librarians and curators rather than the dismissive guardian angels that vexed Woolf's narrator.

Woolf's pre-texts reveal nuanced traces of her approach-avoidance response to cinema. Significant changes and conflicting arguments about cinema surface as we explore the multi-layered loose pages, drafts, published versions and revised published versions and the tensions among them. Her revisions do not end with the first published version of "The Cinema" in June 1926 in *The Arts* in New York; Woolf made major post-publication revisions before the essay was again published a month later as "The Cinema" in the *Nation & Athenaeum* (*N&A*) on July 3, 1926. And, one could argue, bits of the holographs have an afterlife as well, as some ideas edited out of the early drafts may be found recycled in post-texts such as Clive Bell's later essay on film or in Woolf's own essays on literary aesthetics.[1] It is a fascinating tangle.

Just as the possible revisions in the manuscripts of Milton and Thackeray intrigue her narrator in *A Room of One's Own*, Woolf's nineteen pages of pre-texts, with their repetitions and rewritings, knotty sites of contested ideas, and startling alterations invite our attention as twenty-first century scholars. Woolf's holograph working papers on the cinema include two pages of early thoughts and two later partial drafts leading to the published essay "The Cinema." The first two fragmentary pages begin to map, in broad strokes, Woolf's initial response to the new art of cinema; these initial responses to cinema—perhaps significantly—are found at the back of the holograph draft of her first novel, *The Voyage Out*.[2]

---

[1] See Leslie K. Hankins. "Virginia Woolf and Film—the Archival Turn: Bloomsbury, *Vogue*, *Anna Karenina* and Judith Chaplin 'in an Extremely Well-Appointed Library.'" *The Edinburgh Companion to Virginia Woolf and the Arts*, ed. Maggie Humm. Edinburgh University Press, forthcoming 2010.

[2] Though genetic criticism cautions us to temper our tendency to obsess about what came first, it is still tantalizing to speculate about these two pages. The more I ponder these sheets, the more I suspect that the loose sheet is the second sheet of these two, though that would suggest there may be a missing sheet leading up to Woolf's opening of Berg 2, "Nor have we ever found ourselves in an empty house." Yet, the gist of Berg 2 is to celebrate the non-fictional elements of film: the accidents and "photographs of ordinary sights" that Woolf finds "delightful" and that would seem to lead most

Overview of "The Cinema" in the *Nation & Athenaeum*

Before we engage with the holograph pre-texts, an overview of the published essay, "The Cinema," provides a useful context;[3] this summary is based on the *Nation & Athenaeum* version from July 3, 1926. "The Cinema"—like many of Woolf's best essays—defies facile summary. As in her 1929 essay, *A Room of One's Own,* in which, strategically, Woolf invents a narrator who promises "to develop in your presence as fully and freely as I can the train of thought which led me to think this" (*AROO* 4), "The Cinema" traces the narrator's thought process, responding to the idea of cinema from a multitude of perspectives. The essay is rich; in it she exhausted what she had to say about film, as she indicated in a postcard to the editors of the film journal *Close Up*.[4] In a deceptively light way, the text touches on a wide array of issues in film. Woolf rounds up the usual suspects: the need to invent viable conventions for an art, the maturity and immaturity of the medium, the conflict between technical dexterity and immature content, the lure of the exactitude of reality, the potential delights of fantasy, the minefield of literary adaptation, the pluses and minuses of collaboration between film and the other arts, the difficulties of portraying thought and subjective consciousness in film and the possibility of a non-verbal "secret language" of cinema. She also makes gestures toward other film topics: abstraction, suggestiveness, narrative, time, space, the documentary, collision montage, editing, repetition, music, shadow, shape, movement, visual emotion and symbolism.

---

likely to Berg 1, which then moves to investigate fictional films: "It is not so easy to understand why the pictur moving picture versions of famous novels, & imaginary adventures are so popular–" (Berg 1). There is a note of finality at the end of Berg 1: "In the meantime we remain happy, greedy, & indiscriminate" which may imply that it is the second, final sheet. On the other hand, that statement may prompt the "Nor have we ever found ourselves in an empty house" that begins Berg 2. The effort to put first things first here may be not only wasted, but theoretically suspect.

[3] This article uses the version of "The Cinema" as published in the *Nation & Athenaeum*. The version in *E*4 designated as from the *Nation & Athenaeum* differs from the original. Some differences are minor: *N&A* uses American quotation marks and spelling (civilization, generalize), while *E*4 uses British quotation marks and spelling (civilisation, generalise). More significantly, *E*4 prints "an enormous size" (*E*4 593) for "an immense size" (*N&A* 382); "most complete ideas" (*E*4 594) for "most complex ideas" (*N&A* 382); "gesticulations" (*E*4 593) for "gesticulation" (*N&A* 382); "*Doctor Caligari*" (*E*4 593) for "Dr. Caligari" (*N&A* 382); and "in doing so" (*E*4 595) for "in so doing" *(N&A* 383). An amusing typographical error in the *Nation & Athenaeum* mistakenly prints (about thought) "It has speed and lowness" instead of "speed and slowness." I realize how easily errors can slip by, as I was mortified to learn that the version of "The Cinema" I included in my section of *Gender in Modernism* (2007) went to press omitting an entire exquisite sentence of Woolf's: "For a moment it seemed to embody some monstrous, diseased imagination of the lunatic's brain" (Hankins, *Cinéastes* 842).

[4] See Donald, Friedberg and Marcus, 325, note 47, which includes the entire text of Woolf's postcard.

Woolf begins by repudiating critics who suggest that civilization is on the wane, that there is no new terrain for art and that "everything has been said already," suggesting instead that in respect to cinema we may be like the savage men who hit two bars of iron together and heard prophetically "the music of Mozart" (Woolf "The Cinema" *N&A* 381). Film, however, is not there yet, according to Woolf, for now "all is hubble-bubble, swarm, and chaos" (381). To interrogate the cinema, Woolf starts with what might seem its simplest form, the topical short or newsreel. She splits the eye (the pleasure seeking and unthinking perceiver) from the brain (which must make sense of the seen). She considers the effect on viewers of newsreels of ten years ago. Such moving photographs of actuality affect us differently than the experience of actuality, she asserts, because "we see life as it is when we have no part in it" which makes it "more real, or real with a different reality from that which we perceive in daily life" (382). Arguing that film makers have failed to exploit fully the potential of filmed actuality and everyday life, she pens a suggestive list of possible film moments: "the flight of gulls, ships on the Thames, the Prince of Wales, the Mile End Road, Piccadilly Circus" (382).

Woolf then investigates the relationship of film to the other arts, especially literature. That relationship, she finds, unfortunately consists largely of "disastrous" efforts in which "we lurch and lumber through the most famous novels of the world" (382). She directs us away from mainstream narrative films which focus on external verisimilitude, costumes, and plot and toward avant-garde films with their wildly experimental cinematic play. Arguing against film adaptations, the essay casts the relationship between cinema and literature as a predatory one, asserting that the "alliance is unnatural" and that the cinema places all the emphasis on externals ("the eye") rather than on "the inside of the mind" ("the brain") (382). She pens a scathing description of a scene from a purported film of *Anna Karenina* set in "an extremely well-appointed library"; she faults it because "all the emphasis is laid by the cinema upon her teeth, her pearls, and her velvet" (382). Woolf also argues that the cinema simplifies novels in such a way that "we spell them out in words of one syllable, written, too, in the scrawl of an illiterate schoolboy" (382). Hoping instead that film will abandon its parasitic alliance with literature and develop its own devices, she brainstorms about what those devices may come to be.

Here the essay probes most eloquently the intellectual and aesthetic potential of cinema as an artistic medium. Woolf claims to use an accidental distortion projected at a screening of *The Cabinet of Dr. Caligari*, a distortion that seemed to embody the emotion of fear, as the starting point for her brainstorming. Startled by an accidental moving shape-shadow, she extrapolates, "if a shadow at a certain moment can suggest so much more than the actual gestures and words of men and women in a state of fear, it seems plain that the cinema has within its grasp innumerable symbols for emotions that have so far failed to find expression" (382). Considering whether some emotions have remained beyond the scope of the existing media, Woolf wonders whether cinema may fill that gap. She asks if there is an extra-verbal "secret language" that "can be rendered visible without the help of words" (382). In order to attempt an answer to this question, she examines the qualities of thought and argues that thought requires images to convey complex ideas. But, because the visual is only one of the senses, leaving out touch and hearing, for example, she claims that only words can carry fully the suggestiveness of thought.

Though she argues that the poet and painter have priority, Woolf finds that because seeing is related to thought and feeling, "some residue of visual emotion which is of no use either to painter or to poet" may be allotted to the cinema (382). Though the diction and tone here suggest that Woolf is tossing scraps to film, she waxes quite eloquent when she begins to describe the potential of avant-garde cinema. Such cinema would invent a new kind of symbol with which to compose a "controlled and conscious" abstract art (382). This art would be freed from a parasitic dependence on the other arts, though it might rely on "the very slightest help from words or music to make itself intelligible" (382). The defining characteristics of such film would be "movements and abstractions" (382). The task for the film maker, she asserts, is to develop the new symbol for expressing thought; Woolf is at her most brilliant and inspiring as she imagines what this may be. One must take reality and "breathe emotion" into it to "animate the perfect form with thought" (383). The art would capture emotion, incarnate, as it mingled, clashed, and changed. Because film is faster than words, Woolf argues that film could capture "violent changes of emotion produced by their collision" and "fantastic contrasts" (383). Film would also be able to capture fantasies, such as the wild architectural and spatial shifts of dreams and visions, and, because film is not bound by spatial and temporal constraints, it could sport with those. Woolf opens up an intriguing and stimulating vista for film futures. Immediately after this flamboyant and promising gesture toward film futures, however, Woolf abruptly shifts back to the present state of the art and argues that film is not fulfilling that destiny now. It is in fact only in glimpses of real life—in witnessing "a scene waiting a new art to be transfixed"—that one sees a flicker of what reel life might be (383). The essay closes with a significant variation of its opening; this time rather than serving as forerunners or prophets of the art of Mozart, the savage tribe creates cacophonous discord as it encounters an entire orchestra of instruments and begins to "hammer and thump upon them all at the same time" (383).

The text of "The Cinema" is stimulating; scholars and readers have wished to encounter more of the provocative ideas she broaches here; moving to the pre-texts allows us to hear some echoes between the lines, and to engage with significantideas that ended on the cutting room floor. What a lark! What a plunge![5]

[5] After reading of the transcription practices of Susan Dick, J. W. Graham, Stuart Clarke, Beth Rigel Daugherty, Helen Wussow, and Edward Bishop, I opted to keep my editorial marks to a bare minimum for this project. I use ~~strike throughs~~ to signal deletions of various kinds; < > indicates a word or phrase Woolf added between the lines; [ ] indicates a word, phrase or squiggle I could not decipher; { } within a transcription indicates my interpolation. Line breaks are preserved except where the line is too long, in which case it is wrapped and indented in the transcription.

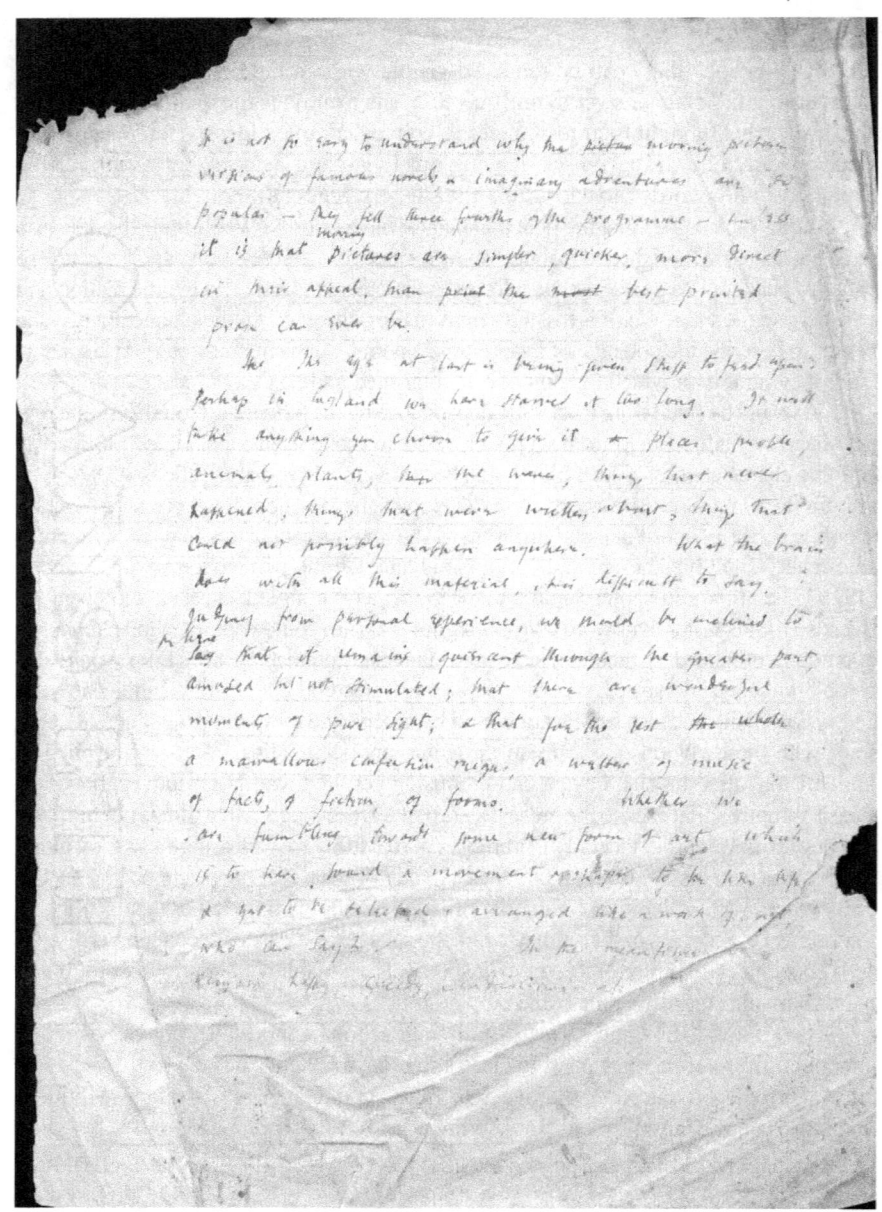

Fig. 1 Berg Fragment 1. At back of her: The voyage out. Holograph draft. Vol. 2 [Captain's death bed and other essays?, The. The cinema] Class distinctions. Holograph fragment. One loose page n.d. ms. 5p.

It is not so easy to understand why the ~~pictur~~ moving picture
versions of famous novels, & imaginary adventures are so
popular -- they fill three fourths of the programme — unless
 it is that < moving> pictures are simpler, quicker, more direct
in their appeal, than ~~print~~ the ~~most~~ best printed
prose can ever be.
    ~~The~~ The eye at last is being given stuff to feed upon.
Perhaps in England we have starved it too long. It will
take anything you choose to give it, & places, people,
animals, plants ~~the~~ the waves, things that never
happened, things that were written about, things that
could not possibly happen anywhere.   What the brain
does with all this material, it is difficult to say.
Judging from personal experience, we would be inclined to
~~say~~ <believe> that it remains quiescent through the greater part,
amused but not stimulated; that there are wonderful
moments of pure sight; & that for the rest ~~the whole~~
 a marvellous confusion reigns, a welter of music
of facts, of fiction, of forms.   Whether we
are fumbling towards some new form of art which
is to have sound & movement & shape, to be like life
& yet to be selected & arranged like a work of art,
who can say?   In the meantime we
remain happy, greedy, & indiscriminate.

Fig. 2   Transcription of Berg Fragment 1

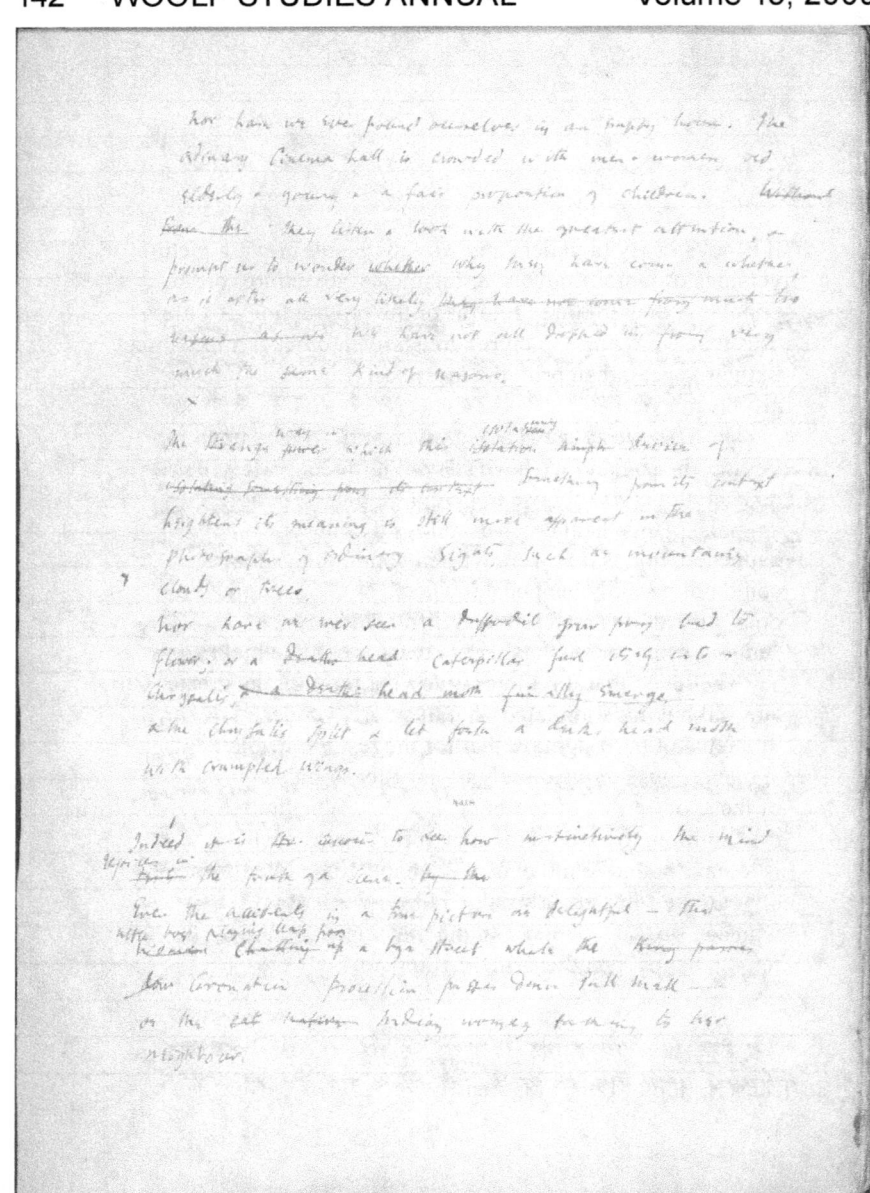

Fig. 3   Berg Fragment 2. At back of her: The voyage out. Holograph draft. Vol. 2 [Captain's death bed and other essays?, The. The cinema] Class distinctions. Holograph fragment. One loose page n.d. ms. 5p.

Nor have we ever found ourselves in an empty house. The
ordinary cinema hall is crowded with men & women, old,
elderly & young & a fair proportion of children. ~~Without
from the~~ They listen & look with the greatest attention, &
prompt us to wonder ~~whether~~ why they have come, & whether,
as is after all very likely ~~they have not come from much the
reasons as we~~ we have not all dropped in from very
much the same kind of reasons.
x
The strange ~~power~~ <way in> which this ~~isolation~~ <isolating> ~~simple device~~ of
~~isolating something from its context~~ something from its context
heightens its meaning is still more apparent in the
photographs of ordinary sights, such as mountains
& clouds or trees.
Nor have we ever seen a daffodil grow from bud to
flower; or a ~~deaths head~~ caterpillar furl itself into a
chrysalis, ~~& a deaths head moth finally emerge~~
& the chrysalis split & let forth a deaths head moth
with crumpled wings.

      Indeed it is ~~str~~ curious to see how instinctively the mind
~~tests~~ <rejoices in> the truth of a scene. ~~by the~~
Even the accidents in a true picture are delightful -- the
~~women chatting~~ <little boys playing leap frog> up a by street while the ~~King passes
down~~ Coronation procession passes down Pall Mall ----
or the ~~cat~~ ~~native~~ Indian woman talking to her
neighbour.

Fig 4 Transcription of Berg Fragment 2

First Fragments About Film: "We remain happy, greedy & indiscriminate"

In Woolf's two initial holograph fragments about film, she makes observations that she returns to in later drafts; she considers how cinema feeds the starved eye, delights in the lure of actuality on film, asks what role the brain plays in processing the visual, notes the popularity of the cinema, and considers some of the opportunities offered by the film as a medium. The tone of the fragments is one of eager questing: she asks questions and seems baffled and curious; dashes convey the immediacy of her thought process. One key component of the complex relationship between literature and film—film adaptation—claims Woolf's attention in the first line of Berg Fragment 1; she speculates about the popularity of fiction films: "It is not so easy to understand why the pictur moving picture versions of famous novels, & imaginary adventures are so popular—they fill three fourths of the programme— unless it is that <moving> pictures are simpler, quicker, more direct in their appeal, than print the most best printed prose can ever be" (Berg 1). Her comment about the program reminds us that the typical film program of her day was made of a variety of different types—and varying lengths—of moving pictures and that spectators dropped in at any time during the program. The Film Society programs were unusual in that they asked spectators to arrive at a particular starting time and to stay through to the end. The other fourth of the programs (even at some of the Film Society screenings) would have been newsreels, travel films, topical shorts, science shorts and other genres that often show actual footage, sometimes exploiting the potential of film to capture or manipulate reality.

Woolf in the fragment is not so sure what to make of fictional pictures, the moving picture versions of famous novels and imaginary adventures; she brainstorms about why such films are appealing, and considers the hunger of the visual sense: "the eye at last is being given stuff to feed upon. Perhaps in England we have starved it too long" (Berg 1). She implies that the eye has been so hungry that it lacks discrimination: "It will take anything you choose to give it, & places, people, animals, plants, the the waves, things that never happened, things that were written about, things that could not possibly happen anywhere" (Berg 1). Though she describes a vast range of input coming to the eye from moving pictures, she undercuts its value by questioning what happens when it gets to the brain: "What the brain does with all this material, it is difficult to say" (Berg 1). Here she shifts to the personal and qualified as she tentatively sketches her opinion: "Judging from personal experience, we would be inclined to say <believe> that it remains quiescent through the greater part, amused but not stimulated" (Berg 1). She describes the result as chaotic: "there are wonderful moments of pure sight; & that for the rest the whole a marvellous confusion reigns, a welter of music of facts, of fiction, of forms" (Berg 1). If confusion might seem negative, "marvellous confusion" conveys a more mixed message; furthermore, the passage is loaded with positive words: "wonderful," "pure," and "marvellous." As Woolf loved to trespass between fiction and fact, and to play with forms, the phrase "a welter of music of facts, of fiction, of forms" may be read as a celebration rather than a condemnation. She projects a question phrased in an open-ended way: "Whether we are fumbling towards some new form of art which is to have sound & movement & shape, to be like life & yet to be selected & arranged like a work of art, who can say?" (Berg 1). It is worth noting that she claims "we" are doing this, and, though the process may be "fumbling," it is not judged harshly.

In Berg Fragment 2, thinking about film popularity and audience, Woolf observes: "Nor have we ever found ourselves in an empty house. The ordinary cinema hall is crowded with men & women, old, elderly and young & a fair proportion of children" (Berg 2). Curious about the audience, she becomes a spectator of the spectators: "They listen & look with the greatest attention, & prompt us to wonder whether why they have come" (Berg 2) and she speculates if "we have not all dropped in from very much the same kind of reasons" (Berg 2).

Woolf groups together "moving picture versions of famous novels" and "imaginary adventures" (Berg 1), contrasting such fictions with film non-fiction recordings of actual sights, such as "<little boys playing leap frog> up a by street while the King passes down Coronation procession passes down Pall Mall---or the eat native Indian woman talking to her neighbour" (Berg 2). She puzzles through the source of her pleasure, wondering about the "strange way" that "isolating { . . . }something from its context heightens its meaning" as she probes the appeal of "photographs of ordinary sights, such as mountains & clouds or trees" (Berg 2). Here she may be referring to popular science shorts by Mary Field and others that showed nature in fast forward by speeding up film to extend vision beyond what unaided eyes could see: "a daffodil grow from bud to flower; or a deaths head caterpillar furl itself into a chrysalis, & a deaths head moth finally emerge & the chrysalis split & let forth a deaths head moth with crumpled wings" (Berg 2). Appreciating the way that cinema extends the senses, Woolf expresses her gratitude (Berg 2); she praises these "true" or actual films wholeheartedly: "Even the accidents in a true picture are delightful" (Berg 2). The "true" pictures please the mind: "Indeed it is str curious to see how instinctively the mind tests rejoices in the truth of a scene" (Berg 2). Overall, these first two fragmentary pages articulate Woolf's early response to cinema in positive terms: "In the meantime we remain happy, greedy & indiscriminate" (Berg 1).

Take One: Holograph Draft 1 of "The Movies"

After the two fragmentary but anticipatory pre-texts, Woolf's two longer holographs, partial drafts entitled "The Movies," move closer to the published versions of "The Cinema" with which we are familiar. If her initial fragmentary pages are full of curiosity and gratitude, however, Woolf's subsequent pre-texts shift her take on cinema from the positive to the qualified and even negative. Generally, in holograph draft 1 her responses are less "indiscriminate" than in her first sheets; she is more critical, especially as she writes about film adaptation. Raising and dismissing various provocative ideas about aesthetics and media, she probes at length the raw material available for film. Though she acknowledges how much we owe to literature, music and painting (personifying those arts through Shakespeare, Beethoven and Titian), she is intrigued by the untamed areas that have not yet been captured by the other arts, and ponders about the artistic potential of sensations that have eluded capture.

Woolf begins holograph draft 1 with a rhetorical move that brooks no contradiction: "No one is likely to deny that the great relief afforded even as things are by the great arts of literature, & music, & painting" (135), as she secures firm footing for the traditional arts of literature, music, and painting. Linking each art with an undisputed iconic master solidifies the established arts' claim to our gratitude: "It would be superfluous to point out how much we owe to Shakespeare, how much to Beethoven, how much to Titian & the rest" (135). Only after she has established the prominence of the traditional arts does she consider the possibility of untapped raw material for another contender: "At the same time things happen, sensations occur, which intimate that even so <that> we are not completely represented even by these great masters" (135). As she brainstorms about such possibilities, she describes a series of outdoor vignettes that affect "us" as spectators:

> Idly dreaming [ ] in a garden lawn the wind blows a feather pirouetting before us < instantly>. A new sensation
> instantly tightens our nerves -- something terrifying & unknown has happened & exciting & inexplicable has happened. or again So, perhaps, a horse feels at the sight of a motor car.
> Or, again, when we are   B something that has never been tamed & familiarized by the genius of man. Or it may be simply the sudden [ ] emergence of an unexpected shadow. <wh. stalks & swells>
> which brandishes a <its> fist at us; & disappears. For fear always accompanies these   Or is the through the door of a city church there echoes & volleys a chaos & dementia of men traffic <taxis & vans hooting> & prayer in which flying [ ] off together in unholy
> combination some how <which> assaults us, as with surprise & [ ] again with surprise & fear (135)

She observes "something that has never been tamed & familiarized by the genius of man" and (most compelling for a reader who has read the published version of the essay) we recognize in the "emergence of an unexpected shadow. <wh. stalks & swells> which brandishes a~~~~ <its> fist at us, & disappears," a forerunner of the figure which she would later develop and claim as an accident emerging from a projection of the film, *The Cabinet of Dr. Caligari*. These "new sensations" are as variable as a feather pirouetting in the wind, or a cacophonous blast of urban sounds through the door of a city church, but they are linked by the response they elicit from spectators; she suggests fear and crosses it out, but as she considers "the unholy combination" (one cannot help thinking of Walter Benjamin's "profane illuminations") she describes how it "assaults us" and evokes "surprise & fear." Calling such phenomena "~~simple~~ trifles," Woolf nevertheless finds them significant because "they testify to a wind blowing ~~somewhere~~ about in us a power of emotion which is still unharnessed to its proper object" (135). As we know from *A Room of One's Own*, the trivial is not merely trivial for Woolf; such moments are often the most significant and powerful ones.

In this draft, Woolf's mixed responses may be read as those of one deeply invested in the competing art of literature; she is intrigued but also perhaps threatened. Most thought-provoking is the trope about a horse and a motorcar that is written and then crossed out (135). If we assume Woolf used this figure as one way to convey the feelings of the writer reacting to film, it is interesting to contemplate whether the horse—or writer—feels merely startled amazement at the new invention, or fears its own obsolescence as the transportation—or art—of the future whizzes by. Though Woolf throughout the draft uses many terms that relate to the horse and carriage image, such as "unharnessed," or "hobbled," she does not develop further the horse and motorcar image, shifting instead to explore anxieties about technology through the trope of the savage in the picture palace (135, 137, 139).

The figure of the savage that she introduces in draft one at the end of page 135 is a figure she returns to again and again to rework throughout her two drafts (135, 137, 139, 145, 151, 175). The figure shifts from "a savage who might have felt when he struck two pieces of iron together" that the sound foretold the music of Mozart and Beethoven, to "the savage in us" (135) and then to the rather conflicted figure of "the English savage of the twentieth century" (137) who is a "polished specimen." This twentieth century savage finds with surprise at the movies "how much he resembles the naked man striking two pieces of iron together" (137). The movies initiate the savage/spectator's identity crisis and a form of future shock; "strangely & terrifyingly" the awed twentieth century savage "feels himself standing on the verge of the future, looking into a cauldron from ~~which~~ whose bubble & steam a new shape will ~~eventually arise~~ one of these centuries arise" (137). We can guess in what direction Woolf's thoughts are moving as we note how she shifts from "eventually" to "one of these centuries," as if even "eventually" were too close for comfort.

Woolf's perplexed and perplexing figure of the savage suits her cultural moment with its conflicted responses to the primitive and to the modern artistic technology of the cinema. As she continues to revise the complex concept of the savage, Woolf notes "but still the savage lurks about somewhere in us" (139) and "makes his presence felt most at the picture palaces" (139) because there the spectators (notably "we") "become aware of ~~these~~ unharnessed emotions, of a crude attempt at expression, of something ~~which will~~ trying to lift itself up out of chaos" (139). Here Woolf brings back into play the concepts of new sensations and untapped raw material that she began to explore earlier on page 135, and links those with the spectator's response: "There we seem to be able to guess at some art" which "in the course of time will harness these ~~queer~~ amorphous sensations" (139). The line of thought suggests that cinema, by filling a gap in the existing arts, would thus prove valuable.

Moving to "disentangle what we feel at the Movies," Woolf finds "we are tripped at every turn" by the gap between the actual and the potential (139). "At first sight" movies are "slick & efficient" with lovers kissing their girls, ships sailing, horses winning their races, the King shaking hands with football teams (139). As Woolf first introduces these images of lovers, ships and horses, they are plural and general, not specific examples culled from actual newsreels. It is only later (the end of page 141) that she adds specifics. Attempting to riddle through the suggestiveness of these sights, she notes and crosses out "~~here is nothing except what we have seen dozens of times for ourselves~~" (139). Woolf pushes herself to explore what lies beyond first sight, or the things she has seen herself, to examine "at second sight" how "these ordinary scenes have taken on a mysterious quality" (139). Attempting to describe this quality, she pens and crosses out "~~some sublimity~~" and "~~sublime~~" before concluding "a quality for which there seems to be no name. Are we to call it reality?" (139). Probing her second sight, considering the "dumb show," her thoughts tangle as she crosses words out five times in a row:

> ~~Things seen in themselves~~ ~~There is an~~
> ~~There is~~ ~~Things seen as~~ ~~It seems as if we saw~~ (139)

Significantly, here Woolf writes and then deletes a familiar phrase from her essays on literary aesthetics: "Things seen in themselves." The rejection of this phrase for her cinema essay may be significant, because that phrase is a touchstone in Woolf's aesthetics, from "Character in Fiction" in 1922 to *A Room of One's Own* in 1929 where she describes what the novelist of the future should do: "Think of things in themselves" (*AROO* 111). Perhaps she is unwilling to offer this option to cinema. At any rate, she decides instead that we become "disinterested observers," a spectator position perhaps indebted to the aesthetics of Roger Fry and Clive Bell, and develops this train of thought: "as we gaze we seem to be removed from the pettiness of actual existence" (141). She probes the complex mélange of emotions as the spectator is "stirred yet at the same time saddened by the revelation of this extraordinary beauty which will continue whether we watch it or not" (141).

At this thought-provoking and poignant point, the draft shifts rather suddenly to castigate the "makers of film" for their "neglect" of "one of the most potent & presumably the cheapest of their resources" (141):

> Rome at 3 o'clock in the afternoon <the [ ]> Mont Blanc, & the ~~flight~~ flight of ducks, & the Thames, ~~the~~ shipping at Greenwich, Mr. Asquith making a speech, ~~a ship sail~~
> clouds moving (141).

Again, as in Berg Fragments 1 and 2, Woolf contrasts the positive potential of these actual sights with the tired productions of adaptations: "all these sights <have a beauty & an interest> are infinitely more exciting than dramatised versions of Oliver Twist or Lorna Doone which cost thousands of pounds to produce" (141). Making a probable reference to the Film Society's Sixth Programme of Sunday March 14, 1926, in which *Williamson's Animated Gazette* of 1910-12 was screened along with other films, Woolf claims that "the film surely proved the other day" that it has the potential to "twist the screw still more effectively" by playing upon "our sense of the past" (141). Reproducing the films "of fifteen years ago" has a dramatic effect on viewers; first Woolf writes and crosses out "~~a curious chaos is produced in the spectator~~" and then she notes how "there is added to the actual picture" (from the spectator) "a cluster of emotion" such as amazement, admiration, anger and surprise (141). She describes the spectator of the 1920s responding to two dated scenes; one is "Lord Salisbury's daughter being married in a gown which no bride could wear to day { . . . } as if there were no such thing as a European war ahead" (141), and another is of the "Suffragettes keeping guard at Holloway—dour looking women, in long skirts, at whom the errand boys are cocking smirks" (141). Unlike the 1910-12 errand boy spectators, the spectator of the mid-1920s adds with hindsight "yet we need not be a suffragette to ~~feel respect~~ <cheer> the dreary old frumps for having won their battle" (141).

Revisiting her earlier lines condemning expensive dramatized versions of *Oliver Twist* or *Lorna Doone*, Woolf expands her critique of adaptation on page 143. Her language is rather strong as she refers to film makers' "neglect," noting how they "are tempted" because "it seems simple enough to take, ~~say~~ Tess of the D'Urbervilles or any other novel with a sufficiently melodramatic plot" and make it into "scenes which any shopgirl or errand boy with half an hour to spare can ~~take in~~ swallow at a gulp" (143). Yet, in a characteristic reversal, she at least momentarily considers puncturing this rant with "Nor is there any reason ~~why we should take up a superior attitude~~" (143). As Woolf rethinks adaptation, she returns to the binary of the "true" film versus fiction film that she set up in Berg 1 and Berg 2; she gives fiction films the backhanded compliment that "the pictures so made, whether from famous novels or ~~from~~ the producers <own> imagination" are somehow "exciting ~~intentionally~~" and "accidentally beautiful" (143). Her overall impression, however, is that something is off:

> But always there seems to be some ~~misfit some waste or~~ misdirection of energy ~~which something~~ misused or ~~some~~ neglected opportunity which reminds us ~~that~~ in the midst of the most gorgeous & ~~competent~~ <spectacles> competent performances of the ~~immaturity of the~~ tentative & immature condition of the art (143).

She finds "at present obviously ~~in these translations &~~ it is leaning far too much of its weight upon literature" (143), and her marginal note adds, "pictures can only follow books in the most halting & clumsy fashion" (145). She deplores the resulting adaptations: "as the eye is in very imperfect accord with the literary sense, ~~what happens is that~~ we get a version say of Oliver Twist which ~~is not only~~ has very little resemblance to the book ~~of that name but is~~ for ever trying to break away from ~~its~~ the connection & give us something ~~entirely of a different entirely different~~" so it "hobbles after the story, is always trying to break away & give us something ~~entirely~~ different, ~~congenial~~ after its own heart," or "off its own bat" (145). She plays with a cricket image of trying to do something "off its own bat" or "cinema's bat" which leads her to ask about the "peculiar gift of the cinema" (145). She terms cinema the "cousin to so many arts" (145), a significant choice, because *cinéastes* of the day claimed for cinema the closer relationship of a sister art.

After describing the problematic situation of cinema, "impeded from taking a stride in any one direction by the multitude of paths" (145), she imports the figure of the affecting shadow she had explored earlier on page 135. As she investigates this image further, she adds in the margin the first reference to a particular film, "At a performance of D. Caligari the other day" (145) and she expands that note in her frenetic jottings:

> Yet Now & again something happens at a movie which
> ~~reminds~~ gives us precisely the sense which we have
> imagined in the savage <when> ~~making~~ his iron bars ~~ring~~ <rang>
>   together
> ~~together & foretelling the~~ & he dimly < foretold> foreboded <the
>   music of > Mozart &
> Beethoven.   At ~~Dr. Caligari~~ a performance of Dr.
> Caligari the other day for instance, a shadow shaped
> something like a tadpole appeared in one corner of the ~~screen~~.
> For a moment it ~~had the   seemed to be   looked intentional~~
> seemed intended, & ~~to be the~~ embodiment of some
> monstrous diseased imagination in the lunatic's brain.
> ~~For a moment~~ Some new expression of an unrealised idea
> [impended?]   with ~~its~~ <the> [signal thrill?] of excitement & relief
>   which
> such realizations bring with them. Then it was gone.
> It was merely accidental. ~~And~~ & seemed to be in process &
> hauled up & ~~presented to be   prod~~ & so produced a thrill of
> ~~excitement & which the realis~~ a sense of expectation &
> wonder & amazement such as attends those strange moments – (145)

Though at this point her thoughts appear fragmented and fairly illegible, the phrases "produced a thrill" and "sense of expectation & wonder & amazement" do carry a positive charge (145). Reaching back to the suggestive outdoor vignettes of page 135, she now projects them onto a screen; "some new expression of an unrealised idea" harks back to "the new sensations" that appeared at random in the garden and city vignettes and "accidental" reintroduces the "delightful accidents" in "true films" in Berg Fragment 2. She reworks this material on page 147, as she explains that what seemed to be a new shape emerging from "the great bubbling cauldron" (147) "was an accident, a shadow which ~~was not~~ had fallen where it was not intended" (147). The suggestive accidental shadow leads her to consider how movies "have within their grasp" "innumerable symbols for ~~that~~ emotions which have ~~yet~~ so far failed to find expression" (147). The pre-texts clarify the track of Woolf's ideas; they alert us that Woolf does not begin with observations of a film, but with a "sense" and only later adds the reference to a film.

In a compelling bracket, Woolf sketches cryptic but provocative thoughts that again recall her jottings in Berg Fragments 1 and 2: "[Vaguely – dimly we are ~~thinking of/have thought of things~~ which are not in words and not in writing & not in shape: we also have a sense of]" (147). Rather than pursuing these tantalizing thoughts, however, after a few more jottings about tadpoles and terror, she switches to an intriguing vignette about a writer put on film:

> Terror, ~~when the~~
> ~~in~~ at the hands of the film makers ~~can prance~~ &
> ~~dance across a film~~, & then fold itself up & disappear
> inside the brain ~~the~~ of a hard faced man wearing a
> pearl tie pin who is dipping his pen into a presentation
> ink pot (147).

This vignette warrants our perusal. The swift and fragmentary writing suggests her enthusiasm, but Woolf's documented disdain for presentation ink pots suggests that this "hard faced man wearing a pearl tie pin who is dipping his pen into a presentation ink pot" cannot compare with her later vision of Shakespeare in *Orlando*: "Orlando stood gazing while the man turned his pen in his fingers, this way and that; and gazed and mused; and then, very quickly, wrote half-a-dozen lines and looked up" (*O* 17). What is the role of the odd hybrid of a writer/film character in Woolf's draft about film? He seems a stimulus to Woolf, who then pours forth orts and fragments of possibilities for capturing thoughts on film:

> Thoughts can pour out of people's brains in a <the wildest fashion>
> stream ~~of now symbolical, now actual~~ Either of shadows or
> of ~~actual shapes; now minute, vast, racing, stationary~~
> A ~~whole part can~~ be They can change dimensions, swell,
> Taper; race, & stand stock still (147).

In a characteristic sidestep, Woolf turns from the enigmatic hard-faced man with a presentation ink pot, to the poet proper. In this, her first discussion of the poet, she posits a handicap the poet labors under compared with the film maker; the film maker has the advantage here, for "the poet must particularize" whereas "the film maker can catch dawn or mist or wave" and "relate these ancient symbols in some new fashion" so it "revives the worn idea afresh" (147). Looking to the future, she urges film makers to distance themselves "from the arts we know" (149) in order to move towards something that can exploit the unique resources of the movies. She celebrates the potential scope of the medium for "speed," "creating astonishing & fantastic forms," for "immensity & minuteness, its capacity for contrasting," "exactitude," and for capturing "the welter & intense world which exists ~~when we have no part in it~~" (149). As the modernists embraced the drive to "make it new," Woolf's description of the innovative technical proficiency of cinema would seem to acknowledge film as a contender as a modern medium. However, after she generates her flurry of possibilities, Woolf punctures that excitement: "Such at least are the ~~glimpses~~ <hints> which ~~peep out~~ emerge/accidentally" and she asks and crosses out "But ~~what art can be made of hints and glimpses~~?" (149).

In holograph draft 1, and persisting to the penultimate published essay, Woolf calls for someone to establish fitting conventions for the cinema, much as her essays on literary aesthetics call for revising literary conventions to fit each historical moment and its pressures. She finds cinema amorphous without traditions to shape it, arguing that someone needs to connect the fragments "to create for the cinema the conventions" which "centuries of experiment" "have created for literature & art & music" (149). This innovator would detach film from "parasitic dependence upon the other arts" (151) and "make us believe" in its "fantasticality and speed" as we accept "the scale in music" or "rhyme & metre in poetry" (151).

Woolf abruptly switches from this futuristic fantasy to the trope of the savage, penning and crossing out "~~Meanwhile we must let the savage in us have his say~~" (151). The savage continues to intrigue and perplex Woolf. Shifting from "we" to "they," she alternately identifies with and distances herself from twentieth century "savage" spectators, as she first writes "we must accept the fact that all the <we must accept the fact that we are all >savages are essential" (151) and then writes, "They do not know what they want" and "are generally dissatisfied with what they are given" (151). Claiming that the savages "have got ideas into their heads" (151), Woolf speculates about the thoughts of one of the savages:

> For instance, Piccadilly Circus--so one of the savages
> may think in a moments pause among the flower
> [baskets?] < its ~~cacophony~~> ~~what~~ how beautiful & [ ] with its floating flags <[ ]> & its immense turmoil of thought <its [ ] & its omnibuses
>   & its
> clouds; the railings beneath it; & the gulls above:
> ~~Oh for a~~   ~~Why not try that on the films?~~   What a
> film ~~they will~~ ~~might~~   they will make of that! (151).

Would the phrase "~~Oh for a~~" have ended with "movie camera" before that thought was deleted? We must wonder, too, why Woolf's narrator projects the suggestion for a film of Piccadilly from the hypothetical perspective of one of the savages, rather than directly from the imagination of the narrator. At any rate, the multi-faceted savage, thus, with suggestions for directing, has the last word in the first holograph draft, but, as holograph draft 2 will demonstrate, the dialogue is far from over.

Take Two: Holograph Draft 2 of "The Movies"

Holograph draft 2 begins with the title, "The Movies," and reintroduces the familiar figure of the savage as a contested one. Woolf first distinguishes between the people/philosophers and savages: "They {the philosophers} have never seen the savages watching the pictures" (175), but she soon blurs the distinction:

> They have never seen the savages watching the pictures in
> They have never sat in the stalls & thought how ~~with a~~
> for all ~~their ornaments &~~ the ~~fur~~ clothes on their backs
> & the carpets at their feet ~~they are precisely the same~~
> no great distance separates them from those ~~eager~~ &
> bright eyed naked men who ~~rang two~~ knocked two
> bars of iron together & heard in that [] clangour ~~a foretaste of~~
> ~~far off~~ all the music of Mozart (175)

First the savages are a spectacle (even if the philosophers are *not* seeing them), but then the philosophers seem to become the savages, or "they." Next, Woolf complicates the figure even more when she strikes through the line "~~they are precisely the same~~" and substitutes "No great distance separates them" (175).

A welter of deletions and fresh starts in the draft indicate that Woolf has hit a snag as she attempts to write with any certainty of the art of cinema in the future:

> it is extremely difficult to ~~make any~~ say what
> is new and what is ~~coming~~ <old>, & what is <~~will~~>to be the art ~~of the~~
> cinema <will become> in the future. ~~As we only. But if our~~
> ~~Only this seems certain-- It seems certain that when the~~
> ~~For the most part one can swallow the pictures~~
> Only it seems ~~certain that from~~ ~~The~~ (175)

The plethora of crossouts and re-beginnings in this bit of the holograph emphasize that she may not be certain at all. Then, rather to our surprise, the next undeleted line asserts boldly, "To begin with it seems a simple, even a stupid art" (175). "Stupid" seems harsh, certainly more so than holograph draft 1's "slick & efficient" (139). The replacement of draft 1's strategy of damning with faint praise with less subtle name-calling marks a significant shift in tone.

Woolf then begins to ask—but interrupts and crosses out—a provocative question, "~~Do we get any exalted emotion from~~" (175), a line that strongly suggests the aesthetics of Roger Fry and Clive Bell, particularly Bell's measuring stick of "aesthetic emotion." This may indicate a trace of conversations between

Woolf and Bell about cinema (conversations I've considered elsewhere)[6] because a very similar question emerges in Clive Bell's later essay, "Cinema Aesthetics": "Has anyone seen a film not merely interesting, not merely decorative, not merely registering emotions and events but carrying emotions and events up to that high world of aesthetic experience?" (Bell 39). As Woolf and Roger Fry commiserated about Bell's tendency to crib their ideas, it would not be surprising to find him borrowing her thoughts. Because Woolf scribbles and abandons this hint here but doesn't include it in the published essay, Bell would have had access to the comments only through reading the pre-texts or through conversations.

Again in holograph draft 2, Woolf lists the newsreel vignettes, but with a significant difference; in this version the images are singular rather than plural, though they remain for the most part general rather than specific: "The King shaking hands, a boat sailing, a horse running" (175). When Woolf revisits the emotions felt by a spectator of dated newsreel footage, she describes the experience in less positive terms than she had used in draft 1. The first draft's "cluster of powerful emotions {...} amusement, admiration, anger, surprise" (141) diminishes in draft 2 to "slightly amused & hypnotized" (175); furthermore, in a deleted marginal note, Woolf downplays the visual, claiming that sight, "unless ~~you are a painter is the most elementary~~ of the senses" (175).

One particularly knotty section attempts to come to terms with the "mysterious quality" of moving photographs in newsreels; a marginal note clarifies that this quality is one "wh. they have not in real life, by being [shown?] in action upon a sheet" (177). Though she argues that they are "not beautiful in the sense in which pictures or buildings are beautiful" (177), she appears at a loss for words as she gropes: "~~possessed of a quality for which there seems to be no name.~~ but <u>real</u>; ~~more~~ but something else. Shall we say that they have become more real? That we behold for the first time life as it is ~~when~~ <when> because we ~~now have~~ no part in it?" (177). The newsreel footage allows for aesthetic distance: "As we gaze we seem to be removed from the pettiness of actual existence, its cares, its conventions, & [ ]~~something less personal & more general enters into our view~~" (177). Though she is still a few inches from the bottom of the sheet, she begins a fresh page and writes:

---

[6] I addressed the intriguing possibility of such a conversation and Clive Bell's takes on film in a June 2006 paper, "Tracking Clive Bell's Takes on the Cinema in the 1920s," for the Sixteenth Annual International Conference on Virginia Woolf at the University of Birmingham, U.K., and also in my chapter in *The Edinburgh Companion to Virginia Woolf and the Arts*, Ed. Maggie Humm (Edinburgh: Edinburgh UP, forthcoming 2010).

> ~~To this queer quality of reality~~ which reality ~~it is possible~~
> Nor is ~~this the only quality that~~ Thus a perfectly literal
> film of a perfectly ordinary sight--~~Piccadilly in the~~
> the traffic in Piccadilly, a flight of ducks, the shipping on the
> Thames, the Prince of Wales, the Prime Minister--has ~~an~~ a
> ~~interest which of~~ quality of its own. To this moreover,
> it is possible to add another quality which is ~~imparted~~
> ~~Place these scenes in the past, moreover~~ (179)

A vertical wavy line then strikes through most of this passage, and she rephrases some of the ideas as "Further the movies can play upon our emotions by bringing into action { . . . } our feeling toward the past" (179). Exploring the contradictions a retro-spectator sees in the scene of the pre-war wedding, she tries out words such as "~~grotesque~~," "innocent pomp," "pathetic credulity," and "pathetic ~~trustful~~ innocence" (179). Then, she describes in more detail how "we" see another newsreel initially glimpsed in draft 1:

> Or we see the suffragettes marching up & down
> before the gates of Holloway. ~~Already they appear~~
> Time has ~~moved so far from them that already they~~ it
> ~~seems already~~ removed them   which has made them
> almost grotesque of [ ] & almost past recognition
> ~~in <with> their long skirts~~) & as women has lent them some
> proud dignity ~~which~~ as the champions of a
> victorious cause (179).

At this juncture in draft 2, just as in draft 1, she suddenly shifts from the newsreels to critique film producers who "seem dissatisfied with these obvious sources of interest" which she here labels (and crosses out) as "~~The Real~~ Plain ~~Reality~~" (179) before settling on "the wonders of the actual world & the curious aspects of contemporary life" (181). Asserting that the film producers prefer "to heighten & season the plain truth" (181) she segues once again to the topic of adaptation and curbs any early optimism about adaptations of literature. She crosses out a good bit in this section; she asserts that "~~the alliance is unfortunate~~" and changes that to "But the results are only moderately & accidentally successful," penning and sometimes crossing out words such as "disastrous" "~~injurious~~" and "~~deadly~~" (twice), and reducing the good points of cinema to "some accidental grouping & happy gesture" (181). Spectators are, Woolf argues, left "utterly failing to connect ~~this~~ this long series of emphatic scenes" (183) with the book and she reworks on pages 181 and 183 her phrasing for her argument (see Figures 5 – 8).

Solving the Riddle of the *Anna Karenina* Film in Holograph Drafts 1 and 2

As Woolf suggests in *A Room of One's Own*, investigating manuscripts may help to solve riddles the published text presents, and the pre-texts of "The Cinema" do oblige us by solving one such riddle posed by the published essay. Because the published versions of the essay refer to only one film adaptation, a film of *Anna Karenina* that she describes in vivid detail, scholars have assumed that her discussion of film adaptation followed a screening of that film, and we have expended considerable energy attempting to track down the specific adaptation that Woolf describes so scathingly and deliciously:

> The cinema fell upon its prey with immense rapacity, and to this moment largely subsists upon the body of its unfortunate victim. But the results are disastrous to both. The alliance is unnatural. Eye and brain are torn asunder ruthlessly as they try vainly to work in couples. The eye says: "Here is Anna Karenina." A voluptuous lady in black velvet wearing pearls comes before us. But the brain says: "That is no more Anna Karenina than it is Queen Victoria." For the brain knows Anna almost entirely by the inside of her mind—her charm, her passion, her despair. All the emphasis is laid by the cinema upon her teeth, her pearls, and her velvet. Then "Anna falls in love with Vronsky"—that is to say, the lady in black velvet falls into the arms of a gentleman in uniform, and they kiss with enormous succulence, great deliberation, and infinite gesticulation on a sofa in an extremely well-appointed library, while a gardener incidentally mows the lawn. So we lurch and lumber through the most famous novels of the world. So we spell them out in words of one syllable written, too, in the scrawl of an illiterate schoolboy. A kiss is love. A broken cup is jealousy. A grin is happiness. Death is a hearse. None of these things has the least connection with the novel that Tolstoy wrote, and it is only when we give up trying to connect the pictures with the book that we guess from some accidental scene—like the gardener mowing the lawn—what the cinema might do if it were left to its own devices (Woolf, "The Cinema" *N&A* 382)

In holograph drafts 1 and 2, eye-opening discoveries undercut any assumptions about a film of *Anna Karenina*. Draft 1, first of all, rather than focusing on film, lists various literary texts as candidates for the harshly judged film adaptation:

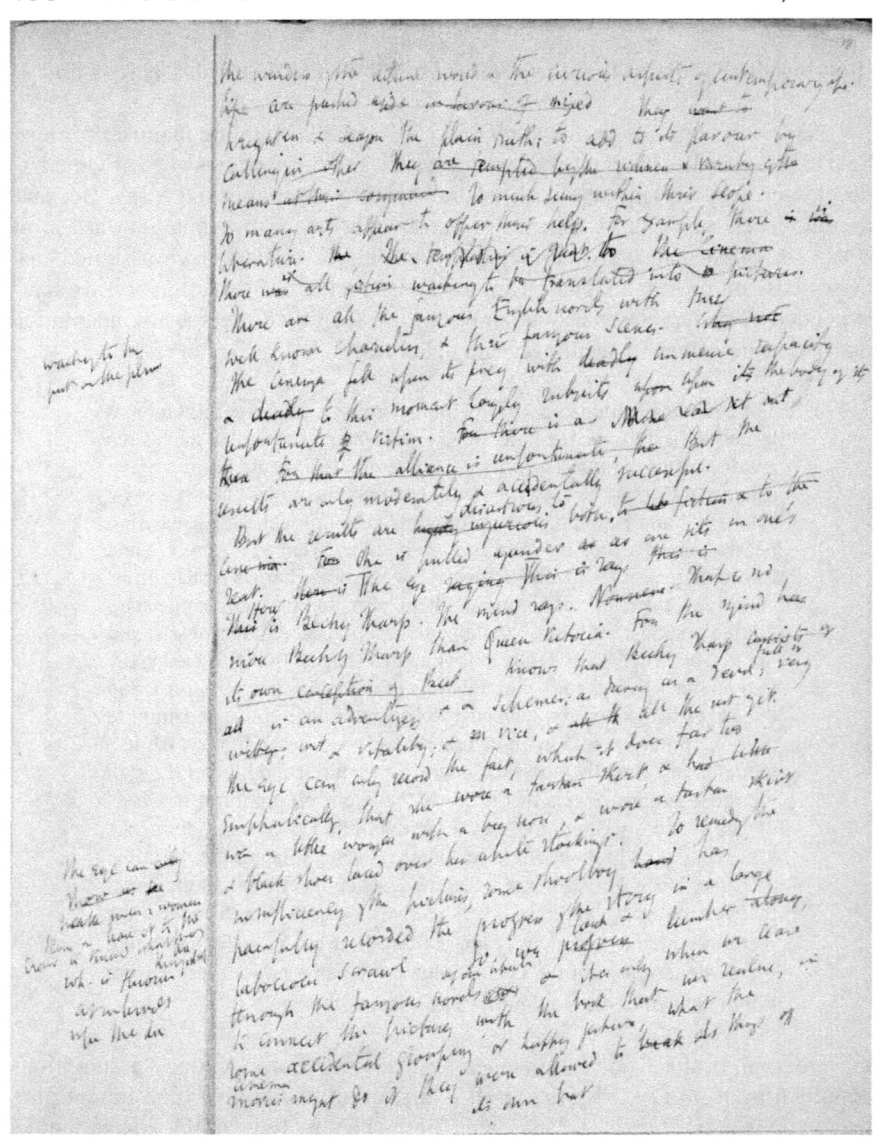

Fig. 5 Page 181 of Woolf's second holograph draft of "The Movies." In her: [Articles, essays, fiction and reviews] vol. 2, May 22, 1925 (Part II of 1925), p. 135-151; 175-189 [Captain's death bed and other essays, The. The cinema] The movies. Holograph n.d. ms. 9 p; 8 pg.

	the wonders of the actual world & the curious aspects of contemporary life ~~Life are pushed aside in favour of mixed~~ They ~~want to~~ heighten & season the plain truth; to add to its flavour by calling in other They ~~are tempted by the richness & variety of the~~ means ~~at their command~~ So much seems within their scope. So many arts appear to offer their help. For example, there ~~is was~~ <is> literature. ~~The The temptation is great to The Cinema~~ There ~~was~~ <is> ~~all fiction waiting to be translated into pictures.~~
waiting to be put on the films	There are all the famous English novels with their well known characters, & their famous scenes. ~~Why not~~ The cinema fell upon its prey with ~~deadly~~ immense rapacity & ~~deadly~~ to this moment largely subsists ~~upon~~ upon ~~its~~ the body of its unfortunate victim. ~~For there is a No one can sit out [The] For that The alliance is unfortunate The~~ But the results are only moderately & accidentally successful. But the results are ~~highly injurious~~ <disastrous to> both.~~to lit fiction & to the cinema.~~ ~~For~~ One is pulled asunder ~~as~~ as one sits in one's seat. ~~There is~~ The eye ~~saying this is~~ says ~~this is this~~ <Here> is Becky Sharp. The mind says. ~~Nonsense~~. That is no more Becky Sharp than Queen Victoria. For the mind ~~has its own conception of Beck~~ knows that Becky Sharp ~~consists of all~~ is an adventuress & a schemer; as daring as a devil; very <full of> ~~witty~~; wit & vitality; & ~~m~~ vice, & ~~all th~~ all the rest of it. The eye can only record the fact, which it does far too emphatically, that she ~~wore~~ a ~~tartan skirt & had little~~
The eye can ~~only show us see~~ [ ] men & women [ ] or leave it to the brain to know what they are thinking Wh. is [shown?] at intervals upon the [ ]	was a little woman with a big nose, & wore a tartan skirt & black shoes laced over her white stockings. To remedy the insufficiency of the pictures, some schoolboy ~~hand~~ has painfully recorded the progress of the story in a large laborious scrawl. So we ~~progress~~ <lurch &> lumber ~~along,~~ through the famous novels ~~;~~ <of our library> & it is only when we cease to connect the pictures with the book that we realise, in some accidental grouping or happy gesture, what the movies <cinema> might do if they were allowed to ~~be at~~ do things off its own bat

Fig. 6 Transcription of Figure 5.

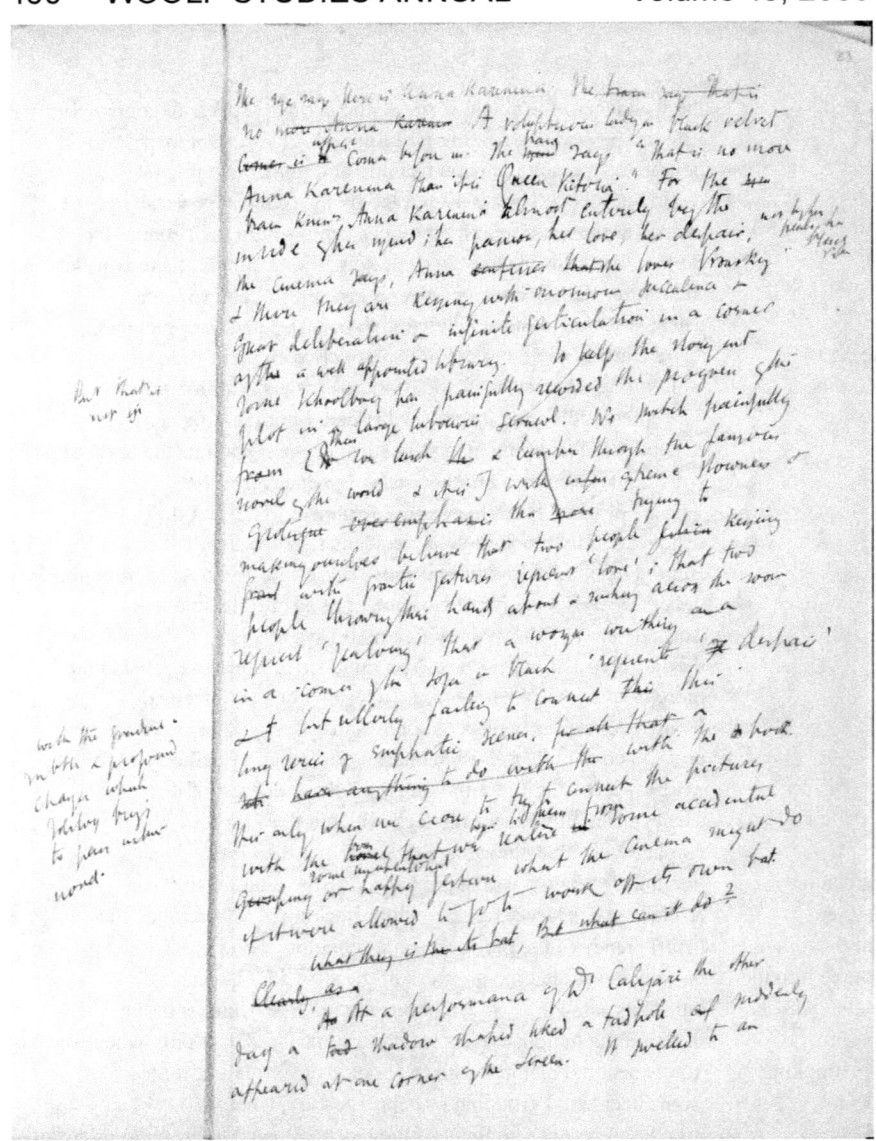

Fig. 7 Page 183 of Woolf's second holograph draft of "The Movies." In her: [Articles, essays, fiction and reviews] vol. 2, May 22, 1925 (Part II of 1925), p. 135-151; 175-189 [Captain's death bed and other essays, The. The cinema] The movies. Holograph n.d. ms. 9 p; 8 pg.

The eye says here is Anna Karenina. ~~The brain says that is no more Anna Karenin~~ A voluptuous lady in black velvet ~~comes in~~ <appears> comes before us. The ~~mind~~ <brain> says "That is no more Anna Karenina than it is Queen Victoria." For the ~~min~~ brain knows Anna Karenina almost entirely by the inside of her mind; her passions, her love, her despair <not by her pearls her black velvet> The cinema says, Anna ~~confesses that she~~ loves Vronsky & there they are kissing with enormous succulence & great deliberation & infinite gesticulation in a corner of ~~the~~ a well appointed library.   To help the story out some schoolboy has painfully recorded the progress of the plot in a large laborious scrawl. We switch painfully ~~from~~ [~~So~~ <Then> we lurch ~~thro~~ & lumber through the famous novels of the world & it is] with ~~infin~~ extreme slowness & ~~grotesque overemphasis~~ the ~~more~~   trying to making ourselves believe that two people ~~gesticu~~ kissing ~~frant~~ with frantic gestures represent 'love'; that two people throwing their hands about & rushing across the room represent 'jealousy' that a woman writhing ~~on a~~ in a corner of the sofa in black represents ' despair' ~~&~~ but utterly failing to connect ~~this~~ this long series of emphatic scenes ~~for all that~~ or ~~wh have anything to do with the~~ with the book. It is only when we cease to try to connect the pictures with the ~~novel~~ <book> that we realise ~~in~~ <begin to guess> <from> some accidental ~~grouping~~ <some unintentional> or happy gesture what the cinema might do if it were allowed to go to work off its own bat.
         ~~What then is the its bat,~~ But ~~what can it do?~~
         ~~Clearly as a~~
               ~~As~~ At a performance of Dr Caligari the other day a ~~tad~~ shadow shaped like a tadpole ~~of~~ suddenly appeared at one corner of the screen.   It swelled to an

But that is not it

'ith the gradual & ubtle & profound hanges which olstoy brings) pass within a novel

Fig. 8   Transcription of Figure 7.

Woolf names *Oliver Twist, Lorna Doone, Tess of the D'Urbervilles* "or any other novel with a sufficiently melodramatic plot" (143). She appears to be choosing a literary title at random, as she notes, "we get a version say of Oliver Twist" (145) and "~~say~~ Tess of the D'Urbervilles" (143). Draft 1 passages about the inadequacies of film adaptation do not even mention *Anna Karenina*: "we get a version say of Oliver Twist" which "has very little resemblance to the book" (145).

Draft 2 provides even more startling evidence about the elusive film adaptation of *Anna Karenina*; we learn that Woolf first drafted the damning passage with another character in mind–one not from Tolstoy's novel at all:

> <Here> is Becky Sharp. The mind says. ~~Nonsense~~. That is no
> more Becky Sharp than Queen Victoria. For the mind ~~has its~~
> ~~own conception of Beck~~ knows that Becky Sharp ~~consists of~~
> ~~all~~ is an adventuress & a schemer; as daring as a devil; very <full of>
> ~~witty~~; wit & vitality; & ~~m~~ vice, & ~~all th~~ all the rest of it.
> The eye can only record the fact, which it does far too
> emphatically, that she ~~wore~~ a ~~tartan sk~~irt & ~~had little~~
> was a little woman with a big nose, & wore a tartan skirt
> & black shoes laced over her white stockings. To remedy the
> insufficiency of the pictures, some schoolboy ~~hand~~ has
> painfully recorded the progress of the story in a large
> laborious scrawl. So we ~~progress~~ <lurch &> lumber ~~along~~,
> through the famous novels ~~;~~ <of our library> (181)

On the next page, Woolf pens her surprising and significant revision:

> The eye says here is Anna Karenina. ~~The brain says that is~~
> ~~no more Anna Karenin~~ A voluptuous lady in black velvet
> ~~comes in~~ < appears> comes before us. The ~~mind~~ <brain> says "That is no more
> Anna Karenina than it is Queen Victoria." For the ~~min~~
> brain knows Anna Karenina almost entirely by the
> inside of her mind; her passions, her love, her despair <not by her pearls
>   her black velvet>
> The cinema says, Anna ~~confesses that she~~ loves Vronsky
> & there they are kissing with enormous succulence &
> great deliberation & infinite gesticulation in a corner
> of ~~the~~ a well appointed library.   To help the story out
> some schoolboy has painfully recorded the progress of the
> plot in a large laborious scrawl. We switch painfully

~~from~~ [S̶o̶ <Then> we lurch t̶h̶r̶o̶ & lumber through the famous novels of the world & it is] (183).

Though Woolf abruptly recasts the starring character of her adaptation from Becky Sharp to Anna Karenina, changing the costume from tartan skirt to black velvet and pearls, she keeps much of the original phrasing, which suggests she was projecting her own imagined adaptation, rather than recalling a specific film. This alerts scholars that we perhaps need no longer seek film adaptations of *Anna Karenina*—though it might be diverting to track down silent versions of *Vanity Fair*, perhaps, featuring Becky Sharp in a tartan skirt. Some scholars (e.g. Rubenstein) have suggested that Woolf chose to refer to the film *Anna Karenina* because she was re-reading that novel at the time, which may very well be true, but it is also amusing to consider that Woolf may have switched the reference in order to associate cinema with an adulteress who commits suicide rather than with a successfully scheming upstart. Ultimately, learning that the reference to *Anna Karenina* was a late revision and the screening perhaps hypothetical is quite significant for understanding Woolf's relationship to cinema because it demonstrates once again that literature is always the pre-text for her discussion of cinema.

"The Imagination is Baulked"

Revealing Woolf's keen interest in the promise of cinema as an art vying to project thoughts, pages 185-189 of draft 2 engage at length with film's potential for expressing thought and how it compares with that of words. These pages of the pre-texts are particularly enlightening because they show Woolf's more complex take on an issue that she treats rather dismissively in the published version. Some *cinéastes* might find fault with Woolf's claim in the published version of the essay that Shakespeare or words alone can fully express thought. That version squelches any discussion of cinema's potential with a blunt imperative: "All this, which is accessible to words, and to words alone, the cinema must avoid" (Woolf, "The Cinema," *N&A* 382). However, Woolf explores this vexing issue in much more nuanced depth in holograph draft 2; tracking her thought process through the holograph is illuminating.

In the draft, she allows more free play for film potential—though she interrupts it. She considers that "the movies have within their grasp innumerable symbols for emotions which have so far failed to find expression" (185), but when she does try to think of what Anna and Vronsky can do besides "scowl" and "grimace" she breaks off: "They might—but here the imagination is baulked" (185). However, as the draft continues to explore Shakespeare's use of images, it raises doubts for *cinéastes*. In a rather tortuous site of revision Woolf raises (and then abandons) the idea that the poet's choices are selected by and right for the poet because they can be best expressed in words and suggests that the film maker could make different, equally valid choices within that medium. She crosses out ideas about connections between sight and thought, and she debates about the different raw material for each medium and the choices the poet or film maker must make. She posits, "No one wishes the cinema to follow parasitically the working of a poet's mind" (187) and her marginal note clarifies that the expressions of the poet's mind are those "wh. have been chosen because they can be expressed in words" (187). The draft continues in a very rough passage that begs for further study: "if so much of our thinking & feeling is connected with seeing, if love a girl is like 'a red red rose that's newly sprung in June' if a then it seems that the cinema ought to be able to follow some trains of thought exactly & beautifully by illustrating them rendering the pictures which compose them" (187), an option which is much more promising than the abrupt dismissal in the published version. In addition, she warns that cinema will have to keep far from "exact representation" (187).

In the last surviving pages of draft 2, Woolf considers that cinema might prove itself through testing; she recommends further studies of sight, motion and emotion: "it remains to be seen how far sight can stimulate our emotions" and "also the effect of motion itself has to be tested" (187) though she then crosses through the entire passage. Draft 2 ends rather abruptly on page 189, still considering how film could bridge dislocations in stories. There are no holograph pages for the ending of drafts 1 or 2; it is possible that when she worked on her revisions, those sheets were lost.

Changes and Outtakes from Holographs to Publication

Tracking what Woolf takes out from drafts to publication can be as suggestive as what she chooses to develop. For example, in draft 1 when she investigates the impact on a viewer of watching a ten year old newsreel, she describes the effect of watching the suffragettes. Though the suffragettes made it to the second draft, they were eliminated from the published version's significantly more patriarchal list of the marriage of Lord Salisbury's daughter, horse-races, the King shaking hands with a football team, and Sir Thomas Lipton's yacht.

Moving from the holographs to the published texts is a rest for the eyes, after the daunting task of deciphering Woolf's penmanship, but we keep the holographs at hand, because the interplay between the pre-texts, the text, and revised texts offers ongoing revelations.

Re-Takes—The Two Published Versions: Text and Revised Text

Changes between the first version of "The Cinema" in *The Arts* and the second version in the *Nation & Athenaeum* are rather startling, especially when we consider that the publication dates are so close.[7] Though *The Arts*' version is somewhat more comprehensive, the later *Nation & Athenaeum* version is more polished and graceful in style, and has been extensively and thoroughly revised, eliminating 148 words out of 2191, for instance, and with entire sections omitted, added, or drastically reworked. The revisions are not solely for style. The most extensive ones are in the section in which Woolf considers the way cinema and literature relate to thought and in which she offers advice to film makers; there the majority of the content is different and shows that she had not only re-written, but re-thought the argument.

The passages in which Woolf wrestles with the concept of visible thought are changed considerably. When she writes of the relationship between thought and the visual in the first published version, she claims that thought has "an inveterate tendency, especially in moments of emotion to make images run side by side with itself, to create a likeness of the thing thought about, as if by so doing it took away its sting, or made it beautiful and comprehensible" (Woolf, "The Cinema," *The Arts* 315). The line about the sting, omitted from the later version, resonates with Woolf's passages in "A Sketch of the Past" about her motivation as a writer: "It is only by putting it into words that I make it whole; this wholeness means that it has lost its power to hurt me; it gives me, perhaps because by doing so I take away the pain, a great delight to put the severed parts together" (*MOB* 72). Because in the pre-texts Woolf claims that various sensations, including some forms of fear, have not been adequately addressed by the other arts, and that they provide appropriate raw material for the cinema, it would be fitting for her to claim here that cinema could operate to take away the sting of these sensations through art as well. However, the second version does not go there. In her revised version of the cinema essay, Woolf writes, "But it [thought] has also, especially in moments of emotion, the picture-making power, the need to lift its burden to another bearer; to let an image run side by side along with it. The likeness of the thought is, for some reason, more beautiful, more comprehensible, more available

---

[7] In *The Arts*, Woolf's essay, "The Cinema," is the first one noted on the journal cover (though a typographical error in the Contents has her as "Virginia Waalf"—a bit of a howler! [297]). The notes on contributors on the contents page identify her: "Virginia Woolf is one of the most prominent of contemporary English novelists and essayists" (297). In McNeillie's *Essays of Virginia Woolf* v4, the version from *The Arts* alters some of the spelling to British spelling, changes a few punctuation marks, and corrects "effecting" (*The Arts* 316) to "affecting" (*E4* 352). My quotations where identified as such are from the version published in *The Arts*.

than the thought itself" (Woolf, "The Cinema" *N&A* 382). The term "picture-making power" which she adds to the revised version, leads us to think of film making, and to expect a discussion of the way cinema could take its place in this process. However, Woolf backs away from this reasonable extension of her argument as she asserts that the suggestive complexity of the image is "accessible to words, and to words alone" ("The Cinema," *N&A* 383). If the pre-texts and—to a degree—the first published text—display some openness and engagement with cinema, the revised *Nation & Athenaeum* version demonstrates a move to contain and undermine its power.

Some of the changes between the published versions are subtle, but evocative. Woolf eliminates passages which posit an engaged spectator, changing "We are peering over the edge of a cauldron in which fragments seem to simmer, and now and again some vast shape heaves and seems about to haul itself up out of chaos and the savage in us starts forward with delight" ("The Cinema," *The Arts* 314), by deleting "and the savage in us starts forward with delight" ("The Cinema," *N&A* 381). In the later version, she removes another line, "The brain adds all this to what the eye sees upon the screen" (*The Arts* 314) thereby toning down an active and participatory role for the spectator. In other passages, she changes assertions such as "So many arts at first stood ready to offer their help. For example, there was literature. All the famous novels of the world with their well known characters and their famous scenes only asked to be put on the films" ("The Cinema," *The Arts* 315) to passages which qualify the readiness of the other arts: "So many arts *seemed* to stand by ready to offer their help. For example, there was literature. All the famous novels of the world, with their well known characters, and their famous scenes, only asked, *it seemed,* to be put on the films" (emphasis added, "The Cinema," *N&A* 381).[8] A similar shift in tone is apparent in the change between the published versions from "there must be some residue of visual emotion *not seized* by artist or painter-poet which may await the cinema" (emphasis added, "The Cinema," *The Arts* 316) to "some residue of visual emotion which is *of no use* either to painter or to poet may still await the cinema" (emphasis added, "The Cinema," *N&A* 382). The first suggests that

---

[8] This is a dynamic example of the intense interplay among pre-texts, texts and post-texts, because Woolf goes back and forth in her decision about qualified and unqualified phrases. In holograph draft 2, she qualifies the help the other arts offer, but in the first published version she changes to assertions. In the second published version, however, she shifts back to the qualified phrasing, as in holograph draft 2:

> So much seems within their scope.
> So many arts appear to offer their help. For example, there ~~was~~ is
> literature. ~~The~~ ~~The temptation is great~~ to ~~The Cinema~~
> There ~~was~~ is all fiction waiting to be translated into pictures (181).]

the cinema may use elements which the other arts have failed actively to seize (which fits with Woolf's assertion in the early holographs that some sensations cannot be captured by the other arts and await new art forms); the second that cinema should have only the scraps for which the other arts have no use, which is a radically different spin. These changes, individually minor perhaps, together work to diminish the role of cinema—and that is telling.

The most significant change between the two published versions is in the endings. The version in *The Arts* ends with a thought-provoking analysis that brings in issues central to the pre-texts:

> All this guessing and clumsy turning over of unknown forces points at any rate away from any art we know in the direction of an art which we can only surmise. It points down a long road strewn with obstacles of every sort. For the film maker must come by his convention, as painters and writers and musicians have done before him. He must make us believe that what he shows us, fantastic though it seems, has some relation with the great veins and arteries of our existence. He must connect it with what we are pleased to call reality. He must make us believe that our loves and hates lie that way too. How slow a process this is bound to be, and attended with what pain and ridicule and indifference can easily be foretold when we remember how painful novelty is, how the smallest twig even upon the oldest tree offends our sense of propriety. And here it is not a question of a new twig, but of a new trunk and new roots from the earth upwards.
>
> Yet remote as it is, intimations are not wanting that the emotions are accumulating, the time is coming, and the art of the cinema is about to be brought to birth. Watching crowds, watching the chaos of the streets in the lazy way in which faculties detached from use watch and wait, it seems sometimes as if movements and colors, shapes and sounds had come together and waited for someone to seize them and convert their energy into art; then, uncaught, they disperse and fly asunder again. At the cinema for a moment through the mists of irrelevant emotions, through the thick counterpane of immense dexterity and enormous efficiency one has glimpses of something vital within. But the kick of life is instantly concealed by more dexterity, further efficiency.
>
> For the cinema has been born the wrong end first. The mechanical skill is far in advance of the art to be expressed. It is as if the savage tribe instead of finding two bars of iron to play with had found scattering the sea shore fiddles, flutes, saxophones, grand pianos by Erard and Bechstein, and had begun with incredible energy but without knowing a note of music to hammer and thump upon them all at the same time. (Woolf, "The Cinema," *The Arts* 316)

The *Nation & Athenaeum* ending is truncated, with these three paragraphs reduced to one paragraph of seven sentences:

> How all this is to be attempted, much less achieved, no one at the moment can tell us. We get intimations only in the chaos of the streets, perhaps, when some momentary assembly of colour, sound, movement suggests that here is a scene waiting a new art to be transfixed. And sometimes at the cinema, in the midst of its immense dexterity and enormous technical proficiency, the curtain parts and we behold, far off, some unknown and unexpected beauty. But it is for a moment only. For a strange thing has happened—while all the other arts were born naked, this, the youngest, has been born fully clothed. It can say everything before it has anything to say. It is as if the savage tribe, instead of finding two bars of iron to play with, had found, scattering the seashore, fiddles, flutes, saxophones, trumpets, grand pianos by Erard and Bechstein, and had begun with incredible energy, but without knowing a note of music, to hammer and thump upon them all at the same time. (Woolf, "The Cinema," *N&A* 383)

From her extensive treatment in the pre-texts to the first published version in *The Arts*, Woolf revises her call for the development of cinematic conventions to a few sentences. And the revised published version of the essay in the *Nation & Athenaeum* omits such passages entirely.

The rhetorical choices in the published versions of "The Cinema" forge radically different relationships between the narrator and the film maker. In the first version, the narrator is more distant and authoritarian; the film maker is often described in the third person and from outside. The narrator speaks of, not to, the film maker, and uses the imperative: "For the film maker *must* come by his convention, as painters and writers and musicians have done before him. *He must* make us believe that what he shows us, fantastic though it seems, has some relation with the great veins and arteries of our existence. *He must* connect it with what we are pleased to call reality. *He must* make us believe that our loves and hates lie that way too" (emphasis added, "The Cinema," *The Arts* 316). The overwhelming "he must" phrases stand out as contrary to Woolf's usual style—and to the tone of the pre-texts. The *Nation & Athenaeum* version is rather altered. The harangue to the film maker is gone; attention focuses on crafting the collaborative camaraderie between narrator and spectator and providing the film maker with more agency. Woolf chooses qualifying terms, such as "when," "if" and "could" rather than imperatives. The second version directs the director less, and expends more energy inventing the film that "we" (the spectator/reader and narrator) would be seeing. Rather than dictating answers, Woolf has "us" raise questions: "Is there, we ask, some secret language which we feel and see, but never speak, and, if so, could this be made visible to the eye?" ("The Cinema," *N&A* 382). In a significant transformation, she changes "his [the filmmaker's] Vronsky and his Anna" ("The Cinema," *The Arts* 316) to "Annas and Vronskys—there they are in the flesh" ("The Cinema," *N&A* 383).

In both published versions of "The Cinema," Woolf creates a place for the spectator—just as she often creates a place for the reader—and she manipulates that spectator position in strategic ways, just as she often does with her reader position. Yet in each she also takes on the role of director as she imagines the possibilities for film:

> We should see these emotions mingling together and effecting [sic] each other. We should see violent changes of emotion produced by their collision. The most fantastic contrasts could be flashed before us with a speed which the writer can only toil after in vain. The past could be unrolled, distances could be annihilated. ("The Cinema," *The Arts* 316)

As she expands this in the revised version, she appears almost carried away with the opportunity to direct; the text races along projecting her vision, leaving her hypothetical toiling writer behind:

> We should see violent changes of emotion produced by their collision. The most fantastic contrasts could be flashed before us with a speed which the writer can only toil after in vain; the dream architecture of arches and battlements, of cascades falling and fountains rising, which sometimes visits us in sleep or shapes itself in half-darkened rooms, could be realised before our waking eyes. No fantasy could be too far-fetched or insubstantial. The past could be unrolled, distances annihilated .... ("The Cinema," *N&A* 383)

The text repeats the mantra: "We should see" as the narrator spins her fantasy and claims a role as a delighted co-spectator alongside the reader. By placing the emphasis on the viewer—and by aligning the reader with the viewer and narrator as "we," she diverts our attention from the fact that she is not only showing, but also creating, the film she purports to describe. Such passages might suggest that Woolf was a closet director. But, reading back through the pre-texts and texts reminds us that all of literature is behind Woolf's take on film, and that, as alluring as directing may be, her heart is elsewhere.

"Hints & Glimpses": Pretexts and Pre-texts on the Threshold of the Library

> Then "Anna falls in love with Vronsky"—that is to say, the lady in black velvet falls into the arms of a gentleman in uniform, and they kiss with enormous succulence, great deliberation, and infinite gesticulation on a sofa in an extremely well-appointed library, while a gardener incidentally mows the lawn. So we lurch and lumber through the most famous novels of the world. ("The Cinema," *N&A* 382).

> in some houses they [books] have become such a company that they have to be accommodated with a room of their own—a reading room, a library, a study. Let us imagine that we are now in such a room; that it is a sunny room, with windows opening on a garden, so that we can hear the trees rustling, the gardener talking, the donkey braying, the old women gossiping at the pump—and all the ordinary processes of life pursuing the casual irregular way which they have pursued these many hundreds of years. ("How Should One Read a Book?" *E4* 388-389)

Woolf's essays are always a delight to read; the fluid prose, the wit and the seductive narrative can smooth over weak links in argument, and dazzle us into accepting her claims. The polished version often erases tell-tale traces of evasions and omissions; it projects a smooth surface that covers the gaps and fissures, the hesitations and failings. The pre-texts offer different, but equally compelling, delights. There, we participate in the struggles of mind, the idea before it has been tamed into an argument. We have the chance to witness where the mind goes, and where it refuses to go. Mesmerized by the bubbling cauldron, hot on the boil, we can let the ideas play. Immersion in the pre-texts allows a reader a much more nuanced take on the published essays. We have an unsettled and unsettling sense of what was developed, lost, refined, eliminated, complicated, or avoided. The holographs enable us to witness key conceptual challenges in contorted cross-outs and to experience the energy of frenetic imaginative flares. The changes, out-takes, shifts in emphasis and missed opportunities we witness in the pre-texts, texts, and revised published versions, provide us with a radically new perspective on "The Cinema."

Reading back through the revised published versions to the pre-texts provides us with the opportunity to raise new questions and deepen our understanding of Woolf's wide-ranging and conflicted thoughts about the cinema. Though we do not wish to bog down in authorial intention, we cannot resist asking about Woolf's pretext for engaging with film. What do her pre-texts and texts and revised texts tell us about this? The wealth of literary allusions in the pre-texts indicates how Woolf's cinema reflections were beholden to literature. Whenever another art threatens to become too much of a contender, Woolf reverts to Shakespeare and the literary canon, and her thoughts on the cinema are no exception. The pre-texts in particular remain much more in a library than in a screening room; she refers to Shakespeare, Robert Burns, *Vanity Fair*, *Tess of the D'Urbervilles*, *Lorna Doone*, *Oliver Twist* and "all the famous English works" of literature, but the two films she mentions, an adaptation of *Anna Karenina* and a revival of *The Cabinet of Dr. Caligari*, may be fictionalized screenings. Her assessment of film is always grounded in literary history, though those literary precursors were omitted from the published essay. In the published versions, though she eliminates traces of the literary titles, she upgrades the well-appointed library to the "extremely" well-appointed library, as if to emphasize the library's presence and role.

Composed and revised in the same sweep of time as "The Cinema," "How Should One Read a Book?" began as a lecture to a school for girls in January 1926 and was published in October of that year. As in the imagined screening scene in "The Cinema," the imagined setting for this essay is a well-stocked library; notably, that library includes *Tess of the D'Urbervilles*, *Paradise Lost*, *Anna Karenina*, *Robinson Crusoe*, *Emma*, *Vanity Fair*, *Clarissa Harlowe*, and texts by Flaubert and Conrad. The overlap with the library in the pre-texts of "The Cinema" suggests that Woolf has the same virtual library in mind. In a pre-text fragment of "How Should One Read a Book?" which Daugherty's sharp sleuthing about the essay dates as January 19, 1926 or later (124), Woolf begins and breaks off a discussion of plays/shows: "Only I would have you notice that it [reading biographies] is not reading in the sense that reading a novel is reading. We are using different faculties; we are getting a different kind of pleasure. And I go on to suggest that a play [show] has its own . . ." (*E4* 597). This thought is abruptly halted and, several spaces down, she begins anew with a different topic. What, one wonders, might have filled the gap here? Did Woolf begin thinking of shows and that led to thinking of cinema and hence to those delicious pre-texts of her ideas about film that have led us to the Berg? That is a provocative question.

Perhaps the most candid and vivid description of how Woolf funnels other arts into the inkpot of the writer is in her 1925 essay "Pictures," which Diane Gillespie tapped for the introduction to *The Multiple Muses of Virginia Woolf*. Woolf's essay, set in an art gallery, boldly admits, "They [writers] are not there to understand the problems of the painter's art. They are after something that may be helpful to themselves. It is only thus that they can turn these long galleries from torture chambers of boredom and despair into smiling avenues, pleasant places filled with birds, sanctuaries where silence reigns supreme" (*E4* 244). Thus, as she finds Cézanne's paintings "provocative to the literary sense" (*E4* 244-45), we can imagine how some movies proved likewise, turning the picture palaces from torture chambers of boredom and despair into smiling avenues leading Woolf back to the writing shed and the library. Do Woolf's pre-texts demonstrate that Woolf's pretext of exploring cinema was another way to provoke the literary sense? And what of the scholars' pretext for studying the pre-texts of Woolf's exploration of the cinema? On that note, we all meet on the threshold of the library, and this essay ends where we began, with an invitation to enter the famous library to explore Woolf's words. What scholarship can be made of hints and glimpses? This essay is a sneak preview of pre-texts of "The Cinema," a teasing trailer to lure scholars into the vaults to follow hints and glimpses of Woolf's holographs and these partial transcripts to continue to bring Woolf's pre-texts into play with the published works we know.

I am very thankful to Anne Garner, Librarian, and Dr. Isaac Gewirtz, Curator, at the Berg Collection, New York Public Library, who proved tireless in their efforts to aid me and locate archival materials. Jeremy Crow of the Society of Authors was gracious and timely as he gave permission to publish the transcripts and illustrations of the holograph drafts, as well as to quote extensively from the essay. My eyes thank Mark Hussey, who rescued me from some of the most daunting tangles when deciphering Woolf's handwriting. Any errors are my own. I would also like to thank Diane Gillespie for kind efforts on my behalf.

Illustrations of Woolf's manuscripts (Figures 1, 3, 5, and 7) are courtesy of the Henry W. and Albert A. Berg Collection of English and American Literature, the New York Public Library, Astor, Lenox and Tilden Foundations.

Quotations from Virginia Woolf's works are Copyright ©2009 The Estate of Virginia Woolf. By permission of the Society of Authors, as the literary representative of the Estate.

Works Cited

Amberg, George. *The Film Society Programmes 1925-1939*, New York: Arno Press, 1972.
Bell, Clive. "Cinema Aesthetics: A Critic of the Arts Assesses the Movies." *Theatre Guild Magazine* (October 1929): 39, 62-3.
Bishop, Edward. "The Alfa and the *Avant-texte*: Transcribing Virginia Woolf's Manuscripts." *Editing Virginia Woolf: Interpreting the Modernist Text*. Eds. James M. Haule and J. H. Stape. New York: Palgrave, 2002: 139-157.
———. *Virginia Woolf's* Jacob's Room. *The Holograph Draft*. NY: Pace UP, 1998.
Clarke, Stuart Nelson. *Virginia Woolf,* Orlando: *The Holograph Draft*. London: S. N. Clarke, 1993.
Daugherty, Beth Rigel. "Virginia Woolf's 'How Should One Read a Book?'." *Woolf Studies Annual* 4 (1998): 123-85.
Dick, Susan. To the Lighthouse: *The Original Holograph Draft*. Toronto: U of Toronto P, 1982.
Donald, James, Anne Friedberg, and Laura Marcus, eds. *Close Up 1927-1933: Cinema and Modernism*. Princeton: Princeton University Press, 1998.
Deppman, Jed, Daniel Ferrer and Michael Groden, eds. *Genetic Criticism: Texts and Avant-Textes*. Philadelphia: University of Pennsylvania Press, 2004.
Froula, Christine. "Modernism, Genetic Texts and Literary Authority in Virginia Woolf's Portraits of the Artist as the Audience." *The Romanic Review*. 86 (1995): 513-526.
Guide to the Virginia Woolf Collection of Papers, 1882-1984 (1919-1940). Berg Coll. MSS Woolf. The Henry W. and Albert A. Berg Collection of English and American Literature. The New York Public Library. Encoded by Lynn Lobash and Nina Schneider, 2006. http://www.nypl.org/research/manuscripts/berg/brgwoolf.xml
Hankins, Leslie Kathleen. "'Across the Screen of my Brain': Virginia Woolf's 'The Cinema' and Film Forums of the Twenties." *The Multiple Muses of Virginia Woolf*. Ed. Diane F. Gillespie. Columbia: University of Missouri Press, 1993: 148-79.
———. "*Cinéastes* and Modernists: Writing about Film in 1920s London." *Gender in Modernism: New Geographies, Complex Intersections*. Ed. Bonnie Kime Scott. Urbana: Illinois University Press, 2007: 808-858.
———. "Virginia Woolf and Film—The Archival Turn: Bloomsbury, *Vogue, Anna Karenina* and Judith Chaplin 'in an Extremely Well-Appointed Library.'" *The Edinburgh Companion to Virginia Woolf and the Arts*.

Ed. Maggie Humm. Edinburgh University Press, forthcoming 2010.
Hay, Louis. "History or Genesis?" Trans. Ingrid Wassenaar. In *Drafts*, special issue of *Yale French Studies* 89 (1996): 191-207. Originally "Histoire ou genèse?" in *Les Leçons du manuscript.* Special issue of *Etudes Françaises* 28, 1 (1992): 11-27.
Humm, Maggie. *Modernist Women and Visual Cultures: Virginia Woolf, Vanessa Bell, Photography and Cinema.* New Brunswick: Rutgers University Press, 2003.
Hussey, Mark, ed. *Virginia Woolf: Major Authors on CD-ROM.* Woodbridge, CT: Primary Source Media, 1997.
Jenny, Laurent. "Genetic Criticism and Its Myths." *Yale French Studies* 89 (1996): 9-25.
Marcus, Laura. "'A new form of true beauty': Aesthetics and Early Film Criticism," *Modernism/modernity* 13.2 (April 2006): 267-289.
———. *The Tenth Muse: Writing about Cinema in the Modernist Period.* Oxford: Oxford UP, 2007.
McNeillie, Andrew, ed. *The Essays of Virginia Woolf.* Volume 4: 1925-1928. London: Hogarth P, 1994.
Rubenstein, Roberta. "Reading Over Her Shoulder: Virginia Woolf Reads *Anna Karenina.*" Eighteenth Annual Virginia Woolf Conference, Denver, 2008.
Trotter, David. "Virginia Woolf and Cinema." *Film Studies* 6 (Summer, 2005): 3-18.
———. *Cinema and Modernism.* Oxford: Blackwell Publishing, 2007: 159-79.
Woolf, Virginia. Berg 1 and Berg 2. The Cinema. At back of her: The voyage out. Holograph draft. Vol. 2. Virginia Woolf Collection of Papers, The Henry W. and Albert A. Berg Collection of English and American Literature. The New York Public Library.
———. "The Cinema." *The Nation & Athenaeum.* 3 July 1926: 381-383.
———. "The Cinema." *The Arts* (New York). June 1926: 314-16.
———. "The Cinema." McNeillie, ed.: 348-54.
———. "The Cinema/The Movies and Reality." McNeillie, ed.: 591-95.
———. Holograph drafts 1 and 2. Holograph. The cinema The movies. Holograph. n.d. ms. 9p; 8p. In her: [Articles, essays, fiction and reviews] vol. 2, May 22, 1925 (Part II of 1925), p. 135-151; 175-189. Virginia Woolf Collection of Papers. The Henry W. and Albert A. Berg Collection of English and American Literature, The New York Public Library.
———. "How Should One Read a Book?" McNeillie, ed.: 388-400.
———. "How Should One Read a Book? – Manuscript Draft." Appendix III. McNeillie, ed.: 597-598.
———. *Orlando.* 1928. Annotated and with an introduction by Maria DiBattista. San Diego: Harcourt, 2006.

———. "Pictures." *The Essays of Virginia Woolf.* Vol. 4: 1925-1928. Ed. Andrew McNeillie. London: The Hogarth Press: 1994: 243-247.

———. *A Room of One's Own.* 1929. Annotated and with an introduction by Susan Gubar. San Diego: Harcourt, 2005.

———. "A Sketch of the Past." *Moments of Being.* Second Edition. Ed. Jeanne Schulkind. New York: Harcourt, 1985.

Wussow, Helen M. *Virginia Woolf's "The Hours": The British Museum Manuscript of* Mrs. Dalloway. NY: Pace UP, 1997.

Guide to Library Special Collections

This guide updates the information in volume 14.

Name of Collection: The Beinecke Rare Book and Manuscript Library

Contact: Kevin Repp, Curator of Modern Books and Manuscripts
Patricia Willis, Curator of American Literature

Address: Yale University Library
P.O. Box 208240
New Haven, CT 06520-8240

URL: www.library.yale.edu/beinecke/brblhome.html

Hours: Mon.–Thu. 8:30 AM–8 PM
Fri. 8:30 AM–5 PM

Access Requirements: Register at the circulation desk on each visit.

Holdings Relevant To Woolf: General Collection includes autograph manuscript of "Notes on Oliver Goldsmith." Comments on Edward Gibbon, William Beckford Collection. Letters from Virginia Woolf in the Bryher Papers, the Louise Morgan and Otto Theis Papers, and the Rebecca West Papers. Related material: 41 letters from Vita Sackville-West to Violet Trefusis; files relating to Robert Manson Myers's *From Beowulf to Virginia Woolf* in the Edmond Pauker Papers.

Yale Collection of American Literature includes typewritten manuscripts of "The Art of Walter Sickert," "Augustine Birrell," "Aurora Leigh," "How Should One Read a Book?" "Letter to a Young Poet," "The Novels of Turgenev," "Street Haunting." Dial/Scofield Thayer Papers: manuscripts of "The Lives of the Obscure," "Miss Ormerod," and "Mrs. Dalloway in Bond Street." Letters from Virginia Woolf in the William Rose Benet Papers, the Benet Family Correspondence, the Henry Seidel Canby Papers, the Seward Collins Papers, the Dial/Scofield Thayer Papers, and the *Yale Review* archive. Material relating to translations of Woolf in the Thornton Wilder papers. Related material: Clive Bell, "Virginia Woolf" (Dial/Scofield Thayer Papers); 43 letters from Leonard Woolf to Helen McAfee (*Yale Review*); 11 letters from Leonard Woolf to Gertrude Stein.

Name of Collection: The Henry W. and Albert A. Berg Collection of English and American Literature

Contact: Isaac Gewirtz, Curator

Address: New York Public Library, Room 320
Fifth Avenue & 42nd Street
New York, NY 10018

Telephone: 212-930-0802
Fax: 212-930-0079
Email: igewirtz@nypl.org

Hours: Tue.–Wed. 11AM–7PM
Thu.–Sat. 11AM–6PM
Closed Sun., Mon. and legal holidays

Access Requirements: Apply for card of admission at Office of Special Collections, Room 316 after first acquiring ACCESS card in room 315. (Online form may be printed). Traceable identification required. Undergraduates working on honors theses need letter from faculty advisor.

Restrictions: Virginia Woolf's MSS are now made available on microfilm and CD. N.B. *All the Berg's Woolf MSS are on microfilm and CD published by Research Publications and available at many research libraries.*

GUIDE TO LIBRARY SPECIAL COLLECTIONS

Holdings Relevant To Woolf: Manuscripts/typescripts of all of the novels except Orlando, including: *Between the Acts, Flush, Jacob's Room, Mrs. Dalloway* (notes and fragments), *Night and Day, To the Lighthouse, The Voyage Out, The Waves, The Years*; 12 notebooks of articles, essays, fiction and reviews, 1924–1940; 36 volumes of diaries; 26 volumes of reading notes; correspondence with Vanessa Bell, Ethel Smyth, Vita Sackville-West and others. Su Hua Ling Chen's Bloomsbury correspondence.

Name of Collection: The British Library Manuscript Collections

Contact: Manuscripts Enquiries

Address: 96 Euston Road
London NW1 2DB
England

Telephone: 0207-412-7513
Fax: 0207-412-7745
Email: mss@bl.uk

Hours: Mon. 10AM–5:00PM
Tue.–Sat.: 9:30AM–5:00PM

Access Requirements: British Library Reader Pass (signed I.D. required and usually proof of post-graduate academic status, or other demonstrable need to use the collections—see www.bl.uk). In addition, access to most literary autograph material only available with letter of recommendation.

Restrictions: Paper Copies, Microfilms, and Photography of selected items available upon receipt of written authorization for photo duplication from the copyright holder.

Holdings Relevant to Diaries 1930–1931 (microfilm); Mrs. Dalloway
Woolf: and other writings (1923–1925) three volumes; letter from Leonard Woolf to H. G. Wells (1941); two letters from Virginia Woolf and three letters from Leonard Woolf to John Lehmann (1941); letter written on behalf of Leonard Woolf to S. S. Koteliansky (1946); notebook in Italian kept by Virginia Woolf; notebook of Virginia Stephen (1906–1909); A sketch of the past revised ts (1940); letters from Virginia Woolf in the correspondence files of Lytton and James Strachey; letter from Virginia Woolf to Mildred Massingberd; letter from Virginia Woolf to Harriet Shaw Weaver (1918); letters from Virginia Woolf to S. S. Koteliansky (1923–1927); letter from Virginia Woolf to Frances Cornford (1929); letter from Virginia Woolf to Ernest Rhys (1930); correspondence of Virginia Woolf in the Society of Authors archive (1934–1937); letter and postcard from Virginia Woolf to Bernard Shaw (1940); three letters (suicide notes) from Virginia Woolf (1941); two letters from Virginia Woolf and three from Leonard Woolf to John Lehmann (1941). "Hyde Park Gate News" 1891–1892, 1895 (add. MSS 70725, 70726). Letters of Virginia and Leonard Woolf to Lady Aberconway, 1927–1941. Letter from Virginia Woolf to Frances Cornford. Letters from Virginia Woolf to Macmillan Co. 1903, 1908. Collection of RPs ("reserved photo copies"– copies of manuscripts exported, some subject to restrictions).

Name of Collection: Harry Ransom Humanities Research Center

Contact: Research Librarian

Address: The University of Texas at Austin
P.O. Box 7219
Austin, TX 78713-7219

GUIDE TO LIBRARY SPECIAL COLLECTIONS

Telephone: 512-471-9119
Fax: 512-471-2899
Email: reference@hrc.utexas.edu

Hours: Mon.–Fri. 9 AM–5 PM
Sat. 9 AM–NOON
Closed holidays; intersession Saturdays; one week each in late May and late August.

Access Requirements: Completed manuscript reader's application; current photo identification.

Holdings Relevant To Woolf: The manuscript collection includes the typed manuscript with autograph revisions of *Kew Gardens*, and the typed manuscript and autograph revisions of "Thoughts on Peace in an Air Raid." The Center holds 571 of Woolf's letters, including correspondence to Elizabeth Bowen, Lady Ottoline Morrell, Mary Hutchinson, William Plomer, Hugh Walpole and others. Further mss. relating to Virginia Woolf include letters to her from T. S. Eliot and reviews of her work. A substantial collection of the first British and American editions of Woolf's published works, as well as 130 volumes from Leonard and Virginia Woolf's library and a collection of books published by the Hogarth Press, is also housed. An art collection holds a landscape painting of Virginia's garden and a series of Cockney cartoons in a sketch book, signed "V.W." The center also has extensive holdings of materials related to Leonard Woolf, Ottoline Morrell, Mary Hutchinson, Lytton Strachey, Dora Carrington, E. M. Forster, Clive Bell, Roger Fry, Vanessa Bell, Bertrand Russell, Elizabeth Bowen, William Plomer, Stephen Spender and Hugh Walpole.

Name of Collection: King's College Archive Centre

Contact: Patricia McGuire, Archivist
King's College

Address: Cambridge CB2 1ST

Telephone: 01223-331444
Fax: 01223-331891
Email: archivist@kings.cam.ac.uk

Hours: Mon.–Thu. 9:30 AM–12:30 PM and 1:30 PM–5:15 PM. *Closed during public holidays and the College's annual periods of closure.*

Access Requirements: Proof of ID, letter of introduction, appointment in advance.

Holdings Relevant To Woolf: Woolf MSS and letters: Minute book, written up by Clive Bell, of the meetings of a play-reading society, with cast lists and comments on performances by CB. Dec. 1907–Jan. 1909, Oct. 1914–Feb. 1915. Players included variously Clive and Vanessa Bell, Roger and Margery Fry, Duncan Grant, Walter Lamb, Molly MacCarthy, Adrian and Virginia Stephen, Saxon Sydney-Turner. *Freshwater, A Comedy*— photocopy of editorial typescript prepared from the MSS at Sussex University and Monk's House; photocopy of covering letter from the publisher to "Robert Silvers," Jan. 29, 1976. Papers relating to the Virginia Woolf Centenary Conference held at Fitzwilliam College, Cambridge, Sept. 20-22, 1982. TS with corrections of "Nurse Lugton's Curtain." Typed transcript of R. Fry's memoir of his schooldays. Correspondence with Clive Bell, Julian Bell, Vanessa Bell, Richard Braithwaite, Rupert Brooke, Mrs. Brooke, Katharine Cox, Julian Fry, Roger Fry, John Davy Hayward, J. M. Keynes, Lydia Keynes, Rosamond Lehmann, Charles Mauron, Raymond Mortimer, G. H. W.

Rylands, J. T. Sheppard, W. J. H. Sprott, Thoby Stephen, Madge Vaughan. Woolf-related archival collections held: Charleston Papers; Rupert Brooke Papers; E. M. Forster Papers; Roger Fry Papers; J. M. Keynes Papers; George Humphrey Wolferstan ('Dadie') Rylands Papers.
J. T. Sheppard Papers; W. J. H. Sprott Papers. Various works of art by Vanessa Bell, Duncan Grant, and Roger Fry, held in various locations around King's College. Access via Second Bursar's secretary.

Name of Collection: The Lilly Library

Contact: Breon Mitchell, Director
Saundra Taylor, Curator of Manuscripts

Address: The Lilly Library, Indiana University
1200 East Seventh Street
Bloomington, IN 47405-5500

Telephone: 812-855-2452
Fax: 812-855-3143
Email: liblilly@indiana.edu, mitchell@indiana.edu
taylors@indiana.edu

Hours: Mon.–Fri. 9AM–6PM; Sat. 9AM–1PM;
Closed Sundays and Major Holidays

Access Requirements: Valid photo-identification; brief registration procedure.

Restrictions: Closed stacks; material use confined to reading room; wheelchair-accessible reading room and exhibitions (but no wheelchair-accessible restroom).

Holdings Relevant To Woolf: Corrected page proofs for the British edition of *Mrs Dalloway*; letters to Woolf from Desmond and Mary (Molly) MacCarthy; 77 letters (published in *Letters*) from Woolf to correspondents including Donald Clifford Brace, Robert Gathorne-Hardy, Barbara (Strachey) Halpern, Richard Arthur Warren Hughes, Desmond MacCarthy and Molly MacCarthy; "Preliminary Scheme for the formation of a Partnership between Mr Leonard Sidney Woolf and Mr John Lehmann to take over The Hogarth Press" (includes contract signed by Lehmann, Leonard Woolf, and Virginia Woolf and receipt for Lehmann's payment to Virginia Woolf to purchase Virginia Woolf's share in the Hogarth Press); photographs of Virginia Woolf, Leonard Woolf, Lytton Strachey, Strachey family, Roger Fry, and Vanessa Bell (Hannah Whitall Smith mss.); (Richard) Kennedy mss. (four hand-colored lithographs of Virginia Woolf: artist's proofs for RK's portfolio, VIRGINIA WOOLF: "AS I KNEW HER"; Sackville-West, V. mss. (10,529 items: includes the correspondence of Vita Sackville-West, and Harold Nicolson); MacCarthy mss. (ca. 10,000 items: papers of Desmond and Molly MacCarthy); correspondence between LW and Mary Gaither regarding publication of *A Checklist of the Hogarth Press* (1976, repr. 1986); Todd Avery, *Close and Affectionate Friends: Desmond and Molly MacCarthy and the Bloomsbury Group* (The Lilly Library / Indiana University Libraries, 1999).

Name of Collection: Archives and Manuscripts, University of Maryland, College Park, Libraries

Contact: Beth Alvarez, Curator of Literary Manuscripts

Address: University of Maryland Libraries
College Park, MD 20742

GUIDE TO LIBRARY SPECIAL COLLECTIONS

Telephone: 310-405-9298
Fax: 301-314-2709
Email: alvarez@umd.edu

Hours: Mon.–Fri. 10 AM–5 PM, extended hours Weds. 8 PM Sat. NOON–5 PM (Fall and Spring semesters).

Access Requirements: Photo ID.

Holdings Relevant To Woolf: Papers of Hope Mirrlees contain five autograph letters and postcards (1919–1928) from Virginia Woolf to Mirrlees. Also in the collection are 113 letters from T. S. Eliot to Mirrlees, and three letters from Lady Ottoline Morrell to Mirrlees. A finding aid is available at http://hdl.handle.net/1903.1/1536.

Name of Collection: Monks House Papers/Leonard Woolf Papers/Charleston Papers/Nicolson Papers

Contact: Fiona Courage, Special Collections Manager

Address: University of Sussex Library
Brighton
Sussex BN1 9QL
England

Telephone: 01273-678157
Fax: 01273-678441
Email: Library.Specialcoll@sussex.ac.uk
URL: www.sussex.ac.uk/library/speccoll

Access Requirements: By appointment
Identification to be presented on arrival. Application for access (including contact details of referee) to be completed on arrival.

Restrictions: Photocopying strictly controlled.

Holdings Relevant To The University of Sussex holds two large archives
Woolf: relating to Leonard and Virginia Woolf: The Monks House Papers, primarily correspondence and MSS of Virginia Woolf, including the three scrapbooks relating to *Three Guineas*; and The Leonard Woolf Papers, primarily correspondence and other papers of Leonard Woolf. (Monks House Papers are available on microfilm in many research libraries.) The Charleston Papers consist in the main of letters written to or by Clive and Vanessa Bell and Duncan Grant which had accumulated in their home; the library houses Quentin Bell's photocopied set; letters from Roger Fry, Maynard Keynes, Lytton Stachey, Virginia Woolf, Vita Sackville-West, E. M. Forster, T. S. Eliot, Frances Partridge and others. The Maria Jackson letters comprise some 900 letters from Maria Jackson to Julia and Leslie Stephen. The Nicolson Papers complement these three Sussex archives relating to the Bloomsbury Group, and consist of Nigel Nicolson's correspondence relating to his editorial work as principal editor of the six-volume *Letters of Virginia Woolf*, published between 1975 and 1980.

The Bell Papers. A. O. Bell's correspondence relating to her editorial work on Virginia Woolf's diaries, a parallel collection to the Nicolson Papers.

Collection level description may be accessed at www.archiveshub.ac.uk

Name of Collection: The Morgan Library & Museum

Contact: Reading Room

Address: 225 Madison Ave.
New York, NY 10016

GUIDE TO LIBRARY SPECIAL COLLECTIONS

Telephone: 212-590-0315
Email: readingroom@themorgan.org
URL: www.themorgan.org

Access Requirements: Admission to the Reading Room is by application and by appointment.

Holdings Relevant To Woolf: Virginia Woolf. Autograph manuscript notebook, 1931 Sept. 24. 1 item (52 p.) ; 265 x 208 mm. Contains drafts of "A Letter to a Young Poet," a brief letter to the press entitled "The Villa Jones" [ff. 3–5] and a monologue by a working-class woman [ff. 44–46]. MA 3333. Purchased on the Fellows Fund with the special assistance of Anne S. Dayton, Enid A. Haupt, Mrs. James H. Ripley, Mr. and Mrs. August H. Schilling, and John S. Thacher, 1979.
Virginia Woolf. Autograph letters signed (2) and typed letter signed, dated London [etc.], to E. McKnight Kauffer, 1931 Apr. 4–23, and undated. 3 items (4 p.). Concerning a drawing of her and a bibliography of her works. MA 1679. Purchased in 1959.
Vanessa Bell. Autograph letters (83) and postcards (3), signed mainly with initials, and a telegram, dated Gordon Square (London), to John Maynard Keynes, 1907–1936. 87 items (147 p.) Concerning Duncan Grant, Roger Fry, Clive Bell, the Bell children, Virginia Woolf, Lytton Strachey, the Keyneses, & David Garnett. MA 3448. Purchased on the Fellows Fund; a Gramercy Park Foundation (Mrs. Michael Tucker), 1980.

Name of Collection: Archives & Manuscripts

Contact: University Archivist

Address: University Museums and Special Collections Service
University of Reading
Redlands Road

Reading RG1 5EX
England
Telephone: 0118-931-8776
Fax: 0118-931-6636
Email: c.l.gould@reading.ac.uk

Access Requirements: Appointment needed to consult material. Permission required to consult or copy material in the Hogarth Press and Chatto & Windus collections from Random House, 20 Vauxhall Bridge Road, London SW1V 2SA, UK. (Jean Rose, Library Mgr. JRose@Randomhouse.co.uk)

Holdings Relevant To Woolf: Hogarth Press (MS2750): editorial and production correspondence relating to publications of the Press including Woolf's own titles. Production ledgers 1920s–1950s. Correspondence between Leonard Woolf and Stanley Unwin about progress with his collected edition of the works of Freud.
Chatto & Windus (MS2444): small number of letters 1915–1925; 1929–1931.
George Bell & Sons (MS1640): 5 letters from Leonard Woolf 1930–1966.
Routledge (MS1489): Reader's report by Leonard Woolf on George Padmore's "Britannia rules the blacks" (1935); "How Britain rules Africa."
Megroz (MS1979/68): 2 letters from Leonard Woolf, 1926.
Allen & Unwin (MS3282): Correspondence with Leonard Woolf 1923–1924; 1939–1940; 1943; 1946; 1950–1951, including letters concerning a reprint of *Empire and Commerce in Africa*, and concerning ill-founded rumors about the Hogarth press.

Name of Collection: Frances Hooper Collection of Virginia Woolf Books and Manuscripts/Elizabeth Power Richardson Bloomsbury Iconography Collection.

Contact: Karen V. Kukil, Associate Curator of Special Collections
Mortimer Rare Book Room

GUIDE TO LIBRARY SPECIAL COLLECTIONS

Address: William Allan Neilson Library
Smith College
Northampton, MA 01063

Telephone: 413-585-2906
Fax: 413-585-4486
Email: kkukil@email.smith.edu
URL: www.smith.edu/libraries/libs/rarebook

Hours: Mon.–Fri. 9 AM–5 PM

Access Requirements: Appointment to be made with the Curator.

Holdings Relevant To Woolf: The Hooper Collection emphasizes Woolf as an essayist but also includes many Hogarth Press first editions, limited editions of Woolf's works, and translations. The collection includes page proofs of *Orlando, To the Lighthouse,* and *The Common Reader,* corrected by Woolf for the first American editions, a proof copy of *The Waves* that Woolf inscribed to Hugh Walpole, and the proof copies of *The Years* and of *Flush.* The Collection also has one of the deluxe editions of *Orlando* that was printed on green paper. Other items include twenty-two pages of reading notes from 1926, three pages of notes on D. H. Lawrence's *Sons and Lovers*, thirty-three pages of notes for *Roger Fry*, a six-page ms. "As to criticism," a five-page ms. of "The Searchlight," and a fourteen-page ms. of "The Patron and The Crocus." The Hooper Collection also owns 140 letters between Woolf and Lytton Strachey as well as other correspondence, including a 13 February [1921] letter to Katherine Mansfield and ten letters to Mela and Robert Spira.

The Richardson Collection is a working collection of books and materials used by Richardson in preparing her *Bloomsbury Iconography*. It includes Leslie Stephen's photograph album, ninety-eight original exhibition catalogs dating back to 1929, clippings and photcopies of such items as reviews of early Woolf works, and Bloomsbury material from British *Vogue* of the 1920s. The Collection also has three preliminary pencil drawings by Vanessa Bell for *Flush*.

The Mortimer Rare Book Room also owns Woolf's 1916 Italian ms. notebook and her corrected typescripts of "Reviewing" and "The Searchlight." In addition, there is a 1923 photograph of Woolf at Garsington. Original cover designs for Hogarth Press publications include *The Common Reader*, *On Being Ill,* and *Duncan Grant*. The Mortimer Rare Book Room also has a Sylvia Plath collection that includes eight of Woolf's books from Plath's library, several of which are underlined and annotated, as well as Plath's notes from her undergraduate English 211 class at Smith (1951–1952) in which she studied *To the Lighthouse*. The collection also includes Woolf's 26 February 1939 letter to Vita Sackville-West, a 1931 bronze bust of Virginia Woolf by Stephen Tomlin, a 1923 Hogarth Press edition of T.S. Eliot's *The Waste Land*, a 1919 Hogarth Press edition of *Paris* by Hope Mirrlees and first editions of Vita Sackville-West publications. Online exhibitions are available on the Mortimer Rare Book Room's web site.

Name of Collection: Woolf/Hogarth Press/Bloomsbury

Contact: Robert C. Brandeis

Address: Victoria University Library
71 Queens Park Crescent E.
Toronto M5S 1K7
Ontario Canada

Email: victoria.library@utoronto.ca

GUIDE TO LIBRARY SPECIAL COLLECTIONS

URL:	http://library.vicu.utoronto.ca/special/bloomsbury.htm
Hours:	Mon.–Fri. 9 AM–5 PM
Access Requirements:	Prior notification; identification.
Restrictions:	Limited photocopying.
Holdings Relevant To Woolf:	This collection, the most comprehensive of its kind in Canada, contains all the work of Virginia and Leonard Woolf in various editions, issues, variants and translations; all the books hand-printed by Leonard and Virginia Woolf at the Hogarth Press, including many variant issues and bindings, association copies and page proofs; a nearly comprehensive collection of Hogarth Press machine printed books to 1946 (the year Leonard Woolf and the Press joined Chatto & Windus) including presentation copies, signed limited editions, page proofs, variants as well as substantial amounts of ephemera. The collection is also very strong in Bloomsbury art, especially the decorative arts, and contains important examples of Omega Workshops publications and exhibition catalogues. Vanessa Bell correspondence/MSS; Leonard Woolf correspondence; Ritchie family materials and correspondence re: Anne Thackeray Ritchie/Stephen family. Vanessa Bell dustwrapper designs for Woolf novels; Quentin Bell correspondence; S. P. Rosenbaum mss. Large Ephemera Collection. Bronze bust of Lytton Strachey by Stephen Tomlin (1901–1937). A companion piece to Tomlin's bronze of Virginia Woolf. More than 150 additional items including Hogarth Press variant bindings and proof copies; translations of Virginia Woolf and Leonard Woolf; ephemera, including Hogarth Press: Complete Catalogue of Publications to 1939 with annotations

by Leonard Woolf; materials relating to Bloomsbury Art and Artists including the catalogue of the second post-impressionist exhibition, 1912, and catalogues relating to Vanessa Bell and Duncan Grant exhibitions. 228 items, including Hogarth Press proof copies; Hogarth Press publication catalogues; bronze medal of Virginia Woolf by Marta Firlet; oil on canvas portrait of Amaryllis Garnett by Vanessa Bell (c.1958); Duncan Grant and Vanessa Bell designed Clarice Cliff dinner plates, 95 additional items.

Name of Collection: Library of Leonard and Virginia Woolf (Washington S U)

Contact: Trevor James Bond
Special Collections Librarian

Address: Washington State University Libraries
Pullman, WA 99164-5610
Email: tjbond@wsu.edu
URL: www.wsulibs.wsu.edu/holland/masc/masc.htm

Hours: Mon.–Fri. 8:30 AM–5 PM

Access Requirements: Letter stating nature of research preferred; student or other identification.

Restrictions: Materials must be used in the MASC area under supervision. Photocopying or photographing is permitted only when it will not harm the materials and is permitted by copyright.

Holdings Relevant To Woolf: WSU has the Woolfs' basic working library including many works which belonged to Woolf's father, Sir Leslie Stephen, and other family members. Over 800 titles came from their Sussex home, Monks House, including some works bought at auction soon after Leonard Woolf died in 1969. Later additions include: 1,875 titles from his house in

Victoria Square, London; 400 titles from his nephew Cecil Woolf; and over 60 titles from Quentin and Anne Olivier Bell. WSU has been actively collecting: all works in all editions by Virginia Woolf; all titles by Leonard Woolf; works published by the Woolfs at the Hogarth Press through 1946; books by their friends and associates, especcially those by Bloomsbury authors and about Bloomsbury artists; relevant correspondence and original works of art. Original artwork by Vanessa Bell; scattered letters by Vanessa Bell, E. M. Forster, Roger Fry, Leslie Stephen, Lytton Strachey, and Leonard Woolf. Original artwork by Richard Kennedy for illustrations in his book *A Boy at the Hogarth Press*; scattered letters by Roger Fry, Leslie Stephen, Ethel Smyth, and Leonard Woolf. Virginia Woolf's initialed copy of *Cornishiana*; Leonard Woolf's annotated copy of *An Anatomy of Poetry* by A. William-Ellis; Leslie Stephen's copy of *Lapsus Calami and Other Verses,* inscribed by James Kenneth Stephen. Several letters from Virginia Woolf, including two written in 1939 to Ronald Heffer, and a letter to Edward McKnight Kauffer. New in the Hogarth Press Collection are a copy of E. M. Forster's *Anonymity, an Enquiry,* bound in cream paper boards, and what Woolmer calls the third label state of Forster's *The Story of the Siren.*

Name of Collection: Yale Center for British Art

Contact: Elisabeth Fairman, Curator of Rare Books and Manuscripts

Address: 1080 Chapel Street
P.O. Box 208280
New Haven, CT 06520-8280

Telephone: 203-432-2814
Fax: 203-432-9613

E-mail:	elisabeth.fairman@yale.edu
Hours:	Tue.-Fri. 10 AM-4:30 PM
Access Requirements:	Call or e-mail for appointment. Permission needed in order to reproduce.
Holdings Relevant To Woolf:	Rare Books & Mss Department: 94 letters from Vanessa Bell and Duncan Grant to Sir Kenneth Clark; Prints & Drawings Department: 4 drawings by Vanessa Bell; 4 drawings by Duncan Grant; 6 drawings by Wyndham Lewis; 1 drawing by Frederick Etchells; Paintings Department: 1 painting by Vanessa Bell, 4 paintings by Duncan Grant (including portrait of Vanessa Bell); 3 paintings by Roger Fry.

Reviews

Imagining Virginia Woolf: An Experiment in Critical Biography. Maria DiBattista (Princeton: Princeton UP, 2009) x +194 pp.

In 1980 a fresh voice appeared in Woolf criticism, bold enough to entitle her work *Virginia Woolf's Major Novels* and to examine the way Woolf's authority was situated in the long tradition of English narrative. The young Maria DiBattista clearly knew her theory: her readings were shaped by Carolyn Heilbrun and Brenda Silver's discoveries, and by Hillis Miller and Harold Bloom's attentiveness to the interplay of narrative inheritance, especially that tradition informed by the Romantics. But the real urgency of her brilliant book came from old fashioned literary values. DiBattista's readings of Woolf"'s "major novels"—*Mrs. Dalloway, To the Lighthouse, Orlando, The Waves*, and (tellingly) *Between the Acts*—were beautiful, and beautifully written. Her insights sprang from centrifugal force, the urge inward, toward paying attention. The book demonstrated a delight in close reading.

Now—almost thirty years later—DiBattista reconsiders the great problems of Woolf's "narrative authority, narrative voice, narrative succession" (*Major Novels* x) which she took up in *Virginia Woolf's Major Novels* from a new slant. As then, she considers "the rhythm of feeling" (*Major Novels* 12), but this time the subject and source are more complex. This "experiment in critical biography" focuses on the permeable boundary between the writer's words and the reader's consciousness, to ask how we can find Woolf in her *oeuvre* and what that discovery might mean for her books and for us. In asking this simple question, *Imagining Virginia Woolf* has moved only a millimeter from DiBattista's first published work, just a slight tap of the kaleidoscope. Her writing has the same lucidity and beauty, her object is still to understand Woolf's voice and her distinctive place in English fiction; she revisits the great novels. But like Woolf, DiBattista has grown into her sensibilities. This is the kind of wise and humane book which only someone who has read Woolf deeply for many years could conceive. That it will speak equally powerfully to undergraduates who first crack open *To the Lighthouse* in a survey course and to seasoned (even geezery) Woolfians who will hear every echo that informs DiBattista's mercurial insights is a testament to the power of the narrative problems, the depth of Woolf's greatness, and the lucidity of DiBattista's ideas and writing.

DiBattista's argument seems commonsensical, in a philosophical sort of way. As readers, we can know a writer only through the medium of language—through her writing. (This is equally true if one is a biographer or a literary critic, though

DiBattista imagines a fascinating mermaid condition between the two.) But, she warns, "we can never know the person who writes *directly* through her writing" (5). Instead, she posits, we can only find Woolf "from the impressions, some more concrete than others, that I collect as I am reading her" (6). These impressions DiBattista christens "the figment of the author," "a subjective creation and not a literary personification" (6). As we "try to become the author" through our reading of her work, then, we are replicating the insight Woolf describes as "learn[ing] through feeling" (Woolf, "How Should One Read a Book," qtd. 7). In other words, a writer's style is a way of learning about the particularities of an author's *persona*, and incidentally about who she is and who we are.

DiBattista is aware that Woolf "leaves [her] text and comes into our life" in an imprecise, kinetic and fractured series of selves. She accepts Barthes' presupposition that "this author has no unity but appears to us as a plural and often discontinuous being" (8). Thirty years ago, this insight was truth enough for DiBattista. In *Virginia Woolf's Major Novels*, the place where Woolf the author existed was called "a transparency of figure [...] like the transparency of that literary ground called tradition, [which] only discloses nakedness, emptiness, an echoless nothing" (238). Now the charm of seeing how Woolf works—in other words, both seeing the magician and feeling the spell—reveals an authorial majesty to DiBattista, not an emptiness. It doesn't matter that we can't find a unified personality in Woolf's work. Instead, she discerns a series of Woolfian *personae*, aspects of her authorship, which she labels and treats thematically in successive chapters, as "The Sibyl of the Drawing Room," "The Author," "The Critic," "The World Writer," and "The Adventurer."

Thus DiBattista brings into focus the ineffable thing which Emily Dickinson called "Myself—the term between"—the place where the writer's personality is limned by the reader's consciousness. The book is (like Woolf's writing) full of surprises, new ways of seeing, lucid writing, and plain humanity. It's not easy to overlook intelligence or the beauty of this book, but it might be possible to fail to recognize its wisdom.

We are ripe for this kind of work in literary studies and Woolf studies now. DiBattista takes us back not only to seeing Woolf afresh, but to the touchstones of our critical training. Here is Erich Auerbach, our *stout Cortes* of Woolf studies, being taken up seriously. (Here are the ghosts of the great readers—Ralph Freedman and Martin Price and Hillis Miller of long ago. Here too the echoes of Julia Briggs, and Hermione Lee; and even, to my ear, the same lucidity and density of D. A. Miller on Austen or of Vendler on Shakespeare.) By trimming the edges of the context to Woolf's fiction and criticism and just a few great close readers of Woolf, DiBattista keeps the focus tight enough for us to see new patterns, and new truths, in the familiar. She also may introduce new readers of Woolf to the pantheon of great close readers. The scholar steeped in Woolfiana will appreciate the magpie eye, the lightness, the peering in unusual corners to find the evidence, the poetry in the structure of her inquiry. The book bears reading at least twice.

Here is where I go to the big questions of subjectivity, sex, and narrative authority. These questions, informed by feminist criticism and the insights of cultural studies which put Woolf into what Alex Zwerdling called *the real world*, are questions for now, urgent and important questions. We are at a moment when learning to read is becoming a lost art, and when reading the newspapers—or even having a newspaper to read—is ever more important for young people. The Woolf who wrote *Between the Acts* faced a no less anxious and weary world. This is why DiBattista's crisp, plain, playful insistence on being careful about interpretation, on piecing together the familiar and the obscure, in *discrimination* seems welcome to me. It is what the power of the humanities is about, and we need it in the fierce urgency of now.

DiBattista does not make ethical claims. But she is exacting in her inquiry. She discovers Woolf the writer (or any writer) "not a literary personification but a subjective creation," and discerns in the voice of a writer speaking to a reader a spell which she calls the "demon of reading" (8). This formulation gives credit to the consciousness of the reader and the writer and celebrates an interest not in "universal truths, but in particular personalities" (11). Her method ("so different from the principles I was officially taught in school") is associative, honest, liberating (10). In practice and in theory it takes up Woolf's big questions. How can we use our imagination to understand and shape the world? What about the interior life tells us about being human? How are women especially fit to convey the "bilocation" of consciousness—both in speech and silence, "ventriloquism" and "soliloquy" (55, 82)? The focus is on the mutuality of this human endeavor of reading the world.

DiBattista's questions are especially useful in untangling the knot of impersonal subjectivity in Woolf's writing, her ability to create consciousness not anchored in narrator or character, the empathy so deep and Keatsian that it inhabits the consciousness of a sparrow, or a cloud. This force DiBattista describes as a kind of female "nonegotistical sublime" (35). Sometimes, when DiBattista is performing these spells of reading—lightly traveling from the obscure (the 1906 short story "Phyllis and Rosamund") to the most hoary passages of *To The Lighthouse* and back—her description of Woolf seems like a polished mirror in which, for a moment, we can get a glimpse of the reflection of the critic/writer DiBattista herself: "A writer whose relationship to words strikes us as either so advanced or so primitive as to confound any settled view we might have of her" (65). To DiBattista, Woolf is a "radical conservative." This appellation could as well apply to her (67). In this book there are new things to learn and new things to see in old things. (Two examples: Woolf planned an essay on "Mr. Byron and Mr. Briggs" which forms a spectral antecedent to "Mr. Bennett and Mrs. Brown" [93]. Or the way that Woolf's power as a critic [not to say empathic friend to the common reader] often springs from "the disarming admission of shared ignorance," like not knowing when to laugh in Greek literature [107].) Like Woolf, DiBattista is alert to "the enormous burden of the unexpressed" (110)—both what can't be said or hadn't been said because saying such things can't be done by women; or the fact that many important things exist in silence, or are so ineffable as to defy expression.

For me, the place where her argument is least successful comes in the chapter entitled "The World Writer." DiBattista makes a case for Woolf's "comparative instinct" (123), despite (or because of) her failure to travel and to know the larger world outside of London. She argues that Woolf is a world writer, because like the exiled Auerbach himself, she felt the "awkward unease in translation" (129). The two thrusts of Woolf's worldliness in this formulation are her treatment of Russian literature and Greek culture. But not knowing Greek, and encountering Chekhov and the Russian novelists in (Constance Garnett's) translation, take us only so far into the world of the World. Not far enough. There may be no frigate like a book, but a frigate does displace your body somewhere where your mind must follow, and Woolf's parochialism has limits that Conrad, Forster, Joyce, Lawrence—yes, yes, I know, all men who were entitled to their adventures—were not constrained by. DiBattista is especially unfair to Conrad, whom she accuses of "subdued tone and ponderous narration" (142). These men's writing, at its strongest, was the better for their peregrination and exiles. DiBattista's defense of Woolf's worldliness in this chapter sounds stout-hearted but defensive to my ear.

The final, and what might seem the outer, ring of the structure of DiBattista's argument, is the *persona* of Woolf the Adventurer. Here we return to DiBattista's strength. "Debarred from adventure" women became inward explorers—at their keenest both Lily Briscoe and Woolf herself look inward to what Woolf called plainly "the human inside." DiBattista argues persuasively that Woolf was "the Columbus of the Human Inside" (165). Her greatest adventures chart Lily's discoveries, Orlando's liberation of the body and the mind, and perhaps the whole conceit of *Between the Acts.*

As a quotidian biographer, I must quibble with the subtitle of this book, *An Experiment in Critical Biography.* It is an experiment, and it is critical, and it concerns Woolf's human individual self. All these are true, yet to paraphrase Forster, *how false a summary of the book.* Only if we put the emphasis on *experiment* can we adequately honor how DiBattista's lightness and her confidence, her playfulness and her sharpness of sensitivity, all adumbrate real solutions to real narrative and critical problems. There *is* a difference between the way one reads an author in that author's published writings and the work of putting the author's body and mind into the culture of her time. What DiBattista does in this book is not really critical *biography*. Or maybe her concept of the biographical self is too experimental for my traditional brain. But the Woolf who lives in our imagination is a real person. She may be described as a demon, a phantom, but I prefer to think of her as an imaginative shaper like Prospero. DiBattista is her Ariel.

—Wendy Moffat, *Dickinson College*

Conversation with Julian Fry. S.P. Rosenbaum. Bloomsbury Heritage Series 43. (London: Cecil Woolf, 2005) 25 pp.

Roger Fry, Apostle of Good Taste, and Venice. John Lello. Illustrated by Sandra Lello. Bloomsbury Heritage Series 44. (London: Cecil Woolf, 2006) 23 pp.

Laura Stephen: A Memoir. Hilary Newman. Bloomsbury Heritage Series 45. (London: Cecil Woolf, 2006) 47 pp.

Julian Bell: The Violent Pacifist. Patricia Laurence. Bloomsbury Heritage Series 46. (London: Cecil Woolf, 2006) 44 pp.

Now in its fifteenth year with nearly fifty volumes offered, the Bloomsbury Heritage Series occupies a cozy niche in the diverse marketplace for work on Bloomsbury. Published by Cecil Woolf (Leonard's nephew) and his wife Jean Moorcroft Wilson, who is the editor of the series, the monographs are among the materials and memoirs produced or endorsed by descendants of Bloomsbury, who remain among the most visible proponents of the group's legacy. The slim volumes declare their "heritage" with a cover design by Robert Campling, which recalls Vanessa Bell's designs for the Hogarth Press, and the topics vary from new scholarship to reflections on less-familiar facts about Bloomsbury, as well as reprintings of work by major and minor figures in and around the group. While some of the volumes are very slight and even sloppy, others offer details and perspectives on Bloomsbury that may be interesting to academics and to enthusiasts of the group. With so much ongoing work on Bloomsbury's relationship to its social and political context, scholars might draw upon the scattered new information about the diverse interests and activities of the Group, which some of the monographs provide. More interestingly, perhaps, given scholarship on issues of celebrity and the literary marketplace by Jane Garrity, Regina Marler, Brenda Silver, and Jennifer Wicke, among others, the Bloomsbury Heritage Series is a revealing contemporary iteration of Bloomsbury's "coterie consumption." It continues the marketing of Bloomsbury and of modernism within the academy and to a broader public, providing easily consumable morsels of scholarship and information that reinforce our vision of Bloomsbury as a coherent if complex cultural phenomenon.

Titles 43 through 46, published in 2005 and 2006, demonstrate the Series' sometimes charming and sometimes frustrating variety of methods and focus. Patricia Laurence's *Julian Bell: The Violent Pacifist* is the most persuasive of the recent volumes, and it draws heavily from Laurence's work on Bell for her *Lily Briscoe's Chinese Eyes: Bloomsbury, Modernism and China* (2003). Laurence traces the tensions between Bell's inclinations as a "man of action" and as a "poet and a pacifist," and she proposes that "the way he lived his life may be read as a dialogue with his community, and particularly with his mother, and aunt, Virginia Woolf" (3, 5). She briefly discusses Bell's childhood and his time at Cambridge, and she lingers over his poetry and his sixteen months spent teaching in China as a way to understand his decision, at age twenty-nine, to reject Bloomsbury's pacifism and to fight in the Spanish Civil War where he died driving an ambulance. She argues that his interest in war was longstanding, offering for example an ironic account of young Julian and Quentin Bell staging mock battles at Charleston with conscientious objectors Duncan Grant and Bunny Garnett during World War I (7). Laurence's focus on the tension between aesthetics and politics in Julian Bell's life reflects recent scholarly concerns with the politics of modernism, but the focus of this slight monograph is not on directly engaging or advancing specific academic debates.

Laurence's research for *Lily Briscoe's Chinese Eyes*, which contributed to current scholarship on the global dimensions of modernism, makes her account of Julian's experiences at Wuhan University in China the most compelling section of her portrait of Bell. As in her book, her Bloomsbury Heritage monograph uses letters, manuscripts, and photographs (some reproduced in the monograph itself) to reconstruct his love affair with Ling Shuhua, the intelligent, charming wife of a leading professor at the university. Bell comes off as callous and sexist, decrying "the feminine taste for honour and complete lack of it," when Shuhua becomes upset about her husband's discovery of their affair and Julian's subsequent decision to leave China (30). By contrast, Shuhua seems a remarkable, progressive woman, a writer and artist who was "part also of the 'new woman' movement in China" (22). As Laurence observes, Julian's sexism is particularly striking given his extremely close bond with his mother and his relationship with his aunt, who—with the other women of Bloomsbury—were among "the most talented, free and progressive women in the early twentieth century" (23).

While Julian described his affair in terms of familiar sexist conceits, Laurence suggests (as she does in her 2003 book) that his time in Wuhan altered and intensified his attitude towards war. China was girding itself for the Sino-Japanese war (1937-1945), and this atmosphere encouraged Julian to embrace the necessity of military action. After returning to England and despite Vanessa's pleas and others' arguments, Julian departed for Spain to serve in a medical support unit in June 1937. He was killed the next month when his ambulance was bombed. Laurence tempers claims for the significance of Bell's short life, admitting the mediocrity of his poetry even as she traces its artistic influences and acknowledging the limits of his insights even as she treats them as representative of larger social and political trends. Indeed, Bell emerges as significant mostly in so far as he throws into relief the art and thought of established Bloomsbury luminaries. His sexism, for example, reminds us how extraordinary and embattled his mother and aunt's claims as artists and individuals were. Given his boorishness, it seems all the more remarkable that Woolf's views have in some ways prevailed over Julian's. Fittingly, Woolf's voice guides the beginning and end of Laurence's brief volume, first describing Julian in his boyhood as a "wild ruffian" and finally observing that "the poet in the thirties was forced to be a politician" (3, 41). As Laurence notes, *Between the Acts* and *Three Guineas* show Woolf struggling eloquently with the challenges that influenced and ended Bell's life.

Laurence's implicit tribute to the authority and insight of Woolf's work is typical of these volumes, which justify their subjects by their relationship to the best known individuals and incidents of Bloomsbury. Hilary Newman's *Laura Stephen: A Memoir* offers a brief, sympathetic biography of Leslie Stephen's mentally disabled daughter by his first wife, Minny Thackeray. It draws heavily on census data about the private homes where Laura boarded, on previously sealed records from the institutions where Laura lived, and on a handful of letters from Laura to her aunt, Anny Thackeray. Yet even as Newman tries to rescue Laura from relative obscurity—a product, in part, of Woolf's purported "rejection" of her mentally disabled half-sister—Woolf's recollections of the "vacant-eyed girl... who would throw the scissors into the fire" give a more vivid image of Laura than Newman can conjure from the scant surviving sources ("Old Bloomsbury" *MOB* 182).

There are other potential virtues of Newman's story, particularly in exploring the changing legal and medical conceptions of mental illness during Laura's lifetime (1873-1945), which Newman duly notes. (In a forty page text, she unfortunately repeats a long quote about Victorian distinctions among "idiots," "lunatics," and "imbeciles".) Strikingly, Leslie Stephen and Anny Thackeray did not record concerns about Laura's apparently congenital disabilities until after her mother's death, when Laura was five. Once married to Leslie, Julia Stephen first cared for Laura at home with the help of a governess, as was then the custom among upper-middle class Victorian families, but as a young woman Laura was sent to board with a family in the country and then to institutions for the mentally disabled, which gained wider acceptance throughout her life. The cost of Laura's care was covered by a trust from William Thackeray, which, Newman reveals, the Stephen sisters borrowed from repeatedly. The intimate details we have about Vanessa Bell and Virginia Woolf's finances are glaring evidence that despite Bloomsbury's status as "the best-documented literary and artistic coterie in twentieth-century Britain," Laura remains a relatively unknown figure (Marler 7). She remains a "tongue-tied" young woman ("Old Bloomsbury" *MOB* 182) largely excluded from narratives of the Stephens' childhood within a "very communicative, literate, letter writing, visiting, articulate, late nineteenth century world" ("Sketch" *MOB* 65).

The repeated passage about Victorian medicine in Newman's biography exemplifies one of the common mistakes that appear throughout the volumes. All contain multiple typos, and John Lello's *Roger Fry, Apostle of Good Taste, and Venice* fits an astounding number of typographical and citation errors into a roughly ten-page document. Lello's is the leanest and least satisfying of the present monographs, and focuses on Roger Fry's sojourns in Venice beginning in 1891. In Italy, Lello tells us, "Roger was able to study at first hand the great paintings of the Renaissance and acquire and develop the skills and knowledge required to equip him for professional life as a critic. These were essential years for him but have been largely overshadowed by his later distinction" (9). Unfortunately, besides a few references to influential friends and educational opportunities, Lello does not give a robust sense of why those years were so formative. Frances Spalding's biography of Fry explores this question more effectively, finding a source of Fry's concept of "significant form" in the writings of the critic Bernard Berenson, whom he met in Italy (68). Lello does give more specific information about Fry's residences, assuring us that "Fry did not live like a hobo in Venice" (16). Lello even describes which of Fry's former abodes survive today, presumably so that the reader can make a pilgrimage to the sites. Some of the residences are included in the series of watercolors of Venice by Sandra Lello, the author's wife, an odd touch given that readers likely would be more interested in seeing Fry's work from the period.

Roger Fry is also the focus of monograph 43, *Conversation with Julian Fry*, which contains a short, previously published 1976 interview with Julian Fry, Roger's son, by the Bloomsbury scholar S. P. Rosenbaum, a letter about Roger from Julian to Woolf as she was writing Roger's biography, and a short anecdote from Clive Bell about Julian Fry as a boy. The interview itself quotes Woolf's biography of Roger Fry, Roger's son, extensively, and the result is a somewhat disjointed array of Bloomsbury voices. The volume's foreword tells us that these three documents are being reprinted to celebrate "The Bloomsbury Workshop's exhibition and sale of Julian and Dulce Fry's collection of Roger Fry's paintings and drawings" (6). The Bloomsbury Workshop is a London gallery that specializes in Bloomsbury artists' work, and its owner, Tony Bradshaw, also has published accessible volumes surveying various Bloomsbury figures with the cooperation of members of the current Bell/Garnett clan. This recent cooperation between the Bloomsbury Heritage Series and Bloomsbury's visual art market (with their various familial connections) is particularly fitting given Vanessa Bell's obvious influence on the cover design for the series. What Regina Marler called the "Bloomsbury boom" may now be more of a steady hum, with Bloomsbury material emerging steadily each year. By issuing its slim monographs in Bloomsbury packaging and offering its volumes upon request, the Bloomsbury Heritage Series combines scholarship and celebrity to echo Bloomsbury's once-ambivalent tradition of self-marketing. In doing so, a number of the Bloomsburg Heritage Series' recent volumes, such as Laurence's, strike a distinct and pleasant note.

—Elizabeth M. Sheehan, *University of Virginia*

Works Cited

Garrity, Jane. "Selling Culture to the 'Civilized': Bloomsbury, British *Vogue*, and the Marketing of National Identity." *Modernism/Modernity* 6.2 (1999): 29-58.

Laurence, Patricia. *Lily Briscoe's Chinese Eyes: Bloomsbury, Modernism and China*. Columbia: University of South Carolina Press, 2003.

Marler, Regina. *Bloomsbury Pie: The Making of the Bloomsbury Boom*. New York: Henry Holt and Company, 1997.

Silver, Brenda. *Virginia Woolf Icon*. Chicago: University of Chicago Press, 1999.

Spalding, Frances. *Roger Fry, Art and Life*. Berkeley: University of California Press, 1980.

Wicke, Jennifer. "*Mrs. Dalloway* Goes to Market: Woolf, Keynes, and Modern Markets." *Novel: A Forum on Fiction* 28.1 (Fall 1994): 5-23.

Woolf, Virginia. "Old Bloomsbury." *Moments of Being: A Collection of Autobiographical Writings*. Ed. Jeanne Schulkind. New York: Harvest, 1985.

———. "Sketch of the Past." *Moments of Being: A Collection of Autobiographical Writings*. Ed. Jeanne Schulkind. New York: Harvest, 1985.

Before Leonard: The Early Suitors of Virginia Woolf. Sarah M. Hall (London and Chester Springs: Peter Owen, 2006) 304 pp.

Adrift in a punt, in the middle of summer holidays, seventeen year old Virginia Stephen muses in her journal: "[a]ctivity of mind ... is the only thing that keeps one's life going, unless one has a larger emotional activity of some other kind" (*PA* 138). Stephen's teenaged self-assessment was prophetic; throughout her life, the intellectual work of reading and writing would be a lifeline through times of mental collapse: from 1905, when taking notes for Frederic Maitland's biography of Leslie Stephen helped her recover from the breakdown she experienced after her father's death, to 1941, when Woolf vowed to "read the whole of English literature through" to counter the bombs of World War Two (*L6* 466). It's safe to say, I think, that for Virginia Woolf, as for young Virginia Stephen, the life of the mind was easier, safer, and saner than the "larger emotional activities" she refers to in this diary entry, her detached tone indicating a fundamental ambivalence about the adult world of love, desire, attachment, courtship, and marriage.

Sarah M. Hall acknowledges Virginia Stephen's antipathy to courtship and marriage by opening her recent book, *Before Leonard: The Early Suitors of Virginia Woolf*, with this quotation, from a 1906 letter to Violet Dickinson: "I wish everyone didn't tell me to marry. Is it crude human nature breaking out? I call it disgusting." It appears that what Virginia Stephen most longed for at age twenty-five was not romance or flirtation, but an ideal reader-critic to respond to her apprentice-work as a reviewer and essayist: "Oh – for some one to tell me whether it is well, very well, or indifferently done" (*PA* 226). Indeed, some of Virginia Stephen's most significant attachments, pre-marriage, were for those people who presented themselves as both readers and lovers, while her most passionate emotional attachments in these years, as has been well documented, were for women like Dickinson and Vanessa Bell. But this is not to say that Virginia Stephen wouldn't entertain, or be entertained by, male suitors for her hand in the five year period between Vanessa's marriage in 1907 and her own marriage to Leonard Woolf in 1912. This is precisely the neglected (and often amusing) terrain that Hall's admirably researched collective biography restores to view.

Hall's book offers eight different men in as many chapters as possible suitors for Virginia Stephen's hand: inappropriate Walter Headlam, married Clive Bell, enigmatic Saxon Sydney-Turner, gay Lytton Strachey, handsome Hilton Young, depressed Walter Lamb, Byronic Rupert Brooke, and officious Sydney Waterlow. We are quite familiar with some of these entanglements, particularly with Bell and Strachey, but others may strike the reader as surprising. Hall interprets "suitors" rather broadly, using the term to denote any male friend who "exhibited 'courting' behavior" (27), up to but not necessarily including an actual proposal. This means that Hall gives us the flirts (Headlam, Bell, and Brooke), the just-friends (Sydney-Turner), the near-misses (Lamb), as well as the actual proposals (Strachey, Young, and Waterlow). It's enough to make one fall in love with Leonard Woolf all over again. Although one might quibble with this list of choices (does nude bathing once with Rupert Brooke qualify as an "affair"?), Hall's decision to cast a broad net allows her to construct a portrait of courtship behavior among the British upper-middle classes at the turn of the twentieth century.

The true critic of biography reads as much from the end matter as she does from the text; and Hall's end matter, over forty pages of family trees and scrupulous documentation, is exemplary. The detective work behind this biography is truly laudable: Hall makes extensive use of unpublished archival sources, as well as interviews with the descendants of Woolf's suitors. This allows her to cast a light on previously overlooked episodes and entanglements in the history of early Bloomsbury. One example, small but neatly observed, concerns the minutes of the Play Reading Society, hosted by Clive Bell from late 1907 until early 1909. Hall's reading of the minutes—which consisted of droll reviews of the players' performances, as recorded by Saxon Sydney-Turner and Bell—allows her to claim persuasively that these dramatic evenings helped foment the risqué tone of early Bloomsbury. The Play Reading Society appears in different guises in the chapters on Bell and Sydney-Turner, as it both illuminates Bell's increasing intimacy with Virginia after his marriage to Vanessa and shows Sydney-Turner at his best, humorous and playful. Sydney-Turner was never a significant romantic interest of Virginia's (or vice-versa), and doesn't give the biographer much to go on, but Hall's portrait of him as obsessive-compulsive (counting street signs), idiosyncratic, yet sweetly feline brings this shadowy Bloomsbury figure to life (Hall makes a case for diagnosing Sydney-Turner with Asperger's syndrome).

Collective biography offers its practitioners and readers an opportunity to make connections between wildly disparate people—here, united in their attraction to the young Virginia Stephen. This can occasionally read like a "six degrees of separation" game, as it does in the chapter on Hilton Young, Virginia's first serious suitor. Hilton Young was the son of Sir George Young, mountaineer friend of Leslie Stephen, and the brother of Geoffrey Winthrop Young, mountaineer mentor to George Mallory (who had a brief and unsuccessful fling with James Strachey). After Virginia's rejection of Young's romantic proposal (from a punt on the river Cam), he went on to a successful military and political career, eventually marrying Kathleen Scott, the widow of polar explorer Robert Scott. So far, so good: these are compelling intersections among a relatively small class of people. But why go on to speculate, as Hall does, about a possible friendship between Virginia and Kathleen? They both kept diaries, hated shopping for clothes, and remained virgins until they were thirty. But the fact of the matter is that they never met, and that Kathleen was not particularly fond of the members of the Bloomsbury Group. The reader can appreciate the random encounter of Virginia Stephen and Kathleen Scott purely through their documented relationships with Hilton Young: ruminations about a possible friendship between them fall into the "should-a, would-a, could-a" school of speculative biography and detract from the substantial scholarship supporting Hall's work. Hall's assertion that "Hilton Young would certainly have been Julia [Stephen]'s favorite" (237) is similarly problematic (although I too found him the most dashing of Virginia's suitors).

I agree with the fundamental premise of Hall's argument—that Virginia Stephen treated her "affairs" as attention-seeking experiments in using feminine "power" in the heterosexual marketplace—as well as the supposition that affairs, proposals, and intrigue all provided the apprentice writer with the raw materials for fiction. I had a much harder time accepting Hall's occasionally uncritical assertion of an analogy between these suitors and Woolf's own fictional characters. It's one thing to claim that Clive Bell and Lytton Strachey were the models for Terence Hewet and St. John Hirst in *The Voyage Out*, as Hall and other scholars have done, particularly given that novel's attention to courtship and engagement rituals. It's another to claim that "*Mrs. Dalloway*'s Clarissa is a diluted version of Virginia" and the novel an imaginary portrait of what a marriage to Hilton Young would have been like (155-156). (Hilton Young also shows up as Hall's pick for *To the Lighthouse*'s William Bankes.) Such assertions may be appealing, but threaten to reduce the rich and strange relationship between "real life" and art into a one-to-one correspondence that flattens both.

Rather than focusing on parallels between the biographical and fictional characters, Hall could have developed some of the socio-cultural implications of her study. Were courtship rituals in the Bloomsbury Group exemplary of courtship rituals among other, less bohemian, members of their social class? What is the difference between modern friendships between young men and women in this time period and modern courtships? And finally, given the significant presence of homosexual men among Woolf's friends and suitors, what can Walter Lamb's sexual confusion or Lytton Strachey's momentarily serious marriage proposal teach us about "gay marriage" among the Edwardians? These are all larger issues generated by Hall's scholarship that would have given the individual portraits offered here more substantive historical and social context.

Despite these reservations, I would recommend this biography to anyone who likes their gossip conscientiously supported with archival evidence. Hall's writing is spirited and intelligent, and she has uncovered a wealth of previously unknown or under-studied documents. I especially appreciate her restraint at letting some mysteries stand: for example, the question of what Walter Headlam could possibly have said or done on a walk at St. Ives in 1893 with Julia Stephen that earned him the permanent suspicion of Stella Hills and Vanessa Bell (and his guest appearance as Charles Tansley in *To the Lighthouse*). Here as elsewhere, Hall surveys all possible sources and suggests hypotheses, but allows the inconclusive evidence to remain just that. Hall's respect for documentary evidence makes this a biography for both academics and common readers, and for anyone who appreciates both front and end matter. At its best, this biography creates a vivid and enjoyable portrait of the intrigue and drama early Bloomsbury is known for, as filtered through the courtship of Miss Virginia Stephen.

—Catherine W. Hollis, *U.C. Berkeley Extension*

Modernism and World War II. Marina MacKay (Cambridge: Cambridge UP, 2007) vii + 192 pp.

In the preface to the 1991 reprint of the influential *Modernism: A Guide to European Literature 1890-1930*, the editors Malcolm Bradbury and James McFarlane confidently stated that "somewhere around the end of the 1930s, Modernism, like much else of the world it was born in, came to a *kind of end*" (emphasis added). They conceded, nevertheless, that many of the issues it grappled with remain "integrally woven into our contemporary awareness" (12). It is true that their book is concerned with a European movement which incorporates, for example, Italian futurism and German expressionism as much as the British version of modernism—the field of inquiry must therefore be restricted to a reasonably well-defined time frame. It is just as true that scholars exploring modernist poetics and politics have often more readily dealt with the beginning of modernism rather than its ending(s), so that it is particularly interesting to see that Marina MacKay's book takes up the challenge of investigating the "kind of end" referred to by Bradbury and McFarlane. She pushes the end of modernism forward, however, to include the Second World War, and identifies it as a key moment in British culture, one in which politics and aesthetics were tangled in a complicated web, resulting, as she puts it, in a "guilty compromise" perpetrated by "all major British writers of the mid-century" (10). While the claim that mid-century British writers all more or less implicitly supported the Second World War in their work may startle, for example, many devoted Woolf readers and scholars, MacKay's work encourages us to rethink late modernist politics as transcending clear-cut left/right oppositions, and provides a stimulating framework within which to reassess the work of canonical figures, such as Woolf and T.S. Eliot, as well as "second wave" (19) modernists such as Henry Green and Evelyn Waugh

Her introduction, "Modernism Beyond the Blitz," firmly establishes the Second World War as a watershed event which is as crucial to our understanding of modernism as the Great War and thus merits greater critical attention. MacKay's study is the first to deal with modernism and World War II at length: recognizing that "we can only read modernism from where we are," MacKay proposes "an alternative history of a long modernism, where modernism is read backwards in an effort to bypass conventional historiographies of origins and emergence" (17). The attempt raises a number of immediate, and decisive, questions: what does Englishness come to mean after a war that stripped Great Britain of its empire, and what does modernism come to mean when it becomes institutionalized and historicized, when writers can still look into it and already look back on it? More importantly, what happens to its politics when modernism "goes public"? The paradox of an institutionalized avant-garde haunts the book as tentative answers are offered—these, however, do not serve so much to clarify as to complicate the picture of late modernism. But this difficult and compelling study's interest lies precisely in its complexity, as well as in its effort to illuminate less well-known texts and broaden the definition of what constitutes "proper war literature" (5)—a redefinition often attempted with regard to the First World War.

If there ever was a writer who truly benefited from such a redefinition, that writer would have to be Virginia Woolf. Readings of her novels as texts seeking to make sense of the war experience have been powerful and productive (from the contributions of *Virginia Woolf and War: Fiction, Reality, and Myth*, edited by Mark Hussey in 1991, to Karen Levenback's *Virginia Woolf and the Great War*, 1999, and Christine Froula's *Virginia Woolf: War, Civilization, and the Bloomsbury Avant-Garde*, 2005, to mention only a few). Perhaps this is why MacKay chooses to begin her analysis with a reading of *Between the Acts*. Here she contends that "Woolf's surprising participation in [...] consolatory cultural memories of the war sheds a useful light on the late politics of a writer once thought apolitical and now routinely presented as a leftwing radical" (23), even going so far as to characterize Woolf's last novel as a "shift to the political centre"; MacKay sees this as part of a collective cultural endeavor to "rebrand" Britain in an effort to persuade the United States to get involved in a war that the British could not win alone. The center of her argument seems to lie in the fact that the novel is set in rural England, and that contemporary idealizations of the English countryside served to locate "a serviceable Englishness to send across the Atlantic" (25); indeed, the novel has often been read as an elegy, the expression of a yearning for a traditional past. Yet, while it is true that Woolf's loathing of Hitler and her increasing fear of an invasion may have prompted her, as MacKay notes, to admit that the idea of defending Britain was "not all claptrap" (11), the notion that *Between the Acts* is any less pacifist than *Three Guineas* seems to me, at best, problematic (an interesting discussion on this point is in Karen Schneider's essay "Re-Plotting the War(s): Virginia Woolf's Radical Legacy"). The picture of rural Englishness that emerges from the novel proves to be anything but peaceful and serene when Woolf's ironic tone is taken into due account; the tradition she looks back on is fraught with contradictions and conflict; the village pageant itself is more parody than celebration. Her depiction of Eliza, the village shop-keeper, standing on a soap-box to play the role of Elizabeth I, does not appear to corroborate the idea that "there seems to be a refusal here to engage questions of social class" (33). This essay, however, is a thought-provoking piece which prompts reflection on the fact that, while recent criticism has stressed Woolf's "uncompromising" pacifism (32), this does not automatically entail that it was also always "uncompromised" in practice. Still, the unequivocal realization in *Between the Acts* that the wall of civilization is made up of "orts, scraps, and fragments" does not seem to support the idea that she endorsed a nostalgic rebuilding of it. MacKay's reading nevertheless serves to problematize Woolf's political identity, adding to the wealth of contributions on her pacifist stance in an original way.

MacKay goes on to chart the journey of another writer "of modernist sympathies" (44), Rebecca West, towards a rethinking of her own politics that eventually led her to rehabilitate the "primacy and inviolability of national sovereignty in years when the demystifying critique of the nation-state had hardened into left-liberal orthodoxy" (45). Reading *Black Lamb and Grey Falcon* as a text which resurrected the modernist mythical method in order to engage with the complex relation between nationhood and imperialism, MacKay sees West's use of Yugoslavian history as an allegorical exhortation to transcend ethnic differences (i.e., Scottish vs. English, Croatian vs. Serbian), so that strategic unity may be preserved. The inherent difficulty, however, lies in the fact that this "appeal to national unity" in the face of totalitarian violence inevitably "sanctions internal injustices" (51). MacKay reads "West's compromised and self-conscious rehabilitation of nationality" (70) as yet another indication that the Second World War definitively caused the disintegration of the 1930s call to take sides between unambiguous left- and right-wing political positions. Accordingly, T. S. Eliot's late texts are also seen as participating in the effort to win the United States over to the cause, and *Four Quartets* is read parallel to his "propaganda" pieces ("Defence of the Islands," "A Note on War Poetry," "To the Indians who died in Africa"). Eliot, typically characterized as a champion of conservative values, is shown in some aspects of his work to be nearer Woolf's politics in *Three Guineas*, for example, than one would suspect: "Even Eliot's ultra-conservative *The Idea of a Christian Society* (1939) argues that there is no reason whatsoever for English smugness when it squares up to the continental totalitarian regimes" (79).

While the sections dedicated to Woolf, West, and Eliot each focus on a single work, though read in constant dialogue with other texts, the chapters dedicated to Henry Green and Evelyn Waugh tend to paint a broader picture of their literary careers, dealing with more than one book in detail. This requires an adjustment of perspective on the reader's part, but it also makes for a revitalizing change in the pace of the book. MacKay manages the difficult feat of speaking effectively both to specialists and common readers who may or may not have stumbled upon what she persuasively demonstrates to be important texts for our understanding of late modernism. Woolf is once again a voice to be reckoned with when reading Henry Green: MacKay points to a similarity between his novel *Party Going* and *Between the Acts*, as they both describe "a festivity turning into a funeral" (93). However, Green's treatment of the war as a levelling force in a class-bound society also seems reminiscent of Eleanor Pargiter's liberating realization in the raid scene of *The Years* that it is much nicer *not* to have servants. This treatment of Green's subtle engagement with class politics is followed by a reading of Evelyn Waugh's involvement in the highbrow vs. middlebrow culture issue, at a time in which, ironically, authors had to deal with the "mainstreaming" of modernism, when the public actually came to expect "difficult" literature (119-120). And it is at this point, MacKay suggests, that we may begin to see the end of modernism—the moment when it can no longer pretend to be wholly independent of the Establishment: "Late modernism in Britain represents with increasing anxiety its sense of being superseded by a world that it had helped make possible, its consciousness of being displaced from its old position near the centres of political authority" (136).

In a sweeping final chapter, "more coda than conclusion" (141), MacKay briefly examines a number of post-war texts which scrutinize the remains of Englishness after the loss of the empire. She proposes readings of McEwan and Ishiguro, among others, as writers who strive to create a twofold historiography, dealing both with the war and the significance and legacy of modernism itself—a fitting conclusion to a book that seeks to show that the two are inextricably intertwined. MacKay's study achieves this end, and will interest readers who have already devoured volumes on modernism and the Great War. This is no easy read: the sheer bulk of the information provided in a book that is not excessively long requires unflinching concentration, and if not all of MacKay's conclusions will be universally shared, the lucid articulation of her case forces one to take it seriously and to think long and hard, once again, about art and politics. The reader's effort is well rewarded, and we can expect the author's work as editor of the forthcoming *Cambridge Companion to the Literature of World War II* to further the debate in rich and stimulating ways.

—Iolanda Plescia, *Sapienza University, Rome*

Works Cited

Bradbury, Malcom, and James McFarlane. *Modernism: A Guide to European Literature 1890-1930*. 2nd ed. London: Penguin, 1991.

Froula, Christine. *Virginia Woolf: War, Civilization, and the Bloomsbury Avant Garde*. New York: Columbia University Press, 2005.

Hussey, Mark, ed. *Virginia Woolf and War: Fiction, Reality, and Myth*. Syracuse: Syracuse University Press, 1991.

Levenback, Karen. *Virginia Woolf and the Great War*. Syracuse: Syracuse University Press, 1999.

Schneider, Karen. *Loving Arms: British Women Writing the Second World War*. Lexington: University Press of Kentucky, 1997.

Narrative Form and Chaos Theory in Sterne, Proust, Woolf, and Faulkner.
Jo Alyson Parker (New York: Palgrave Macmillan, 2007) v + 187 pp.

Certain scientific discoveries captivate the critical as well as the popular imagination. Since it was first identified in the 1980s, chaos theory has sparked interest across a wide array of scientific, cultural, and academic fields, providing fruitful (if at times controversial) analogies for describing the ways in which different aspects of our world operate according to systems that are both dynamic and deterministic. Following in the footsteps of other scholars who have applied principles of chaos theory to the study of literature since the early 1990s, in *Narrative Form and Chaos Theory* Jo Alyson Parker examines how four texts—Sterne's *Tristram Shandy*, Proust's *In Search of Lost Time*, Woolf's *Mrs. Dalloway*, and Faulkner's *Absalom, Absalom!*—demonstrate an analogous chaotic response to particular narrative problems by connecting form and content, writer and reader, undermining a linear and absolute conception of time and space, and revealing an order inherent to disorder.

"Chaos theory" is a general term that refers to chaotic systems in a variety of disciplines. Parker uses chaos theory as it particularly applies to the field of physics—called "dynamical systems theory"—to create the literary analogies she applies to the four texts under study here. She focuses this analogous relationship around two fundamental elements of dynamical systems theory: the strange attractor and the fractal. At their most basic levels, strange attractors function as the behaviors of a chaotic system, and fractals as the geometrical properties of that system. Narratologically speaking, strange attractors are analogous to narrative content and fractals to form; the narrative to the system, and both the writer and reader as the dynamicists creating order and meaning out of the system. In each novel examined here, Parker identifies a different dynamical system of strange attractors and fractals being worked upon by writers and readers to create what she calls "a bounded randomness, infinitely evolving within certain constraints" (26).

Parker begins with Laurence Sterne's *Tristram Shandy*. Hundreds of years before the science of dynamical systems, Sterne's novel explores nonlinearity and disorderly order in a narrative that is a "reaction to the grand linear narratives of the eighteenth century" (33). Identifying the "strange attractors" of sex and death in the novel, the non-linear temporality of the novel combines the time of events, the time of writing, and the time of reading in a complex narrative system that undermines notions of linear and absolute time. In her analysis of Proust's *In Search of Lost Time*, Parker emphasizes the ways in which Proust subverts the conventions of autobiography as well as of narrative temporality in order to accomplish a thematic goal of the novel: "to retard time's forward march and to recapture lost time" (Parker 62). By shifting between different kinds of temporal experience through iteration and scale, Proust creates a narrative world where reality exists only in individual memory. Parker continues her interest in the vagaries of individual memory in the last chapter on Faulkner's *Absalom, Absalom!* There, Parker explains that the character Shreve McCaslin illustrates how a variety of internal narrators contribute to a pattern of narrative that emerges from what appears to be a chaotic and ultimately indeterminate system. As what Parker calls "both the model reader and the model for the reader" (128), Shreve McCaslin contributes to the construction of meaning in the novel by collecting and ordering the various strains of a narrative in which he plays no direct part. McCaslin, like the reader, can only follow the attractor (or meaning) of these narrative strains towards an infinitely receding, attracting point of meaning in a constantly evolving chaotic system.

Parker finds the "bounded randomness" to be an especially prominent aspect of *Mrs. Dalloway*, and Woolf's "emphasis on creating a self-contained world" a "testimony to Woolf's admiration for both Sterne and Proust" (88, 89). Within Woolf's self-contained world, the writer's "disordering of traditional narrative structure" creates a dynamical system that Parker explains is indicative of the desire "to address the thoughts and concerns of women" in particular (90).

Parker compares the "certain constraints" of the structure of *Mrs. Dalloway* to "a fractal, which, created from a simple algorithm, displays infinite complexity" (91). The algorithm of the novel limits Woolf to seventeen hours on a single day, a handful of main characters, a small section of London, and a party. The results—the "strange attractors" of the dynamical system—are much greater than the sum of their relatively simple parts:

> Within these global limits that she sets for herself, Woolf manages to suggest that the potential for an infinite amount of local variations exists. A strange attractor exists within a fractal dimension, and, like the dynamic of the attractor, the overall narrative trajectory of *Mrs. Dalloway* simulates ongoing evolution within a bounded area. Woolf thus manages both to adhere to the constraints she has set for herself and to give us the sense that she has burst them. (91)

Woolf bursts her formal constraints through a combination of what Parker refers to as a "roving trajectory of focalization" and the "temporal trajectory" of the novel (91). The "roving trajectory of focalization" is Parker's term for the shifts between the points of view of more than forty characters. She argues that the fluidity and connectivity between the consciousnesses of multiple characters defies both social hegemonies and the "essential separateness of the human condition," uniting the chaos of division and separateness within an ordered system of shifting perspectives and leading to what Patricia Matson calls a "communal protagonist" (99; Matson 171).

The "temporal trajectory" of the novel, like the "roving trajectory of focalization," resists the hegemonic values of traditional, linear narrative temporalities, and unites otherwise divided and fragmented temporal experiences. The characters move backward and forward through time and memory as the city and novel are filled with the sound of London's many chiming clocks. The clocks—associated with traditional, linear time and hegemonic, authoritarian values—underscore the resistance of the characters' consciousnesses and the narrative to conform to a static order as well as uniting the various non-linear temporalities on a linear trajectory. Parker is also careful to remind her reader that the "roving trajectory of focalization" and the "temporal trajectory" are mutually dependent in the analogy of the dynamic system:

> As we move from character to character, we are moving throughout the temporal grid. The spatial and temporal are intertwined, as in the strange attractor, whose temporal evolution is charted in state space. Like the strange attractor, *Mrs. Dalloway*, in its very boundlessness, makes a good approximation of showing us "everything, everything!" (109)

Woolf's desire to expose the infinite within the finite and the boundless possibilities within the carefully limited is made a reality in *Mrs. Dalloway* through an ordered system of disordered perspectives and temporalities.

Parker is careful to point out that not every narrative benefits from the chaos theory, and the texts to which she applies the analogy in this study are carefully chosen for the ways in which they particularly exemplify aspects of a dynamical systems theory. The crafting and consideration of this analogy and its implications for literary analysis is an excellent model for applying theories, systems, discoveries, and principles from diverse disciplines to others. Rather than forcing the square peg of a scientific theory to fit the round hole of literary narratology, Parker seeks and finds the common and mutually beneficial ground between two fields. Dynamical systems may be found in libraries or laboratories, and both readers and research scientists are dynamicists, making meaning out of the infinite variations in their particular corner of the bounded randomness.

—Erin D. Sells, *Emory University*

Work Cited

Matson, Patricia. "The Terror and the Ecstasy: The Textual Politics of Virginia Woolf's *Mrs. Dalloway*." *Ambiguous Discourse: Feminist Narratology and British Women Writers*. Ed. Kathy Mezei. Chapel Hill: U of N Carolina P, 1996.

Modernism and the Locations of Literary Heritage. Andrea Zemgulys (Cambridge: Cambridge UP, 2008) viii + 247 pp.

Imagine the thrill of walking into a favorite author's drawing room, sitting on the horsehair settee, and *knowing* that the site was the very location where she wrote her masterpieces. For scholars of literature, there is something mystical about connecting with a piece of tangible evidence touched by a dead writer—a garden bench, a torn letter, even an old hat. Somehow, these moments of contact bring the past into the present and shatter perceptions of time and space. However, Andrea Zemgulys's *Modernism and the Locations of Literary Heritage* reveals that our enjoyment of a writer's past life is amateur at best and can breed harmful nostalgia. For her, "heritage" is the term that best describes the ideological and nostalgic creation of the past she explores in her book. "Heritage" serves to create a hegemonic story about England's writers and their surroundings, a narrative Virginia Woolf sought to dismantle. Zemgulys subtly reveals that modernist scholarship focused on "locating" and "mapping" combined with the popular currency of terms like "space" and "place" is empty if it does not offer its reader a better understanding of the relationship between literature and the site of its production.

In a sea of books and articles linking modernism's attempts to "make it new" on paper to rapidly modernizing urban landscapes, Zemgulys's book makes an intriguing foray backward, analyzing how the Victorian project of a carefully constructed literary heritage made by urban house-museums and literary walks informs writings on London by E. M. Forster, T. S. Eliot, and Woolf. These modernists, she claims, were interested in London's literary past just as much as an ordinary middlebrow tourist, and by reading the archive of heritage texts and sites Zemgulys attempts to situate modernist writing in relation to an "ostentatiously mediated past" (2). She argues from the outset that exploring modernism's attempts to break ties with a Victorian past elides some of the above-mentioned writers' deepest tensions within their early work about a past re-invented by heritage. By situating Forster, Eliot, and Woolf within this context, she is able to show that modernists did actively engage with a metropolitan and middlebrow consumer culture of tourism.

The book is a timely example of scholarly interest in the urban environment's effects on the production of modernist literature and the arts, and Zemgulys is deftly conscious of the layers of history contained in a city such as London and how they affected writers, especially Woolf. Compelling archival research underpins her argument and enables her to enter into the conversation on the significance of space and place without becoming esoteric. Zemgulys's work joins that of cultural theorists, such as Jed Esty and Ian Baucom, interested in tracing the development of "a metropolitan English imaginary" (8). There are two major tasks at work within *Modernism and the Locations of Literary Heritage*. The first is to provide a place-based historical account of the creation of a British literary heritage, a project that Zemgulys claims occurred roughly between 1840 and 1930, to show how city government, citizens, and tourists actively created and maintained the afterlives of writers. The second is to explore the ways in which literary heritage works into the writing of Forster, Eliot, and Woolf.

The first three chapters of the book cover enormous ground as Zemgulys moves us through Stratford, "Dickens' London," Haworth, and London. In this section, she offers a comprehensive historical account of literary heritage-making, which she defines as the construction of a narrative about the past that is "fitted to the present" and serves to rationalize "unsettling social change" (1). According to Zemgulys, "literary heritage" is the combined result of three practices: *literary geography*, the practice of writing about authors' lives shaped by their surroundings, *literary memorialization*, the practice of opening house-museums that preserved or replicated an author's belongings within the rooms of his or her house, and finally, *literary tourism*, the practice of visiting memorialized sites and reading literary geographies. Zemgulys claims that the production of literary heritage surged at the end of the nineteenth century and the beginning of the twentieth because it provided a panacea against the chaos of modernity and urban gentrification's destruction of places with historical value. To combat the loss of place, literary heritage manifested itself in house-museums full of "relics" and literary "pilgrimages" aided by maps and guidebooks. Literary tourism offered a hegemonic, collective, unified version of Britain's literary past that appealed to British and American visitors alike. Zemgulys observes that the seemingly harmless recreational and profitable practice of purchasing dead writers' homes and possessions served to reinforce the narrative of Empire as it faced its dissolution. The writer's house told the physically tangible story that "great literature" was produced by "great men" for the benefit of the nation in this very place. Furthermore, the invitation to visit the homes of "great men" (and "good women") appealed to a middle-class, middlebrow, and metropolitan population (14). What's more, the literary tourist did not even have to be literate at all. Anyone could come into the home of Thomas Carlyle or Charlotte and Emily Brontë without knowledge of the texts these writers produced. Thus, to modernists like Woolf, literary tourism becomes problematic in that it provides the visitor with plenty of incidental knowledge about a writer but does not teach him or her anything of value about the author's literary achievement. With a successful emphasis on domestic city spaces, Zemgulys shows that literary heritage does not manifest itself through grand monuments, statuary, or estates of the upper class but that the production of literature happens in humble settings. Literary heritage capitalizes on this notion and ironically attracts the less literate, the tourist who desires to identify with the daily life rather than the mind of a writer.

Though she explores literary heritage throughout England in the first section of the book, Zemgulys maintains that the production of heritage sites is a particularly metropolitan phenomenon. The first section of *Modernism and the Locations of Literary Heritage* ends with a particularly engaging discussion of the idea of a "Vanishing London" in which urban modernization paved over old landmarks and unclaimed historical sites (71). To combat the trauma of such change, she notes that establishing an ethos of heritage in a large, bustling city "transmuted urban 'shock' in to palpable continuity and transmuted crowds into friendly ghosts" (87). In other words, creating a narrative of literary heritage that preserved an "Old London" made it possible to ignore real urban problems such as poverty and over-crowding that plagued 1920s and '30s London. The literary tourist, guidebook in hand, could wander among alleys and old tenements and believe that the life present there was all part of a very convincing act. Scholars interested in how a city contends with gentrification and historical preservation will find Zemgulys's discussion of London's "blue plaque" project illuminating (88). Not only do plaques mark the places where dead authors ate chips and drank a pint, but also, they serve as a marker of a government-modulated reinforcement of "'bettered' citizenry" (89). Only virtuous and upstanding people warranted a blue plaque, Zemgulys aptly notes, because should London suffer "cataclysmic dissolution" and vanish, the plaques will survive and tell the tale of English civilization's greatest contributors (90).

However, Zemgulys's argument could be strengthened by asserting that the plaques also keep the tourist's focus on the constructed past rather than the current conditions of daily life in such historically marked areas of the city. Yet, her work in this section contributes to a greater understanding of how government heritage projects built up an elitist narrative about British greatness. Unfortunately, her over-reliance on the term "collective memory" to explain how the narratives of the past affect everyone, ignores complications in using the phrase. Critics like Susan Sontag teach us that there can be no such thing as "collective memory" because class, race, and religion, among other factors, affect how one processes narrative; thus, a "literary heritage" and its universalizing story does the same damage that the term "collective memory" does. Zemgulys essentially undercuts her own critique of heritage-making by not completely defining her use of "collective memory."

The second section of *Modernism and the Locations of Literary Heritage* seeks to explore how Forster, Eliot, and Woolf engaged with the shifting, malleable cityscape of London. Though Zemgulys states that her intentions with Forster and Eliot are to trace very narrowly how literary heritage operates in *Howards End* and *The Waste Land* respectively, her chapters on both pale next to her lively and innovative reading of a collection of lesser studied Woolf texts. She even claims that next to Woolf, Forster and Eliot's interest in literary heritage is "passing" (189). It is clear that Zemgulys senses the most potential in Woolf, who employs a critique of literary heritage over a span of writings that "serve [. . .] as a platform for [her] to make literature modern" (144). Though the reading of *Howards End* is extraordinarily tight, and her discussion of Eliot's relation to City of London churches sheds significant light on *The Waste Land*, these chapters seem unnecessary, because the book's main theoretical argument about a created literary heritage set up in the first half is for the benefit of Zemgulys's discussion of Woolf.

As with most universalizing narratives of a nation's grand past, literary heritage produced significant gender bias, despite the fact that many of Britain's important writers are women. This component of Zemgulys' argument becomes especially crucial in the Woolf chapter. Zemgulys begins with an examination of a cluster of essays on literary tourism and geography and moves into *A Room of One's Own* to show how English literary heritage permanently genders and embodies writers, promoting interest in their clothing or chairs rather than their writing. Zemgulys points out that Woolf's claim in *A Room of One's Own* that masterpieces can only come from writers we cannot ever know (like Shakespeare and Austen) is a direct result of her considerations of how literary heritage projects shape an image of a writer in his or her surroundings. As Zemgulys sees it, Woolf embarks on a critical project of her own to unravel the hegemonic and sexist narrative of literary heritage and its practices by developing a systematic method of using them as "disciplined exercises of [...] base readerly tendencies" and turning them into "impersonal and judgmental explorations" (161). Woolf succeeds in turning the focus from the writer's gendered and embodied person to the writer's actual house and haunts which, as Zemgulys articulates, makes it possible for Woolf to show the house as a space that provides a backdrop to the *writing* rather than the writer. Zemgulys offers a particularly insightful reading of "Great Men's Houses" to show that once Woolf turns to the "voices" of the house and its material contents, such as broken tea cups, she effectively critiques the promotion of "great men" by exposing the house as a "domestic battleground" where inhabitants male and female occupy the private sphere (167). It is the women—the mistress, the scullery maid, the cook—who maintain and support the success of the house, and this is a piece of the narrative often left out of literary heritage created by the house-museum.

Finally, Zemgulys analyzes two city novels, *Orlando* and *Night and Day*, to explore how the mutable modernizing city full of taxis and apartment complexes collides with the literary memorialization of the past. The two novels represent, for Zemgulys, Woolf's insistence on critiquing middlebrow, middle-class, metropolitan creation, and the sustenance of a false literary heritage. Furthermore, Woolf's active engagement with themes of heritage and its manufacture made her writing distinctly modernist at a level that pushed beyond innovative sentence patterns and impressionistic images. *Modernism and the Locations of Literary Heritage* is an impressively ambitious piece of scholarship and offers something to readers looking for insight not only into some of Woolf's less canonical writings but also a more concrete rendering of the fraught relationship between Victorian London and its modern metropolitan manifestation in the early twentieth century.

—Sarah E. Cornish, *Fordham University*

Modernism, Memory, and Desire: T. S. Eliot and Virginia Woolf. Gabrielle McIntire (Cambridge: Cambridge U P, 2008) x + 264 pp.

For both Eliot and Woolf, according to Gabrielle McIntire, memory is always already tangled up with the body because both writers eroticize reminiscence: "to remember is to desire; to desire *is* to remember" (9). The erotics of this desire are different in each writer's case. McIntire's Eliot is not the dry old High Modernist stick of much received critical wisdom, but a man who is "sexy, dangerous, and crucially *uneven* in his investments and pronouncements" (7), whereas her Woolf is one whose desire is as much textual as sexual.

Little has yet been written on the scatological, homophobic, misogynist and racist verses Eliot composed between about 1909 and 1929 on the adventures of "Columbo" (Christopher Columbus) and his encounters with King Bolo of Cuba and "his Big Black Bassturd Kween," but McIntire opens her absorbing, illuminating analysis of Eliot, Woolf, modernist memory and desire with the argument that these works cannot be dismissed as mere juvenilia. Some of these verses were published in Valerie Eliot's edition of *The Letters of T. S. Eliot*, others in Christopher Ricks's *The Inventions of the March Hare*, but many remain in the archive. McIntire has consulted them all, but she has not been permitted to quote from all of them. Although she tends to overuse it, the word "astonishing" is an apt description of these works' effect on readers familiar only with Eliot's canonical work. For example:

> Now while Columbo and his men
> Were drinking ice cream soda
> In burst King Bolo's big black queen
> That famous old breech l(oader).
> Just then they rang the bell for lunch
> And served up—Fried Hyenas;
> And Columbo said "Will you take tail?
> Or just a bit of p(enis)?"

McIntire characterizes the Columbo and Bolo poems as "pornotropic," seeming to mean Eliot used them as figures by which to negotiate his very conflicted feelings about sexuality; the precise meaning of this term, which is explained in a note as emphasizing the "*tropological* nature of Eliot's very self-conscious use of pornography," never quite became clear to me, however.

Eliot incorporated many of these verses in letters to a male coterie that included Conrad Aiken, Clive Bell, James Joyce, Wyndham Lewis, and Ezra Pound. Retelling the early history of colonial expansion as "an orgy of uncontrollable desire and deviant sexuality" (11), the poems form what McIntire describes in her first chapter's title as an "unexpected beginning" to Eliot's lifelong concern with the mixing of memory and desire. Eliot himself, in a letter to Aiken that includes the first of the Columbo and Bolo poems, mocked and parodied academic discourse that might consider seriously these smutty works (27). Given how typical the poems are of a genre familiar to any Anglo schoolboy of a certain class and time, it takes something of a willing suspension of skepticism to see them as staging and negotiating a "permanent state of cultural hybridity" through their "transatlantic sexual mélange" (32). Nevertheless, McIntire is convincing that as *parergon* (38), the Columbo and Bolo poems do serve to validate our "scandalous suspicions" about Eliot's investments in representing sexuality (85).

"Mixing memory and desire" is a dead metaphor that is evocatively reanimated by McIntire's nuanced and exemplary close reading of Eliot's poetry. It not only is reanimated but becomes fruitful as McIntire argues persuasively that for Eliot the past was tangible and could never die. Corpses "sprout" as the act of remembering stirs "dull roots" into renewed life. A zeugmatic relation between two different categories of human experience—one looking back and the other projecting into futurity—becomes central to the modernism that is implicitly the larger context of McIntire's study. She notes that "modernist writers tended to conflate history and memory, intertwining the facts and acts of the past with the conscious and unconscious narrations and renditions of such events. For their part, Eliot and Woolf both blurred the distinction between recollection and the historical, and the boundaries between memory and history are frequently slight in their work" (48).

It is surprising that there has been so little work directly reading Eliot and Woolf alongside one another, and although McIntire could have gone further in synthesizing her readings of both writers, this work should prompt future studies of the long, rich and complex interrelations between these two important modernists. One point of contact that bears further exploration is the thought of Henri Bergson. In Woolf studies there has been much debate about the extent of Woolf's exposure to Bergson's ideas about time and memory. McIntire points out that Eliot attended his weekly lectures at the Sorbonne in 1911. Bergson's ideas about the materiality of the past clearly inform Eliot's thinking, and when such ideas are deployed in McIntire's argument they imply a specific context for a well-known passage in Woolf's "Sketch of the Past" that became for me an undercurrent to McIntire's book as a whole:

> is it not possible—I often wonder—that things we have felt with great intensity have an existence independent of our minds; are in fact still in existence? And if so, will it not be possible, in time, that some device will be invented by which we can tap them? I see it—the past—as an avenue lying behind; a long ribbon of scenes,

emotions. There at the end of the avenue still, are the garden and the nursery. Instead of remembering here a scene and there a sound, I shall fit a plug into the wall; and listen in to the past. I shall turn up August 1890. I feel that strong emotion must leave its trace; and it is only a question of discovering how we can get ourselves again attached to it, so that we shall be able to live our lives through from the start. (*MOB* 67)

McIntire links Eliot's notion of the past as a body beneath the earth that can be stirred by memory with both Freud's "working through" and Cathy Caruth's explanation of trauma, which "produces a repeated desire to return to and re-experience the scene of abjection to try to grasp cognitively what only the body and the unconscious have come to know" (63). In *The Waste Land*, Eliot emphasizes the *corporeal* aspect of memory, wanting readers "to think of desire and history through nothing less than the body" (73).

For Eliot, in this reading, memory is inextricable from a desire that has to be worked through. McIntire argues that the poet compulsively writes out his repulsion from physical desire "as though by returning to the most visceral aspects of the sensual he might, through poetic intellection, 'work through' his corporeal disgust" (90). Like many of his contemporaries caught in the paradox of an urge to "make it new" so often leading to a return to the past, Eliot runs up against the limits of language and—again like many of his contemporaries—confronts a situation where "language as the vehicle of enunciation betrays a semantic barrenness that parallels Prufrock's (sexualized) dilemmas" (89). In arguing that at times "we must abandon language altogether in our search for iterability" (89), McIntire points out how Eliot allows signification to "break down altogether" in *The Waste Land*'s song of the three Thames daughters, but she does not make the obvious connection to similar moments in Woolf: the song of the "rusty pump" in *Mrs. Dalloway*, that of the caretaker's children in *The Years*, and even the "little language" that Bernard longs for in *The Waves*. And again, where she describes Eliot's "positing a kind of 'third space' beyond the unpleasure of language's confines" I looked for but did not find a concomitant discussion of the "third voice" Woolf refers to in both "A Sketch" and *Between the Acts*.

In turning her attention to Woolf, McIntire focuses on a very different kind of erotics than was the case in her discussion of Eliot's attachment to the past, somewhat narrowing the sweep of her narrative as she considers Woolf's desire for Vita Sackville-West and its embodiment in *Orlando*. In that novel, Woolf plays with the equivalence of writing and birthing a life and seems interested in exploring the "dialogue between recollection, revision, imagination, and desire" (123). *Orlando* here is seen as the culmination of a longstanding interest of Woolf's in the "interpenetration between life and fictionality" (124), fully realized when *Orlando* brings Sackville-West "near to the fold of the same by claiming the power to write her life as a form of textual seduction" (123). Thus, Vita can be both that "radical Other one seeks to know in the encounter of loving, and a more fully knowable facet of the self" (123) through Woolf's art. Like Eliot's, Woolf's writing embodies the notion of the self's fundamental instability that became a "hallmark of modernist writing" (124). McIntire argues that in *Orlando* Woolf was "making the case that to write Vita Sackville-West's personal past was also to write national memory" (133), and in this chapter the relations between personal memory and history that were hinted at but not as explicit in the preceding chapters on Eliot are brought into the foreground. *Orlando*, McIntire contends, suggests "that the contours of personal history might be physically traceable" and by embodying *Orlando*'s history in a single "undying, nearly unaging body," Woolf suggests that the body carries the "residue" of history "in the form of memory" (133). Again, Bergson's ideas about the persistence of history are relevant here, and McIntire points out—correctly, I believe—that although Woolf may not have read Bergson's works his ideas were certainly familiar enough in her milieu to have affected her thinking about history, memory and their physical duration.

For Woolf, Eliot, Freud, Proust and other modernist writers, memory is inscribed with "the indelible ink of desire," the past "leav[ing] its traces in our bodies and on our psyches" (145). Both Eliot and Woolf fought against cultural amnesia at the end of World War I, and in pondering why Woolf, in writing "A Sketch of the Past," might have found a return to the time of her mother's death a "respite," McIntire again refers to Caruth's explanation of trauma as something not experienced *in time* (153); it is returned to endlessly "to find a way in to its testimony" (153). Like Eliot, Woolf regarded the past as a still-living body "which one was charged—ethically and even politically—with avowing and remaking in order to find the new" (160). This body is continually remade in Woolf's fiction through her continual piecing together, gathering up, scraps of memory. McIntire points out the prevalence of domestic metaphors for memory employed by Woolf, noting that as for Eliot, there is a licentiousness about that "hussy, Memory" for Woolf too: "Time [. . .] is a torn tissue [. . .] Woolf is the careful hoarder. With her pen she stores the scraps, hoping, perhaps, one day to piece them together to make a new kind of restored patchwork that would heal the fractured relation between fragments and wholes that haunted Woolf throughout her life" (139).

Woolf's idea of history precedes by decades feminist "gestures of retrieval and valorization" (189), gestures that still engage scholars of modernism in debate today. According to McIntire, Woolf reiterates Eliot's point in "Tradition and the Individual Talent" that "the difference between the past and the present is that the conscious present is an awareness of the past in a way and to an extent which the past's unawareness of itself cannot show" (191). Perceptively, McIntire notes the fragility of the present for Woolf, explaining that it must be so "because it has not yet met the signifying system of an anterior representation" (186). *Between the Acts* gets rather shorter shrift in this study than its subject would seem to warrant, and this may be one area that scholars wish to take up and develop, nurturing what McIntire has planted.

Between the Acts is full of echoes from *The Four Quartets* that remain to be explored. For example, McIntire sees both "East Coker" and Woolf's last work of fiction as "gesturing toward a kind of *logos*, a beginning-again through the word, that would startlingly supervene beyond temporality and text" (208). The compelling argument of this excellent book is that, contrary to the typical view of modernist writers' postures toward the past as emphasizing rupture and discontinuity, "modernism's looking to the past denotes *both* a return and a departure" (209). Woolf in *To the Lighthouse* proposes that every voyage is a return, as does Eliot in "Little Gidding" when he writes that "the end of all our exploring/Will be to arrive where we started/And know the place for the first time" (172). *Modernism, Memory, and Desire* brings Eliot and Woolf into fruitful contact to explain how both writers understood that the "wounded temporality" that is the present needs the "healing" of a narration that can only become available once present is past. This study deserves a wide audience: I hope the exorbitant price charged by its publisher will not limit that audience too much.

—Mark Hussey, *Pace University*

The Letters of Lytton Strachey. Ed. Paul Levy (NY: Farrar, Straus and Giroux, 2005) xxi + 698pp.

In the preface to his 1918 *Eminent Victorians,* Lytton Strachey noted that one of the greatest problems concerning his biographical subjects was their sheer garrulousness. "Concerning the Age which has just passed," he wrote, "our fathers and our grandfathers have poured forth and accumulated so vast a quantity of information that the industry of a Ranke would be submerged by it, and the perspicacity of a Gibbon would quail before it" (Penguin, 1986: 9). The task of a biographer, he wrote, was "to preserve [...] a becoming brevity" (ibid.); that, too, was the task of Paul Levy, the compiler of this new selected edition of Strachey's own letters, for Strachey himself had a remarkable loquacity when it came to letter writing that was easily the match of his Victorian forebears. "If Strachey's letters were to be collected," notes Levy, "they would run to nearly the six volumes needed for Virginia Woolf's, though she lived a decade longer than he" (xiv). As Levy, who is the co-executor of Strachey's literary estate, notes, such a complete collection would be "in the present publishing climate [...] an obvious impossibility"; and so Bloomsbury scholars and aficionados must console themselves with this lively selected edition of Strachey's letters.

Physically ungainly, Lytton Strachey revealed his elegance of mind primarily through his own letter writing, where he chose to construct himself anew in his missives for the benefit of his large and equally vociferous family and his friends, particularly the circle of close friends he made at Cambridge in the "Apostles," the secret society who later became the linchpins of the Bloomsbury Group. Although Lytton Strachey from an early age felt a strong calling to be a writer, he found his own skills at playwriting and poetry to be severely limited, despite his many attempts throughout his life at crafting ribald doggerel to amuse his friends throughout these letters. "I wish I could write poetry," a middle-aged Strachey writes his friend Mary Hutchinson on July 4th, 1929, "but the mould seems to be lacking into which to pour the curious fluid—melted silver? Porridge? Gilded sealing-wax?—of my emotions" (603). While finding himself similarly greatly frustrated by an academic career during the Edwardian decade, when his four hundred page thesis on Warren Hastings was ultimately rejected by Trinity College, he found, almost unawares, a more appropriate "mould" in his letters to his undergraduate friends. It was here that Strachey could show to a smaller world his great intelligence, his wit, and his ability to strike poses both to amuse and to shock his correspondents, who numbered among them such important thinkers and figures as Leonard Woolf (his most frequent correspondent in his early years), G. E. Moore, Bertrand Russell, and John Maynard Keynes. It was during this time, when Strachey tried to supplement his income by reviewing for journals and newspapers, that he began to show his great flair for writing about his own life to his absent Cambridge circle. What often surprises most while reading these early letters is Strachey's endless capacity for self-invention. For example, when Keynes had struck up an affair with Strachey's own previous lover, the painter Duncan Grant, Strachey, stung by jealousy, struck back by writing up in his letters to them wild amorous encounters with a handsome rural swain—improbably named "Horry Townshend"–he claimed to have met in Scotland. Although both Keynes and Grant suspected Horry to be a hoax ("…not a very nice name," wrote Keynes, "does his character absolutely require it?" [158]), they both allowed Strachey to continue with his vivid descriptions to them of his *amour fou*. Ultimately Strachey ended the practical joke when Keynes insisted on meeting the young man by claiming that his new love had drowned; when Keynes complained of his bad taste in perpetrating a hoax over the feigned lover's corpse, Strachey apologized, but added mischievously, "I wonder how much of it you really *did* believe" (160). Life-writing, Strachey found, could be used to beguile as well as to amuse, and he found it as much of an outlet for fantasies as drama or poetry. It is thus no wonder that he became himself such an inveterate reader of letters, in which he found the raw materials for his biographer's art. While reading the letters of Thomas Creevey to research his life of Queen Victoria in February of 1919, he commented to Clive Bell, "How can anyone read novels when there are Creevey Papers to be had—in which there is every variety of human, political, and historical interest, sur le vif—I don't understand" (427).

The same might be said for Strachey's own letters. Always filled with amusing gossip (as anyone who has read his biographies knows, the amusing behaviors of the great in private was always the source of great capital for him), here we see incisive portraits of all his circle. These range from the young Virginia Stephen, whom he describes to Leonard Woolf in December of 1904 as "rather wonderful—quite witty, full of things to say, and absolutely out of rapport with reality" (43), to the mountaineer George Mallory, whose beauty inspires his absolute ecstasies in a May 21st, 1909 letter to Clive and Vanessa Bell: "…he's six foot high, with the body of an athlete by Praxiteles, and a face—ah, incredible—the mystery of Botticelli, the refinement and delicacy of a Chinese print, the youth and piquancy of an unimaginable English boy" (179). Illuminating incidents concerning other more minor figures in Strachey's life are also to be found here, including everyone from Henry James to the Prince of Wales, whom Strachey mistakenly attempts to cruise in the National Gallery in 1930 before fleeing in a panic after noticing the scraping docent at his side. The familiar events of Strachey's life are also all here written down for the first time: his proposal to Virginia Stephen (and his subsequent relief when she turned him down); his early encounters with the painter Dora Carrington; his shock when she married their mutual friend Ralph

Partridge; his great successes with his biographies *Eminent Victorians*, the 1921 *Queen Victoria*, and the 1928 *Elizabeth and Essex*; and, finally, his slow decline from his fatal cancer of the stomach. So, too, do we find Strachey's incisive judgments of many of the books of his day, including those by both Leonard and Virginia Woolf and by E. M. Forster, whose novel *Maurice* Strachey notoriously critiqued ("I really think the whole conception of male copulation in the book rather diseased—in fact morbid and unnatural") in March of 1915 after receiving the circulated unpublished manuscript (247). And finally, here too can we find many of Strachey's observations on the politics of his day, including in particular his impassioned defenses of his strong belief in pacifism, a persuasion that had to be rigorously proved during the First World War when he sought conscientious objector status from the British government.

The figure of Strachey that emerges from the letters, while endearing, is often too much like that of most of his own biographical subjects: flawed, mercurial, and often quite dark and querulous (he retained a lifelong fascination with the figure of Lord Byron). Although Strachey complains incessantly about his friends' personalities and their hospitality, Levy shrewdly includes in this selected edition a typed letter that Clive Bell (often the target of Strachey's ill-will) wrote to his friend after one too many house-visits that itemizes all of Strachey's good qualities while noting simultaneously what an ungrateful and unwelcome tyrant he could be as a Man Who Came to Dinner. (Bell's letter, Levy surmises, was ultimately never sent.) Strachey's cruelties to his friends and benefactors are always on display here, and he is sometimes merciless to the society hostesses, such as Lady Ottoline Morrell, of whose generosities he freely took advantage. It thus comes as little surprise when towards the end of his life Strachey finds an outlet for his causticity in a relationship with the young Roger Senhouse that partakes of sado-masochism, whether real or (lovingly) imagined.

Given the riches available in Levy's selection, it might seem ungallant to complain about omissions; yet there are some here that are quite dismaying, despite the limited space allowed. To his credit, Levy refuses to censor any of Strachey's prejudices, and his frequent expostulations of anti-Semitism (which Levy persuasively surmises were mostly composed for shock purposes) are quite evident here, for indeed they must be a part of our overall picture of who Lytton Strachey was. Unhappily missing, however, are several important letters describing the composition of Strachey's three great biographical achievements, *Eminent Victorians, Queen Victoria,* and *Elizabeth and Essex*, any of which are of inestimable value to Strachey and Bloomsbury scholars. The selection omits, for example, several of the letters Strachey writes to his friends in 1919 and 1920 describing his increasingly adversarial role regarding his biographical subject as he struggled to complete his manuscript of Victoria's life, as well as many similar letters written during the composition of the Elizabeth Tudor biography between 1926 and 1928. Excerpts from these letters appear throughout Michael Holroyd's highly praised biography of Lytton Strachey (*Lytton Strachey: The New Biography* [New York: Farrar, Straus and Giroux, 1994], 460-77 and 567-96), yet only a few of these are to be found in this collection. Although Levy describes his two central criteria for inclusion in this book to be "literary merit" and telling incidents familiar to readers from Holroyd's life or its adaptation into the film *Carrington*, it seems inconceivable he has decided to leave out such important documents detailing Strachey's artistic aims, especially given that this might be the only comprehensive selection of the letters we will see for decades. Levy, it seems, has had to make an unfortunate choice ultimately between Strachey's art and his life—a choice that Lytton Strachey himself might not have been able to make.

—Jay Dickson, *Reed College*

Virginia Woolf, Jean Rhys, and the Aesthetics of Trauma. Patricia Moran (New York: Palgrave MacMillan, 2007) ix + 217 pp.

Patricia Moran's *Virginia Woolf, Jean Rhys, and the Aesthetics of Trauma* examines exactly what a reader might expect upon reading its clear and provocative title: the influence of trauma on Virginia Woolf's and Jean Rhys's representational choices, particularly in their later works. Moran notes a split in the career of each writer—for Woolf marked by *A Room of One's Own*, for Rhys marked by *Good Morning, Midnight*—in which each moves toward an "aesthetics of trauma" in which formal narrative choices reflect the dissociation, depression, gaps in memory, and fragmentation of identity associated with the experience of trauma. Turning first to Woolf in the first half of the monograph and then to Rhys in the second half, Moran's analysis notably succeeds in preserving the differences between these two writers' approaches to fiction, while at the same time it traces their different aesthetic experiments to the common root of traumatic experience.

For Moran, trauma serves as the impetus that propels the radical experimentation with form that typifies the writing of Woolf and Rhys, and each author translates her lived traumatic experience—Woolf's childhood sexual abuse and the death of her mother; Rhys's physical, emotional, and mental abuse by her mother in childhood and her seduction at 14 by a much older family friend—into an aesthetic mode through which readers can experience trauma vicariously. For Woolf, this aesthetics of trauma that emerges in her writing of the 1930s "posits an evolutionary model of traumatic affect, whereby other female family members seem to 'inherit' unconscious memory traces—and with those traces, a concomitant atrophy of sexuality and physicality" (68). In positing this "evolutionary model," Woolf seeks "fictional methods" capable of "convey[ing] the process of repression that turned women's sexual desires into the shameful and guilty emotions she described as 'subterranean instincts'" (68). In contrast, the trauma that Rhys experiences in her youth, according to Moran, results in a "masochistic aesthetic," in which Rhys "moved from depicting masochistic characters to embodying masochism and trauma within literary form itself: portraits of romantic thralldom and erotic domination give way to a masochistic aesthetic, one that deploys repetition, suspends and disavows climax, blurs reality and fantasy, and enacts patterns of reversal—an aesthetic that, in dramatizing and exaggerating the relations of submission and dominance, sets up an oppositional site within power hierarchies" (128). Thus, while each writer gets different results from her formal experiments of the 1930s, each conceives the need for a formal style that embodies trauma.

Moran emphasizes that both Woolf and Rhys engage trauma as a way of seeing or a way of representing: neither merely recounts traumatic experiences in the content of their writing, but rather each uses a language and formal structure of trauma as the means of representation. This sophisticated approach to trauma as linked to narrative experimentation contributes to scholarship on trauma in literature as well as persuades the reader of Moran's readings of the primary texts that she examines. As Moran writes, "What Woolf's and Rhys's texts show is that female modernism takes up female subjectivity at precisely the point that Freud abandoned it, and that women modernists' retrieval and reworking of traumatic stories not only provides motivation for their artistry but enriches considerably our currently impoverished understanding of the uses of and competing claims involved in traumatic memory" (17). Among the greatest strengths of Moran's book is her precision in situating both Woolf and Rhys in relation to theories of trauma, shame, and submission. She offers a powerful explanation for readers' vague sense that there is a split between the early works of these writers and their later ones, and Moran succeeds here in no small part because of the depth of her research, her meticulous attention to detail, and her thorough investigation of both the lives and works of Woolf and Rhys. Moran effortlessly interweaves historical and archival material, literary criticism, and theory. The prose of the monograph is both conversational and engaging, while at the same time it effectively communicates deeply complex and nuanced readings of each of the authors under consideration.

Nevertheless, Moran could have gone further than she does to situate her claims, as she indicates that she will in her introductory chapter, within the current critical conversation about modernist aesthetics and gender and representation in modernism. Moran claims that both Woolf and Rhys should be regarded as playing a central role "in the genesis and elaboration of modernist female aesthetics" and "at the center of modernist debates about female subjectivity and aesthetics" (13). While I agree with this assertion, Moran does not substantiate her claim by situating these two writers in the context of other modernist writers. Does the fact that both Woolf and Rhys experienced sexual trauma fully account for their literary experiments? Could trauma theory account for similar narrative attempts to represent dissociation, depression, gaps in memory, and fragmentation of identity in the work of male authors of the period? Are Woolf's and Rhys's experiments particular to modernism, or are those experiments particular to the experience of trauma, and thus transhistorical in nature?

Moran's book does not answer these questions, but it does inspire readers to ask them. A fuller exploration of these issues would have enhanced the sophisticated analysis of trauma and form that the monograph offers. Moreover, in exploring these issues, Moran might have found it possible to temper her argument about trauma in the works of Woolf and Rhys to the extent that she could admit other factors that work with trauma in informing the aesthetic concerns of these writers. For example, Moran pays little attention to the ways in which class informs both Woolf's and Rhys's writing, in choices related both to content and to form. Ultimately, were such factors admitted into the book's analysis, Moran's argument about trauma would have been even more compelling.

In its consideration of Woolf, *Virginia Woolf, Jean Rhys, and the Aesthetics of Trauma* works best when it interweaves biographical material from Woolf's life, analysis of Woolf's literary writing, and theoretical perspectives about trauma and women's writing. Moran's analysis of *A Room of One's Own* as a transitional text in Woolf's oeuvre and her analysis of *The Years* as evidence of the turn in Woolf's aesthetics are especially strong. Ultimately, Moran argues that *A Room of One's Own* signals a rupture, in which "Woolf shifts her focus to the ways in which the middle-class woman's acculturation teaches her to censor her physicality, a censorship that typically results not only in female silence about physical experience, but in an atrophied or attenuated relationship to physicality altogether. These texts [after *A Room of One's Own*] are also marked by increasingly negative assessments of maternity and female heterosexuality; and while Woolf at times condemns the cult of chastity in *The Years* and *Three Guineas*, she herself moves toward a valorization of the single or asexual woman—or the aged woman who Woolf imagines has outlived her sexuality—in her essays and fiction" (68). Moreover, Moran's discussion of the intersections of Woolf's writing with sexological accounts of female sexuality and creativity, in particular those of Havelock Ellis, proves especially illuminating and well argued. In these areas, the book artfully and clearly situates Woolf within theories of trauma and shame and shows how Woolf's articulations of trauma and shame illuminate current theoretical conversations about trauma and literature.

The reader does wonder, however, how Moran might have handled a further consideration of those moments and characters in Woolf's novels that might not adhere as neatly to the aesthetic model that Moran so persuasively suggests. By focusing attention almost exclusively on Woolf's autobiographical material, including "A Sketch of the Past," *A Room of One's Own,* and *The Years,* the monograph fails to account for Woolf's aesthetics in a way that is exhaustive. In particular, a more extensive consideration of Woolf's *Between the Acts* would have been a welcome addition to the monograph. In addition, the monograph does not give more than passing mention to Woolf's novels of the 1920s, and the split that Moran argues that *A Room of One's Own* marks would have been more clearly drawn if a deeper analysis of at least one of the early works been included.

In sum, *Virginia Woolf, Jean Rhys, and the Aesthetics of Trauma* constitutes a provocative study that contributes not only to Woolf studies but also to scholarship on Jean Rhys and to scholarship on literature and trauma. In pairing Woolf and Rhys, the book offers a path toward reconsidering modernist aesthetics generally and modernist female aesthetics specifically. As Moran convincingly concludes in her epilogue, "For both, writing is a way of managing pain and sorrow, and for both later traumatic experiences are mapped onto the mother-daughter matrix: the maternal idiom informs the narrative aesthetic" (160-161). Moran's masterful integration of biographical material, literary critical analysis, and theoretical context focuses particular attention on aesthetic concerns of late modernism, which so often are marginalized in mainstream modernist studies. The clarity of the analysis throughout the book, and the clarity of descriptions, is exemplary. This book offers original insight into these authors' lives, into these authors' writing, into modernism's formal experiments, and into the ways in which trauma informs aesthetic production.

—Tonya Krouse, *Northern Kentucky University*

Notes on Contributors

Jacqueline Doyle is Professor of English at California State University, East Bay, where she teaches American literature and women's literature. She has published essays on ethnic American women writers in a number of journals, among them *MELUS, Women's Studies, Frontiers, Critique, Hitting Critical Mass*, and *a/b: Auto/Biography Studies*, and in several anthologies, including *Things of the Spirit*, ed. Kristina K. Groover, *Women, America, and Movement*, ed. Susan L. Roberson, and *The Immigrant Experience in North American Literature*, ed. Katherine B. Payant and Toby Rose. Her most recent work on ethnic women's memoir is forthcoming in *Lifewriting Annual*.

Leslie Kathleen Hankins is Professor of English at Cornell College in Iowa. She has presented about Woolf and the cinema at almost all of the annual Virginia Woolf conferences, and has publications on the topic in the Selected Papers from the 2nd, 4th, 7th, 9th, 11th, and 18th conferences, as well as in *Criticism*, in Diane Gillespie's *Multiple Muses of Virginia Woolf* (1993), Bonnie Kime Scott's *Gender in Modernism* (2007), Eileen Barrett's and Ruth Saxton's forthcoming *MLA Approaches to Teaching* Mrs. Dalloway, Maggie Humm's forthcoming *The Edinburgh Companion to Virginia Woolf and the Arts*, and the pamphlet of essays for the Flicker Alley DVD restoration of Abel Gance's 1919 film, *J'accuse* (2008).

Georgia Johnston is Professor of English at Saint Louis University and the current President of the International Virginia Woolf Society. Her recent book, *The Formation of 20th-Century Queer Autobiography*, reads lesbian modernists challenging, through autobiography, the scientifically constructed figure of the lesbian.

Leah Leone is a candidate in both the Ph.D. program in Spanish American Literature and the MFA program in Literary Translation at the University of Iowa. Her doctoral dissertation deals with shifts in narrative structure in Jorge Luis Borges's translations from English into Spanish. Her MFA thesis is the translation and critical introduction of Enrique Jardiel Poncela's *¡Espérame em Sibéria, vida mia!*

NOTES ON CONTRIBUTORS

Jane Lilienfeld is Professor of English at Lincoln University, an historically Black college in Jefferson City, MO. In 2000 her *Reading Alcoholisms* was a CHOICE award winner. She has published essays in *Tulsa Studies in Women's Literature, Modern Fiction Studies, Twentieth Century Literature* and in numerous anthologies, including the essay, "'Could They Tell One What They Knew?': Modes of Disclosure in *To the Lighthouse*" in *Virginia Woolf and Trauma* edited by Suzette Henke and David Eberly. Her essay included here is dedicated to Mark Hussey with thanks for his friendship and extensive service to the study of the works of Virginia Woolf.

Vicki Tromanhauser is an assistant professor of English at the State University of New York at New Paltz. She has published essays on Woolf's London, on Woolf and the classics, and more generally on the present state of the humanities. She is currently working on a book about modernism and human sacrifice.

Virginia Woolf
An *MFS* Reader
EDITED BY MAREN LINETT

As the most canonical woman writer of modern English literature, Virginia Woolf has become central to our conceptions of literature, modernist theory, the arts, feminism, and social analysis. The interdisciplinary examinations in this anthology explore Woolf's major novels, her key essays, and the literary tropes that unify her writings.

A Modern Fiction Studies Book
$25.00 paperback

THE JOHNS HOPKINS UNIVERSITY PRESS
1-800-537-5487 • www.press.jhu.edu

Imagining Virginia Woolf
An Experiment in Critical Biography
Maria DiBattista

"This book is a lively, original, and very interesting personal reading of Virginia Woolf, sensitively done and well-written. It is clever and illuminating to approach Woolf through the idea of the writerly personae, rather than biographically or in more conventionally critical ways. I enjoyed this book very much and was impressed and refreshed by it."
—Hermione Lee, author of *Virginia Woolf* and *Edith Wharton*

Cloth $19.95 978-0-691-13812-1

PRINCETON UNIVERSITY PRESS
800.777.4726
press.princeton.edu

Policy

Woolf Studies Annual invites articles on the work and life of Virginia Woolf and her milieu. The Annual intends to represent the breadth and eclecticism of critical approaches to Woolf, and particularly welcomes new perspectives and contexts of inquiry. Articles discussing relations between Woolf and other writers and artists are also welcome.

Articles are sent for review anonymously to a member of the Editorial Board and at least one other reader. Manuscripts should not be under consideration elsewhere or have been previously published. It is strongly advised that those submitting work to WSA be familiar with the journal's content. Among criteria on which evaluation of submissions depends are whether an article demonstrates familiarity with scholarship already published in the field, whether the article is written clearly and effectively, and whether it makes a genuine contribution to Woolf studies.

Preparation of Copy

1. Articles are typically between 25 and 30 pages, and do not exceed 8000 words. Inquiries about significantly shorter or longer submissions should be sent to the Editor at woolfstudiesannual@gmail.com.

2. A separate page should include the article's title, author's name, address, telephone & fax numbers, and e-mail address. The author's name and identifying references should not appear on the manuscript to preserve anonymity for our readers.

3. All submissions must include an abstract of no more than 250 words.

4. Manuscripts should be prepared according to most recent MLA style.

5. Submissions may be sent *either* by email to woolfstudiesannual@gmail.com *or* by mail to Mark Hussey, English Dept., Pace University, One Pace Plaza, New York NY 10038. For email submissions ONE hardcopy must also be mailed; for mailed submissions, please send **three** copies of the article and abstract.

6. Authors of accepted manuscripts are responsible for any necessary permissions fees and for securing any necessary permissions.

All editorial inquiries should be addressed to woolfstudiesannual@gmail.com. Inquiries concerning orders, advertising, reviews, etc. should be addressed to PaceUP@pace.edu.

www.ingramcontent.com/pod-product-compliance
Lightning Source LLC
Chambersburg PA
CBHW061440300426
44114CB00014B/1769